Is Marx's Theory of Profit Right?

Heterodox Studies in the Critique of Political Economy

Series Editor: Andrew Kliman

The outbreak of the global economic crisis in 2007 has led to renewed discussion of heterodox economics and Karl Marx's contributions. Heterodox Studies in the Critique of Political Economy contributes to and seeks to broaden the focus of these discussions. It welcomes proposals from authors working within various heterodox traditions. Contributions to the critique of political economy in the tradition founded by Marx are strongly encouraged, as are other marginalized voices and perspectives. Thus, non-academics, scholars from Asia and the global South, and proponents of perspectives that are under-represented in the existing academic heterodox literature are encouraged to submit proposals. Both single-authored works and edited collections are welcome.

Recent Titles in This Series

Is Marx's Theory of Profit Right? The Simultaneist-Temporalist Debate, Edited by Andrew Kliman and Nick Potts.

The Dissolution of the Financial State: A Marxian Examination of the Political Economy of Contemporary Money with Case Studies of the United Kingdom and Germany since the 1930s, By Simon Mouatt.

Is Marx's Theory of Profit Right?

The Simultaneist–Temporalist Debate

Edited by
Nick Potts and Andrew Kliman

LEXINGTON BOOKS
Lanham • Boulder • New York • London

Published by Lexington Books
An imprint of The Rowman & Littlefield Publishing Group, Inc.
4501 Forbes Boulevard, Suite 200, Lanham, Maryland 20706
www.rowman.com

Unit A, Whitacre Mews, 26-34 Stannary Street, London SE11 4AB

British Library Cataloguing in Publication Information Available

Library of Congress Cataloging-in-Publication Data Available

ISBN 978-0-7391-9631-1 (cloth : alk. paper)
ISBN 978-0-7391-9632-8 (electronic)

∞™ The paper used in this publication meets the minimum requirements of American National Standard for Information Sciences—Permanence of Paper for Printed Library Materials, ANSI/NISO Z39.48-1992.

Printed in the United States of America

To our mothers,
Janet Potts (1937–1999)
Esther B. ("Itsy") Kliman

Contents

Editors' Note

This volume brings together all of the major contributions to a recent, decade-long controversy over Karl Marx's theory that exploitation of workers is the exclusive source of capitalists' profit. The authors whose works are republished here include Andrew Kliman, Alan Freeman, Simon Mohun, and Roberto Veneziani. The first two are proponents of the temporal single-system interpretation of Marx's value theory, while the latter two are critics. These contributions are preceded by Nick Potts's introduction to and commentary on the debate, which appears here for the first time.

Also included in this volume is a very recent exchange in which several of the same themes resurfaced. It appears here in print for the first time. The protagonists in the latter exchange were the philosopher Robert Paul Wolff on one hand, and Kliman, Freeman, and Chris Byron on the other.

All contributions are presented in chronological order and without amendment or revision. Editors' notes have been inserted inside braces (curly brackets); all material inside parentheses and square brackets was part of the texts as originally published. Typographical errors have been corrected and stylistic changes have been made. References to other works have been moved from the end of individual texts to a consolidated bibliography at the end of the book.

—Nick Potts and Andrew Kliman

Acknowledgments

The editors wish to thank:

The Conference of Socialist Economists, for providing funding that made the publication of this volume possible.

The Institute for Social Sciences of Gyeongsang National University (South Korea), for permission to republish the following articles, which originally appeared in *Marxism 21*:

Kliman, Andrew, and Alan Freeman. 2009. "The Truthiness of Veneziani's Critique of Marx and the TSSI," *Marxism 21*, vol. 6, no. 2, 335–66.

Mohun, Simon, and Roberto Veneziani. 2009. "The Temporal Single-System Interpretation: Underdetermination and Inconsistency," *Marxism 21*, vol. 6, no. 3, 277–301.

Freeman, Alan, and Andrew Kliman. 2009. "No Longer a Question of Truth? The Knell of Scientific Bourgeois Marxian Economics and a Positive Alternative," *Marxism 21*, vol. 6, no. 3, 302–17.

John Wiley & Sons, for permission to republish section 3 (pp. 104–7) of Veneziani, Roberto. 2004. "The Temporal Single-System Interpretation of Marx's Economics: A Critical Evaluation," *Metroeconomica*, vol. 55, no. 1, 96–114. © Blackwell Publishing Ltd 2004.

Marxist-Humanist Initiative, for permission to republish Byron, Chris, Alan Freeman, and Andrew Kliman, "Physicalism and the Exploitation Theory of Profit are Incompatible: A Response to Robert Paul Wolff," which was first published in its web journal *With Sober Senses* (www.marxisthumanistinitiative.org/our-publication) on May 9, 2014.

Sage Publications, for permission to republish the following articles, which originally appeared in *Capital & Class*:

Kliman, Andrew. 2001. "Simultaneous Valuation vs. the Exploitation Theory of Profit," *Capital & Class*, Spring, vol. 25, no. 1, 97–112.

Mohun, Simon. 2003. "On the TSSI and the Exploitation Theory of Profit," *Capital & Class,* Autumn, vol. 27, no. 3, 85–102.
Kliman, Andrew, and Freeman, Alan. 2006. "Replicating Marx: A Reply to Mohun," *Capital & Class,* Spring, vol. 30, no. 1, 117–26.
Mohun, Simon, and Veneziani, Roberto. 2007. "The Incoherence of the TSSI: A Reply to Kliman and Freeman," *Capital & Class,* Summer, vol. 31, no. 2, 139–45.
Kliman, Andrew, and Freeman, Alan. 2008. "Simultaneous Valuation vs. the Exploitation Theory of Profit: A Summing Up," *Capital & Class,* Spring, vol. 32, no. 1, 107–17.

Robert Paul Wolff, for permission to republish his blog posts and e-mail messages that appear here. The blog posts were first published on *The Philosopher's Stone* www.robertpaulwolff.blogspot.com/, on May 4, 10, 11, 12, and 14, 2014.

Abbreviations

BVWW	Botox-value of workers' wages
CSE	Conference of Socialist Economists
FMT	Fundamental Marxian Theorem
FMST	Fundamental Magic Stick Theorem
MELT	monetary expression of labor-time
NI	New Interpretation
PNP	price of the net product
SSSI	simultaneous single-system interpretations
TSS	temporal single-system
TSSI	temporal single-system interpretation

Chapter 1

A Sad Story

An Introduction to and Commentary on the Debate

Nick Potts

Karl Marx argued that exploitation of workers is the exclusive source of capitalists' profit. The first of the two debates contained in this volume—between Andrew Kliman and Alan Freeman on one hand, and Simon Mohun and Roberto Veneziani on the other—initially focused on a logical issue: is it possible to deduce Marx's conclusion in a logically valid way? Which, if any, of the different interpretations of his value theory succeeds in doing so? In the course of the debate, however, issues of pluralism, truth, and scientificity increasingly assumed center stage. As I shall document below, behavior that I regard as suppressive and contrary to scientific norms was engaged in with some frequency, and I personally suffered from it.

Let me make clear from the outset that I was not personally engaged in this debate. For that reason, and because I have set aside my theoretical commitments as much as possible when drawing conclusions about the debate, this introduction to it is reasonably objective. Although some of my conclusions may unfortunately seem a bit harsh, I think other disinterested but knowledgeable parties would draw similar conclusions, and I certainly do not mean to be disrespectful of any individual. This introduction criticizes certain *practices and texts*, not *authors as persons*.

MARX'S THEORY OF PROFIT

A main purpose of volume 1 of Marx's *Capital* is to reveal the shocking secret of where profit (surplus-value) comes from. Although he thought that the classical economists Adam Smith and David Ricardo had come close to having solved the problem, Marx regarded their efforts as ultimately unsuccessful.

He first argued that—in the economy as a whole—profit cannot be the result of cheating, buying things for less than they are worth or selling them for more than they are worth. Particular capitalists can get profit in this way, but only at the expense of other capitalists. One's gain is the other's loss. "The capitalist class of a given country, taken as a whole, cannot defraud itself" (Marx 1990a: 266).

However, the classical economists' proposition that commodities' values are determined by the amount of labor needed to produce them seems to make it impossible for profit to arise in the absence of cheating. Consider a worker who sells her labor on the market for $500 per week, and assume that this sum is the full value of her labor; she is not being cheated. If commodities' values are determined by the amount of labor needed to produce them, then $500 is also the amount of value her labor adds to the products she produces during the week. Now, if the capitalist sells the products at their value—so that the buyers are also not being cheated—he merely recoups the $500 he paid the worker. There is no profit.

We therefore seem to have an insoluble dilemma:

> [Profit] cannot therefore arise from circulation, and it is equally impossible for it to arise apart from circulation. It must have its origin both in circulation and not in circulation.[1]
>
> We therefore have a double result.
>
> The transformation of money into capital has to be developed on the basis of the immanent laws of the exchange of commodities, in such a way that the starting-point is the exchange of equivalents. The money-owner, who is as yet only a capitalist in larval form, must buy his commodities at their value, sell them at their value, and yet at the end of the process withdraw more value from circulation than he threw into it at the beginning. His emergence as a butterfly must, and yet must not, take place in the sphere of circulation. These are the conditions of the problem. *Hic Rhodus, hic salta!*[2]

Yet, Marx argued, there is indeed a solution. Contrary to what the classical economists assumed, workers' labor is not a commodity bought in the "labor market." Labor is the activity that workers engage in. What capitalists buy when they hire workers is instead their labor-power, or ability to work. The worker we introduced above was hired to be *at work* for a week, but how much actual *work* she did during the week is another matter.

Thus, profit arises because the worker's labor creates more value than the value of her labor-power. Although the $500 the worker was paid is the full value of her *labor-power*, the amount of new value created during a week's worth of her *labor* will be greater, say $1,000. During the first half of the week, the worker creates the first $500 of new value, which replaces the amount of value she was paid. At this point, the capitalist has recouped the money he paid out in wages. However, the worker is compelled to work beyond this point—to perform *surplus labor.* She did, after all, contract to work for a *whole* week. Her labor during the remaining half-week creates an additional $500 of new value—*surplus-value.* It does not replace anything; the capitalist obtains it for free. This is the source of the profit and, according to Marx (1991a: 270), it is "the exclusive source of [the] profit."

Marx (1990a: 731) stressed that no cheating, and no violation of property rights, are involved in this process:

> If . . . the amount of value advanced in wages is not merely found again in the product, but [is] augmented by a surplus-value, this is not because the seller [the worker] has been defrauded, for he has really received the value of his commodity. . . .
>
> [The process] takes place in the most exact accordance with the economic laws of commodity production and with the rights of property derived from them. Nevertheless, its result is:
>
> 1. that the product belongs to the capitalist and not to the worker;
> 2. that the value of this product includes, apart from the value of the capital advanced, a surplus-value which costs the worker labour but the capitalist nothing, and which none the less becomes the legitimate property of the capitalist;
> 3. that the worker has retained his labour-power and can sell it anew if he finds another buyer.

Marx's conclusion that profit comes solely from exploiting workers has a number of further implications. One particularly important implication, discussed in volume 3 of *Capital,* is that there is a tendency for the rate of profit to fall as capital accumulates and the economy grows. Capitalists minimize their costs in order to compete successfully, and introduction of labor-saving technological change is an effective way for capitalists to reduce costs. Yet by conserving on labor, they are conserving on the exclusive source of their profit and thereby creating a tendency for their profit rate to fall. It is this that makes capitalism a self-negating system, a phoenix that has to renew itself in crisis.

MARX OR NOT?

Let us be clear about what is actually at stake in the debate presented in this book. The central question is: How do we relate to Marx's theory of value? Do we take it seriously and teach it as a viable alternative theory of value to the theory of value of mainstream economics? Do we explore it? Is our research guided by its actual content? Does the behavior it predicts occur?

If Marx's theory of value best enables us to understand our world, then we must conclude, on purely scientific grounds, that we probably do live in a society where profit results from the exploitation of labor, and that this exploitation does not occur smoothly, but in bouts of growth and crisis that stretch both our planet's resources and our own personal resources to and beyond the breaking point.

Marx has something vitally important to say with his theory of value. Critics of capitalism, like the Occupy movement, who have not developed a fully fledged understanding of the economy, are easily dismissed as good-hearted but naïve dreamers. Such radicals need access to capitalism's greatest critic instead of being left on their own to reinvent the revolutionary wheel.

But access to Marx's economics has effectively been denied to all in academia throughout the developed world. Marxist economists do exist, but what is called "Marxian economics" today differs in crucial respects from Marx's own economics. In particular, the Marxist economists of our day themselves promulgate and enforce the notion that Marx's theory of value, in the form in which he put it forward, is not a logically consistent theory. But if it is not consistent, it is not a viable way to understand our world.

The publication of Paul M. Sweezy's (1970) book, *The Theory of Capitalist Development,* in 1942 was perhaps the key moment in this transformation of Marxian economics into its opposite. But why did this transformation occur? First, Marxist economists copied a number of methodological practices from what was a self-confident and quickly growing mainstream of the economics profession. Crucially, they copied the mainstream's simultaneous general equilibrium approach, which, as we shall explain below, leads to a *physicalist* concept of value.

Second, they copied a number of unscientific academic practices that were, and still are, prevalent in social science in general and economics in particular. These included an inbuilt preference for novelty and uniqueness for its own sake (to obtain PhDs and publish in journals), buttressed by a cavalier attitude toward previous writers in their field—that is, those whose work preceded the latest fashions and fads. Economics departments do not require their students to take courses in the history of economic thought; this has long been the normal state of affairs. Any great economist unlucky enough to be dead is deemed to be worthy of study only insofar as the current generation can improvise on and "improve" them in diverse ways.

In the general equilibrium approach that Marxist economists adopted as their own, prices are solved for "simultaneously." That is, the prices of inputs into production and the prices of the outputs that are produced are set equal to one another. This leads to a physicalist concept of value because, when inputs and outputs are valued simultaneously, it turns out that one needs no information other than the physical quantities of inputs (including the goods that workers consume) and the physical quantities of outputs to determine all goods' relative prices and values, as well as the profit rate.

The basic picture of the economy that emerges is that we start with so many things, then use them in production, and end up with more things. Profit is conceived of as the difference between these two sets of things—*physical* surplus. This leads naturally to the following conclusion: improvements in technology that increase the surplus of things, relative to the amount of things used as inputs, raise the profit rate. This theorem was put forward by Nobuo Okishio (1961), a Japanese Marxist economist. But it flies in the face of what Marx (1973: 748 and 1991b: 104) called the "most important law" of political economy, the tendency for labor-saving technology to depress the profit rate. Because of this tendency, economic crises that restore the profit rate are inevitably needed under capitalism.

If Marxist economists could accept the Okishio theorem, then their work would cease to have a revolutionary edge, as the theorem implies that there is potentially always plenty to go round under capitalism. Workers should let the capitalists (helped by their Keynesian-inspired industrial planning governments) invest lots of the surplus to ensure a rosy future for all. The only thing that is at stake politically is how the fruits of success are distributed. But how can one call oneself a *Marxist* economist while working within a physicalist framework whose concepts and results are so different from Marx's?

To answer this question, the Marxist economists had to find a justification for their embrace of physicalism, and the justification could not be that they wanted an approach that is close to that of the rest of the economics department, lacking any genuine revolutionary edge. They had to present physicalism as being true to the "spirit" of Marx, appearances to the contrary notwithstanding. They argued that Marx's value theory is demonstrably wrong and inconsistent, but that its essential conclusions are rescued when his arguments are reformulated along physicalist lines. What Marx *wanted* to say is therefore better captured by their own models than by what Marx *actually* said.

"CORRECTING" MARX

Conveniently for this project, Marx's key "error" had been spotted and "corrected" in a physicalist manner by Ladislaus von Bortkiewicz (a non-Marxist economist) at the beginning of the twentieth century. What was at issue, above all, is whether workers' surplus labor is really the exclusive source of surplus-value. In light of Marx's "error," the answer seems to be "no"; but Sweezy and later commentators argued that, in the course of correcting Marx, Bortkiewicz had actually vindicated his exploitation theory of profit.

What is the supposed error and how was it supposedly corrected?

In volume 3 of *Capital*, Marx sought to explain a phenomenon that seems incompatible with his value theory: because competition among capitalists tends to equalize rates of profit, different capitalists who invest the same amount of money tend to obtain the same amount of profit. This seems to contradict an implication of Marx's theory that workers' labor is the sole source of new value: the amount of surplus-value produced is relatively greater in industries that employ a relatively large number of workers than in industries that employ relatively large amounts of machinery and other means of production. Marx resolved the apparent contradiction by arguing that, although prices and profits in each industry differ from the corresponding amounts of value and surplus-value that are produced, the differences cancel out. When the economy is considered as a whole,

- total profit equals the total surplus-value extracted from workers (this is Marx's exploitation theory of profit)
- the total price of commodities equals the total value of those commodities
- the aggregate profit rate based on profit equals the aggregate profit rate based on surplus-value

However, Bortkiewicz (1952: 9) claimed that Marx's solution produced an imaginary disequilibrium in the economy, and that this "proved that we would involve ourselves in internal contradictions by deducing prices from values in the way in which this is done by Marx." The root of Marx's supposed error was that the prices of his inputs differed from the prices of his outputs.[3]

Bortkiewicz went on to "correct" Marx by valuing inputs and outputs simultaneously. His values of his inputs equal the values of his outputs, and the prices of his inputs equal the prices of his outputs. Yet in Bortkiewicz's supposedly correct account, the numbers no longer add up. Only one of Marx's three aggregate equalities (the first or the second, but never the third) can hold true. Bortkiewicz's inability to obtain all three aggregate equalities is a consequence of the fact that his procedure, unlike Marx's, splits values and prices into two distinct systems. The fact that Bortkiewicz's revision failed to show the main thing that Marx had tried to show might well have been understood as a signal that his interpretation of Marx's argument was defective. Yet that is not how the Marxist economists understood it. Bortkiewicz's failure to obtain all of the aggregate equalities was instead regarded as one more proof that Marx's own theory of value was inconsistent or wrong!

After Sweezy endorsed and publicized it, Bortkiewicz's solution or slight variations of it became the standard interpretation of Marx's value theory.

The variations were also simultaneist and dualist. That is, input and output prices (and values) were determined simultaneously, and values and prices were held apart in two different systems. In the 1980s, the New Interpretation and simultaneous single-system interpretations appeared. They dropped the dualistic approach to price and value but retained simultaneism.

THE "FUNDAMENTAL MARXIAN THEOREM" AND KLIMAN'S CRITIQUE

After ditching Marx's value theory, Marxist economists needed to stress their link with Marx—how else could they continue to call their work Marxist? Once again, Okishio provided an answer. His answer became widely known in the West in 1973, when Michio Morishima (1973) publicized it and named it the Fundamental Marxian Theorem (FMT). Never mind that the numbers don't add up, Okishio argued. It's not important that total price fails to equal total value or that total profit fails to equal total surplus-value. What's important is that total profit is *positive* if, and only if, workers perform a *positive* amount of surplus labor and thereby create a positive amount of surplus-value. Nothing more is needed to confirm Marx's theory that surplus labor is the exclusive source of profit.

The purpose of Okishio's FMT was therefore to prove that the simultaneist and dualistic model inherited from Bortkiewicz does indeed yield the conclusion that profit is positive if and only if surplus labor is positive—not only in certain instances, but in general. The link between Marxian economics and Marx was evidently now secure. And the task for students of Marxist economics was clear: understand where Marx went wrong and move forward, following the physicalist norms and methods of Marxian economics.

The strategy employed by Marxist economics had an inevitable limitation. Some people might not be particularly interested in becoming part of the "Marxian economics" tradition. They might be more interested in understanding and learning from Marx's work, and they might recognize how dissimilar his own theory was from what Bortkiewicz and his successors had turned it into. And if, upon further investigation, they found that there was a way to interpret Marx such that his results followed from his premises, without any inconsistency, then the notion that Marx's logical errors compel us to adopt the inherited "Marxist approach," and abandon his actual approach, would be exposed as a myth.

A number of authors (e.g., Ernst 1982; Kliman and McGlone 1988; Giussani 1991–1992; Freeman and Carchedi 1996; and Maldonado-Filho 1997) independently came to the conclusion that "Marxist economics" did indeed have little to do with Marx's own work. Their temporal single-system interpretation (TSSI) of Marx's value theory finally freed it from all false allegations of inconsistency.[4] Marx's central conclusions do consistently follow from his premises.

Andrew Kliman's 2001 paper—republished as chapter 2 of the present volume—is a key part of this attempt to reclaim Marx's theory of value and have the study of Marx's economics conform to scientific norms. His paper demonstrated that neither Okishio's FMT nor the FMTs of more recent simultaneist interpretations actually confirm Marx's conclusion that surplus labor is the exclusive source of profit. The FMTs *seem* to succeed only because their authors do not consider all possible cases. They impose restrictions on the problem (e.g., they restrict their investigation to situations in which there is always a positive physical surplus or positive physical net product of every good). As a result, they consider only a subset of the logically possible cases.

In the cases they choose to consider, profit is positive when surplus labor is positive and profit is negative when surplus labor is negative. But this leaves open the possibility that, in other logically possible cases that have not been considered, profit is negative although surplus labor is positive (which means that surplus labor is not sufficient for profit to exist) and/or profit is positive although surplus labor is negative (which means that surplus labor is not necessary for profit to exist). Kliman showed that these kinds of cases do indeed exist. But if surplus labor is not sufficient for profit, something more is needed in order for profit to arise, so it is not the *exclusive* source of profit. And if surplus labor is not necessary for profit, profit can arise even in the absence of surplus labor, so again, it is not the *exclusive* source of profit. It follows that none of the simultaneist interpretations of Marx's theory are compatible with his exploitation theory of profit.

In contrast, Kliman went on to argue, the TSSI of Marx does ensure that the existence of workers' surplus labor is both necessary and sufficient for profit to exist. The TSSI does not require any restrictions that enable it to sweep "perverse" cases under the rug. In particular, because it is not a physicalist interpretation—that is, because its values and prices are not determined by physical quantities—it does not require any of the restrictions on physical surpluses or physical net products that are part and parcel of simultaneist FMTs.

These results are no trick; Kliman did not falsely represent other Marxist approaches. In contrast to the TSSI, the simultaneist FMTs do not successfully provide the link to Marx's exploitation theory of profit that they claim to provide. Kliman's paper thus supports and forms an important part of the TSSI's scientific claim to be an interpretation of Marx's value theory that is superior to the simultaneous interpretations.

THE CRITICS' RESPONSES

The chapters that follow Kliman's paper consist of critical responses to it written by Mohun and Veneziani—at first separately, then as co-authors—as well as counterresponses by Kliman and Freeman. The main importance of the contributions by Mohun and Veneziani is that they show how the "Marxian economics" orthodoxy responded to a fact that was inconvenient to them, namely the fact that simultaneist interpretations had been shown to be incompatible with Marx's theory of profit. Although the issue of compatibility had been the central focus of both Okishio's FMT and Kliman's critique, Mohun and Veneziani's contributions serve to sweep this crucial issue under the rug.

For instance, Veneziani's initial contribution to this debate—a section of a longer paper that is republished here in chapter 5—managed to circumvent the incompatibility issue entirely. He referred to a key example of Kliman's as a "trivially true, and rather uninteresting, algebraic statement that there are arbitrary combinations of the variables such that $\Pi_t > 0$ while $S_t < 0$ [profit is positive while surplus labor is negative], and vice versa." The *implication* of this demonstration is that simultaneist interpretations fail to confirm Marx's theory of profit, but Veneziani refrained from evaluating it as a demonstration of that fact, instead dismissing it as "uninteresting"!

To the extent that Mohun and Veneziani discussed the incompatibility issue at all, they argued that cases in which profit is negative while surplus labor is positive (or vice versa) had not been demonstrated to be what Mohun called "economically possible." When Kliman then provided such a demonstration (chapter 4 of the present volume), the goalpost was moved—the cases now had to be not just economically *possible,* but "empirically *plausible*" (emphasis added) as well, and Mohun and Veneziani left it to "the interested reader" to decide whether Kliman had satisfied this additional demand! Freeman and Kliman's objection to this whole line of argument was that Mohun and Veneziani were ignoring the logical point at stake: a theorem such as "surplus labor is sufficient for profit to exist"

> is true only if it holds universally, i.e., only if no *logically possible* exceptions exist. (Whether the exceptions are "economically possible" is irrelevant. After all, most sufficiency theorems have nothing to do with economics.) . . . To suggest that the theorem does hold true once one ignores the inconvenient ("arbitrary") exceptions is to commit a grave offense against logic.

Mohun and Veneziani never addressed this objection.

The main way in which they tried to get out from under the incompatibility critique was to resort to the "ad hominem tu quoque," or "you too," fallacy. In other words, they argued that the TSSI was also unable to "replicate" Marx's results in the general case (i.e., without any exceptions). This is a logical fallacy since, even if we assume that Mohun and Veneziani were right, this would do nothing to nullify the fact that simultaneist interpretations are incompatible with Marx.

But the point of their line of argument was to find a way to get this issue off the table. They clearly disliked being compelled to evaluate different interpretations of Marx in terms of their adequacy *as interpretations*. They wanted to evaluate them in terms of their merits as "contemporary theory for today," as Mohun put it. And if the TSSI could be shown to be just as poor as simultaneist interpretations at replicating Marx, then evaluation of different interpretations would have to invoke some such alternative criterion. This appears to reflect the attitudes I discussed above, which Marxian economists had imported from the mainstream of the profession—the preference for novelty and uniqueness and the cavalier attitude toward previous writers.

Mohun and Veneziani went to great lengths in their efforts to show that the TSSI is no better than simultaneist interpretations at replicating Marx's results. They had to go to great lengths because their attempts were shown again and again to be unsuccessful. For example, in Mohun's initial paper—republished here in chapter 3—an equation (3.26) is derived in order to show that, if the "price of the net product" is negative, then the TSSI implies that profit is negative although surplus labor is positive. If this were true, the TSSI would fail to replicate Marx for the exact same reason that the New Interpretation and simultaneist single-system interpretations fail. Yet the equation in question has nothing to do with the price of the net product, and Kliman and Freeman later showed that the TSSI replicates Marx's theory of profit even if the price of the net product is negative.

In another instance, Mohun and Veneziani tried to demonstrate that the temporalist monetary expression of labor-time (MELT) can be negative.[5] (If that were true, it would mean that the TSSI fails to replicate Marx's theory of profit, since a negative MELT implies that profit is negative, even though workers perform surplus labor.) They took an equation of Kliman and Freeman's that pertains to the case in which the price of the net product is negative, assumed that the MELT is constant in this case, and arrived at the conclusion that the MELT is negative as well. But this exercise simply does not demonstrate that the MELT can be negative. It merely tells us that, *if* the MELT were constant, *then* it would also be negative. Mohun and Veneziani needed to prove that the MELT could be constant in the case they considered, but instead, they merely assumed it. In other words, their argument begs the question.

There are many other examples like these. It would be tedious to review them all. Suffice it to say that the efforts to show that the TSSI fails to replicate Marx's theory of profit in the general case became increasingly strained and nitpicky. At one point, Mohun and Veneziani went so far as to claim that it had not been shown that the TSSI's FMT holds true in the general case because it would not hold true if the total price of all commodities were zero, and Kliman and Freeman had supposedly not shown that this is impossible!

Mohun and Veneziani's contributions also repeatedly employed several methods of arguing that I regard as contrary to scholarly norms.[6] Space does not allow me to list all the instances in which these methods are used, so please keep the general categories in mind as you read the chapters yourself.

1. *Dismissive language* was used to suggest that the TSSI of Marx is odd and extremist, definitely something to avoid. For example, Mohun warned that "*value is being defined [by the TSSI] differently from how it is conventionally understood* (emphasis in original), and he suggested that the very existence of this difference might be grounds for rejecting the TSSI as meaningless: "Proponents of the interpretation that value and price systems are distinct and different will not be able to attribute any meaning to [the TSSI's] aggregate proportionalities" between the value and the price of constant and variable capital. He and Veneziani also dismissed Freeman and Kliman's concerns that their attempts to discredit the TSSI served to "rule Marx himself out of court while keeping it free for his Marxist economist critics," writing that these and similar statements were "merely polemical tropes."
2. *Technical jargon* was used to make what was being said seem reasonable when it would not seem so reasonable if it were expressed in simple terms. (This is another practice common among mainstream economics.) The way in which Mohun and Venenziani argued that Kliman and Freeman failed to show that the total price of all commodities could not be zero is an example of this strategy: "That p and x are semi-positive vectors does not imply that their product P is strictly positive."
3. *Disguised concessions*. When points were conceded, the concessions were almost always tucked inside damning criticisms that made them easy to miss. For instance, Veneziani wrote that "by showing that all [of] Marx's propositions are *assumed* to be correct, the analysis of TSS models suggests that, *as an interpretation of Marx's theory*, the TSS approach is not particularly enlightening, even though, unsurprisingly, it 'corresponds to the original in a way that others do not.'" This sentence seems to be his way of conceding that the TSSI is superior—"as an interpretation of Marx's theory"—because it is able to replicate Marx's theory in cases in which simultaneist interpretations cannot.
4. *Moving the goalposts*. Mohun and Veneziani's demand for "empirically plausible" counterexamples on top of Mohun's demand for "economically possible" counterexamples is one example of this strategy. In addition,

after Freeman and Kliman had disposed of objections they had raised, they frequently responded just by making new objections.

5. *Denial* that claims have been refuted and arguments have been shown to be flawed. The foremost example of this strategy appears in Mohun and Veneziani's final contribution: "All of our previous criticisms stand and need not be reiterated." Their multiple errors and misrepresentations, only a few of which I have discussed here, evidently count for nothing at all!
6. *Methodological monism*. This is the main vice imported from mainstream economics. According to standard scientific norms, theories should be judged on the basis of their empirical accuracy and logical consistency. Yet almost all of economics would be relegated to the dustbin if these norms were applied, so economists typically defend their turf and instead judge theories on the basis of whether they conform to "proper" *methodo*logical norms—that is, their own particular norms. Mohun and Veneziani's contributions display their commitment to methodological monism at almost every turn. Every time that they object that some example or assumption is arbitrary, or that some aspect of the TSSI is incoherent, underdetermined, undefined, inconsistent, uninteresting, trivial, not compelling, not a "reproducible solution," an "infinite regress," and so on, they are merely insisting that "it's my way or the highway." When Marx's value theory is understood in a way that makes it internally consistent—that is, when it is understood as the TSSI understands it—it is just too different from Marxian economics. It must therefore be rejected and dismissed.

UNACCEPTABLE ACADEMIC PRACTICES

In a paper republished here as chapter 9, Kliman and Freeman provide an explanation for all this unscientific practice, this rushing into print with any criticisms of the TSSI, irrespective of their accuracy or relevance. Their paper seeks to explain why Veneziani's (2004) article was published in *Metroeconomica* despite being filled with what Kliman and Freeman call "so many unrelated mistakes." They are "unwilling to believe that Veneziani set out to do a hatchet job on Marx and the TSSI, or that *Metroeconomica* . . . intended to promote one." Instead, they suggest that the problem is that the author and the journal "employed *truthiness*"—truth that comes from the gut, not from the head—"as their standard of evaluation." Veneziani's paper told them what their guts had told them all along: Marx was internally inconsistent and the contrary findings of the TSSI are the result of trickery and/or error. "And, in order to decide whether [Veneziani's paper] really [was] the long-awaited proof, they appeal[ed] to their guts" {all quotes in the paragraph appear on pp. 80–81 of this book}."

Consider also the review procedures employed by *Capital & Class*, the journal in which chapters 2, 3, 6, 7, and 8 of the present volume were first published. It is clear from Kliman's initial contribution that he was obliged to respond to objections of critical referees. That is all well and good. So why were no critical referees assigned to review Mohun's response to Kliman, which seriously misrepresents the TSSI and is replete with mistakes? No critical referee—indeed, no competent referee other than one whose standards of truth come from the gut rather than the head—would have allowed Mohun's response to be published until it was extensively revised.

This is no trivial matter. I directly suffered as a result of this piece. It was used as an unscientific gatekeeper.

In 2005, I completed my PhD dissertation at the University of London under the supervision of Lord Meghnad Desai. I am not claiming that my dissertation changed the world; indeed, I have moved on from its treatment of rentiers and the financial system. But it was a high-quality piece of economics, as indicated by the fact that it was accepted as a PhD dissertation. Yet when I submitted a summary of it to the *Cambridge Journal of Economics* (as Lord Desai had advised), it was summarily rejected. One reviewer simply said that it adhered to the TSSI and that the TSSI was of no interest. The other reviewer laid out the "issues" that Mohun's response to Kliman had raised, and stipulated that these issues had to be specifically addressed before anything that adhered to the TSSI could be accepted, even though my paper was on a quite different topic.

So my paper was rejected by appealing to false claims and invalid arguments that should have never been published in the first place. I was a young economist in need of good publications as much as anyone else, but my research efforts and my ability to attract funding to focus on my research were held back for unscientific reasons. Not only did I have to contend with the unscientific nature of the mainstream of economics; I had to somehow overcome the unscientific practices of the guardians of Marxist orthodoxy as well.

Sometime later, I joined the editorial board of *Capital & Class* specifically to address the issue of Kliman's right to reply to Mohun's piece. Thankfully, *Capital & Class* is the journal of the Conference of Socialist Economists (CSE), which uncharacteristically chooses its editorial board in a democratic matter. So I attended the annual general meeting of the CSE to make my case. I was elected.

I then attended an editorial board meeting and explained my view of the matter. What had happened is that a Marxian economist serving as an anonymous reviewer had not liked Kliman rocking the Marxist boat in the first place. But since he had succeeded in doing so, Mohun attempted to put this upstart TSSI in its place. Because no one on the *Capital & Class* editorial board had the expertise needed to recognize that Mohun's paper was marred by serious errors, they did not accept that Kliman should be granted the right of reply. (Yet the reason no one had the needed expertise is that Freeman resigned from the editorial board over this issue just before I joined it. I do not know why the editorial board decided not to follow Freeman's expert recommendation.)

So I explained to the editorial board that Mohun's paper was marred by serious errors. No one attempted to argue against any of the points I raised. Kliman was granted the right of reply, which he exercised with the help of Freeman. All members of the editorial board had full access to this piece during the review process, and they were able to discuss it at the editorial board before it was accepted and published.

The sad story now gets a lot worse. A response to Kliman and Freeman, co-authored by Mohun and Veneziani, was subsequently published in *Capital & Class*. But in this instance, the review process was far from open and transparent. A minority on the editorial board received Mohun and Veneziani's response, kept its existence secret from the other editorial board members, including me, and then approved it secretly themselves, in violation of editorial board policy and practice. So this response was published, but only because of the quite exceptional behavior of a minority of editorial board members!

I first became aware of their response when I received my copy of *Capital & Class* in the mail. I was flabbergasted. I immediately registered my disgust by e-mail and turned up at the next editorial board meeting, fully prepared to go through all of Mohun and Veneziani's arguments and point out that no reasonably informed reviewer would ever have agreed to publish this very inaccurate piece.

No one on the editorial board argued against any of my points as to why the piece was inaccurate and should not have been published. Nor did they offer any explanation as to why the existence of Mohun and Veneziani's response had been kept secret or why their piece was "reviewed" in such an underhanded and unscholarly way. All accepted that it had been plainly wrong for the editorial board members in question to act in this way, and all agreed that Kliman and Freeman should have the right to reply to Mohun and Veneziani as soon as possible.

The editorial board members responsible for this unacceptable behavior have never apologized to me for their actions. Yet at least no one has ever tried to do anything like that again!

HOW DEBATE SHOULD BE CONDUCTED

How can such unscholarly behavior be halted? As Kliman and Freeman argued, "[t]he only way to prevent those who control the journals—and, behind them, those who fund the graduate schools—from dictating what is 'true' and 'false,' 'natural' and 'arbitrary,' is to accept and *consistently apply* a clear, evidence-based criterion of decidability." At the end of their final contribution to this debate (republished here as chapter 11), they followed this up with a detailed set of rules that scholarly debate should follow, to ensure that the debate proceeds in a scientific manner and makes progress. I recommend these rules to you, and I aspire to live by them myself.

The cause of knowledge is not well served by proceeding without rules that separate sound from unsound arguments, enable unpopular ideas and views to be heard, and ensure that they are engaged with in a serious fashion. This is not difficult to understand. What does need to be stressed is that the cause of *pluralism* is likewise not well served by proceeding without such rules, letting everyone say whatever they want in "their own" journals and on "their own" blogs and letting the chips fall where they may. The debate I have discussed here was conducted in the latter manner, and the results are unenviable. It was no model of pluralism but merely a "parody of pluralism," as Freeman and Kliman put it. "[A] more dominant school of thought [was allowed] to level a host of egregiously incorrect criticisms against a less dominant one, and . . . the latter school [was 'allowed'] to devote much, if not most, of its limited time and resources to defensively replying to this host of unfounded criticisms." The most positive thing I can say about this debate is that we can study it in order to understand how power and privilege are exercised under the guise of scholarship and how debate should *not* be conducted.

The opportunity for Marxists to unite behind Marx in order to explain capitalism's latest economic crisis to those willing to listen has been lost. We can but hope that science will triumph in the end and that, at some point in the future, Marxists will base their work on Marx's theory of value. In the meantime, we must document what is actually going on, leaving a legacy to a hopefully wiser future generation.

NOTES

1. Marx (1990a: 268–69). "Circulation" refers to the exchange of commodities for money followed by the exchange of the money for other commodities.
2. *Hic Rhodus, hic salta*! (Rhodes is here. Leap here!) can be loosely rendered as "put up or shut up."
3. Specifically, Bortkiewicz construed Marx's solution as one in which the prices of inputs and outputs differ because the inputs' prices equal their values while the outputs are sold at prices of production that differ from values.
4. In the TSSI of Marx, the creation of value is temporal, or sequential; production takes time, so inputs into production can potentially have unit prices and values that differ from the unit prices and value of the outputs that later emerge from production.

The interpretation is also a single-system, or non-dualist, interpretation because values and prices are not held apart in different systems; total *value* and surplus-value determine total *price* and profit, while the sum of *value* transferred to products from used-up means of production depends on the *prices* of these means of production at the start of the period of production. (The latter relation between value and price does not imply that value has been redefined to equal price. The TSSI recognizes that, for numerous reasons, such as the tendency of the rate of profit to equalize, the price of a particular commodity will almost always differ from its value.)

5. The MELT is the ratio of the total money price of commodities to the total value of commodities in terms of labor-time. This ratio is implicit in Marx's work, though he never called it the MELT or formulated it in this exact manner. Using the MELT, we can convert value and price variables measured in terms of labor-time into their monetary equivalents, and vice versa. For instance, according to the TSSI, the ratio of the monetary cost of the used-up means of production (at the moment when they entered into the production process) to the MELT (of that moment) is the labor-time equivalent of the constant-capital portion of a commodity's value. Similarly, the ratio of money wages (at the moment when they are advanced) to the MELT (of that moment) is the labor-time equivalent of variable capital.

6. But Mohun and Veneziani's conduct is not the most problematic in this respect. The *Review of Radical Political Economics'* publication of Ajit Sinha's (2009) book review of Kliman (2007) is. Fifteen scholars from around the world published an open letter to the journal, in which they decried its decision to publish a piece that "willful[ly]" contained several "misrepresentations and falsehoods about the work under review" and requested that the journal retract it (Freeman et al. 2010). It refused to do so. Potts (2014), a detailed analysis of these and other problems with Sinha's review, was first submitted to the *Review of Radical Political Economics*. It rejected my article on the grounds that it is not the journal's policy to publish responses to book reviews!

Part I

THE SIMULTANEIST–TEMPORALIST DEBATE

Chapter 2

Simultaneous Valuation vs. the Exploitation Theory of Profit

Andrew J. Kliman

This paper shows that interpretations of Marx's value theory which value inputs and outputs simultaneously imply that surplus-labor is not the sole source of profit—even in the absence of joint production. Contrary results, such as the Fundamental Marxian Theorem, rely crucially on restrictive and implausible conditions that are shown to be unnecessary for reproduction. In contrast, the temporal single-system interpretation conforms to the exploitation theory of profit under completely general conditions.

I. INTRODUCTION

Despite their other differences, all interpretations of Marx's value theory agree that it identifies the exploitation of workers, that is, the extraction of surplus labor, as the sole source of profit. Proponents of the various interpretations, moreover, all claim to have replicated this feature of his value theory. Yet the mathematics of their systems often tells a different story. As I will show, in those systems in which the prices and values of inputs are determined simultaneously with the prices and values of outputs, the extraction of surplus labor is insufficient and, generally, unnecessary for the existence of positive profit. In these "simultaneist" interpretations, then, surplus labor is not the sole source of profit.

It is well known that, when joint products are produced, certain specifications of the standard interpretation are incompatible with Marx's theory of profit (see Steedman 1977).

As section II will show, however, all simultaneist interpretations (not only the standard one) are incompatible with his theory, even in the absence of joint production.[1]

Because theorists have failed to study the problem in a general setting, this incompatibility has not received attention. In some special cases—those in which a positive physical surplus or positive net product of every good is produced in every period—simultaneist interpretations do imply that surplus labor and positive profit go hand in hand. Yet section III will demonstrate that this result cannot be generalized. I will argue, moreover, that these special cases impose conditions that are much more restrictive and less plausible than is usually thought. In particular, economies can easily reproduce themselves physically without satisfying these conditions.

Section IV will show that an alternative, non-simultaneous, interpretation of Marx's value theory does imply that surplus labor is both necessary and sufficient for positive profit, even under the most general conditions. A brief summary and conclusion follow in section V.

Before proceeding, a few methodological comments are in order. At various points, I will note that the attempts to reconcile simultaneous valuation with the exploitation theory of profit rely on unrealistic postulates—positive physical surpluses of all goods, equalized profit rates, and so forth. These comments are *not* intended as criticisms of any economic theory or model for a lack of realism. I take no position here on whether a theory's postulates should be realistic. The reason I will discuss realism is instead simply to demonstrate that simultaneist definitions imply that surplus labor is not necessary or sufficient for profit to exist in the real world in which we live. If these demonstrations are valid, they are valid even if it is appropriate for formal theories to employ unrealistic postulates, and even if theorems pertaining to imaginary economies are interesting and useful.

The point is that, whether or not it is appropriate to employ unrealistic postulates for other purposes, it would be logically impermissible to use them to draw deductive inferences about real-world situations. Conclusions that are derived validly from a postulated world may or may not hold in the real world. To determine whether they do hold, one can sometimes test the conclusions empirically. That, however, is impossible in this case. Empirical evidence can tell us whether surplus labor and profit in fact coexist. It cannot tell us whether simultaneous valuation is compatible with the theory that they coexist because surplus labor is *necessary and sufficient* for profit to exist. This question can only be answered deductively, by ascertaining whether there exist conditions under which simultaneous valuation leads to the contrary conclusion. It is to this task that I now turn.

II. THE INCOMPATIBILITY

A. The Fundamental Marxian Theorem

In the standard interpretation of Marx's value theory, distinct price and value systems exist, and the inputs and outputs in each are valued simultaneously. Another distinctive feature of this interpretation is that it construes wages in the price system as the price of the wage goods workers receive, and wages in the value system as the value of these wage goods.

Employing this interpretation, Okishio (1993a, 1993b) discovered a set of theorems that Morishima (1973) later dubbed the "fundamental Marxian theorem" (FMT). The FMT is often said to have shown that surplus labor is necessary and sufficient for positive profit when no joint products are produced (see, e.g., Howard and King, 1992: 230, 239).

Yet some versions of the FMT hold only if all producers' profit rates are equal in every period. This is a very particular case; if profit rates are only approximately equal, or only equalized over a span of time longer than one period (two days instead of one, for instance), these versions of the FMT no longer hold. The analysis below considers instead the *general versions* of the FMT (e.g., Okishio 1993a: 33; Okishio 1993b: 80–81; Roemer 1981: 47–50), which prove that the theorem holds for any set of positive *market prices*, not just for "normal" prices. Yet these versions of the FMT rely crucially on an equally restrictive condition: in every period, a positive physical surplus of every good must be produced.

Physical surplus is output net of both consumed inputs and workers' consumption, and, in this interpretation, profit is simply the vector of physical surpluses valued at end-of-period (replacement) prices. Using the usual input-output notation,[2] the column vector of physical surpluses is $\varphi = (I - A - b\ell)x$, so profit is

$$\pi = p\varphi \tag{2.1}$$

where p is a row vector of unit market prices. Unit values are defined as the row vector of vertically integrated labor coefficients λ, so surplus labor, s, is the living labor extracted minus the value of wage goods: $s = \ell x - \lambda b\ell x$. But since $\lambda = \ell(I - A)^{-1}$, it follows that $\ell = \lambda(I - A)$ and thus that $\ell x = \lambda(I - A)x$. Surplus labor can thus be expressed as $s = \lambda(I - A)x - \lambda b\ell x = \lambda(I - A - b\ell)x$, or simply as

$$s = \lambda\varphi \tag{2.2}$$

In the standard interpretation, then, profit and surplus labor are simply the same vector of physical surpluses valued in two different ways. When all elements of φ are positive, that is, when a positive physical surplus of every use-value is produced, it is obvious that the FMT holds. Both π and s must then be positive, given only that no prices or values are negative and that some of both are positive. Because all physical surpluses are positive, it does not matter that prices and values differ, or by how much; a set of strictly positive physical surpluses valued according to either must be positive.

It is, however, equally obvious that the FMT fails to hold unless all physical surpluses are positive. Once there is a negative physical surplus of some good, it matters that values and prices differ. The total "worth" of the physical surplus vector can then be negative when valued at market prices and positive when valued at values, or vice versa.[3] Assume, for instance, a two-good economy, in which $\varphi_1 = -1$ and $\varphi_2 = 2$. If $\lambda_1 = 19$, $\lambda_2 = 10$, $p_1 = 21$, and $p_2 = 10$, then $s = 19(-1) + 10 \cdot 2 = 1$ but $\pi = 21(-1) + 10 \cdot 2 = -1$. If, however, $\lambda_1 = 21$ and $p_1 = 19$, then $s = -1$ but $\pi = 1$. This proves that, under the standard interpretation, surplus labor is neither sufficient nor necessary for profit to exist.

Although the prices in this example were indeed chosen arbitrarily, not derived from other conditions, the proof is valid nonetheless. Again, the general versions of the FMT under consideration examine the relation between profit and surplus labor under all possible market prices, and the market prices of the above example are certainly possible ones.

B. The "New Interpretation" and Simultaneous Single-System Interpretations

During the past two decades, other simultaneist interpretations of Marx's value theory have also emerged. One key difference between the standard interpretation, on one hand, and both the "New Interpretation" (e.g., Duménil 1983; Foley 1982) and the simultaneous single-system interpretations (e.g., Lee 1993; Moseley 1993), on the other, concerns their definitions of wages and surplus labor.

Rather than defining wages as the price or value of wage goods, the latter interpretations construe wages as the sum of money paid to workers. To assess whether surplus labor is extracted, money wages are converted into the equivalent sum of labor-time (or living labor is converted into a monetary equivalent). The ratio of the aggregate net product, $(I - A)x$, valued at end-of-period (replacement) prices, to living labor,

$$\sigma = \frac{p(I - A)x}{\ell x} \tag{2.3}$$

is used to convert monetary sums into labor-time sums. I call this ratio σ to indicate the "simultaneist monetary expression of labor-time." It is held to be the ratio between the monetary and labor-time measures of value added.

In these interpretations, profit is thus defined as the vector of physical net products, valued at end-of-period prices, minus the wage bill:

$$\pi = p(I - A)x - w\ell x \tag{2.4}$$

where w is the money wage per unit of living labor extracted, and surplus labor is defined as living labor minus the labor-time equivalent of the money wage:

$$s = \ell x - \left(\frac{1}{\sigma}\right)w\ell x \tag{2.5}$$

Multiplication of (2.5) by σ yields $\sigma s = \sigma\ell x - w\ell x = p(I - A)x - w\ell x$, or, equivalently,

$$\pi = \sigma s \tag{2.6}$$

This result has led proponents of the "New" and simultaneous single-system interpretations to claim that they yield an exact correspondence between surplus-value and profit. Not only is surplus labor necessary and sufficient for positive profit, but the magnitudes of surplus labor and profit are strictly proportional.

Yet it simply does not follow from this proportionality that surplus labor is sufficient for positive profit. Indeed, it is not sufficient. Equation (2.3) implies that, if the net product valued at end-of-period market prices is negative, then so is σ. Profit is therefore negative although surplus labor is positive.

Unless the net products of all goods are non-negative, the aggregate price of the net product, and thus σ, can be negative, even in highly productive economies. Imagine that net products of almost all goods are positive and large, and only a few are slightly negative. If the prices of the latter group are sufficiently high, the aggregate price of the net product will be negative. Thus, an economy that would have a positive σ under certain prices could have a negative σ under different prices. Even a slight change in prices could lead to such a reversal.

A couple of other perverse implications of these interpretations are noteworthy. When σ is negative, equation (2.5) implies that a fall in the money wage rate will lead to a fall, rather than a rise, in the amount of surplus labor extracted. As an anonymous referee has noted, moreover, necessary labor (the labor-time equivalent of money wages) is defined here as $(1/\sigma)w\ell x$, so it is negative when σ is negative. Workers supposedly produce an equivalent of their wages in less than no time! No oddity of the labor market or technology underlies this result—workers' wages and the amount of work needed to reproduce their means of subsistence are both positive, and necessary labor might well be positive if only relative prices were different.

All of these paradoxes disclose a serious conceptual flaw in the claim that the monetary expression of the value added by living labor can be measured by the price of the net product.[4]

The proportionality of surplus labor and profit also fails to imply that surplus labor is necessary for profit to exist. As Dmitriev (1974) discovered, if we imagine a fully automated economy that produces a positive net product of all goods—and if, in addition, prices in such an economy exist and are positive—then profit as defined above is positive, even though no labor or surplus labor is extracted.

Apart from this case, the interpretations in question do imply that, when the price of the net product happens to be positive, positive profit and positive surplus labor will coexist. The relevant issue, however, is not *whether* they coexist, but *why*. Unless a theory denies that profit could be positive if no human labor were employed—and those under consideration seem not to do so—then we must conclude that it admits the possibility of positive profit without surplus labor. Putting the same point differently, the only way to refute Dmitriev's challenge to Marx's theory of profit is to deny that the physical surplus of a fully automated economy is effectively the same thing as profit under capitalism. This requires that one deny either that the price of the physical surplus constitutes profit, or that this surplus could have a positive price under complete automation. The definitions of profit given above do not do so.

III. REPRODUCTION

Perhaps the main reason that the obvious points made in section II have not received attention is that theorists have been interested in economies that are able to reproduce themselves physically. Negative physical surpluses or net products have been thought to imply an economy incapable of long-run reproduction, and have therefore been ignored.

Yet the appeal to physical reproducibility is either an evasion of the issue at hand or the result of a logical fallacy. Assume for the sake of argument that *if* an economy is capable of reproduction, *then* surplus labor and profit as defined in the simultaneist models are both positive (or both negative or zero). It does not follow that surplus labor is either necessary or sufficient for positive profit. Analogously, *if* I am a man, *then* I am both male and adult. Yet not all males are adults, nor are all adults males.

In any case, it is simply not true that long-run reproduction requires positive physical surpluses or net products of all goods. All actual economies produce some negative net products, and therefore negative physical surpluses, because some goods (386 computers, for instance) are used as inputs without being reproduced. The economies sustain themselves and even grow by producing, instead, similar but not identical goods (586 computers).[5] Yet, as was noted above, simultaneist theorems that surplus labor is sufficient for positive profit do require the postulate that all net products are positive. Since this postulate is violated in every actual economy, it follows that the theorems do not apply to the real world.[6]

It is impossible, moreover, for simultaneists to construct comparable theorems to cover real-world situations, because simultaneous valuation is impossible when some inputs are not reproduced as outputs. To compute the aggregate price of the net product, one takes the gross price of the outputs and subtracts the *replacement* cost of the inputs, that is, the vector of inputs pre-multiplied by their end-of-period prices. Yet inputs that have been used up without being reproduced do not have end-of-period prices, so this is impossible.

One could, of course, use their prices when they entered production, but then one would not be valuing inputs and outputs simultaneously. The only other alternative is to impute end-of-period prices to the inputs by trying to establish an equivalence between them and goods that have replaced them as outputs. Yet any attempt to homogenize heterogeneous things is not only conceptually dubious; it also leads to arbitrary results. One estimate may conclude that the price of the aggregate net product is positive, while another, even slightly different, estimate may conclude that it is negative. The truth of a theorem that surplus labor is necessary and/or sufficient for positive "profit" would then depend on the idiosyncrasies of the estimators!

Yet even if we ignore non-reproduced inputs, it is very probable that actual economies, even highly productive ones that do reproduce themselves over time, fail to satisfy the received definition of "reproducibility" (e.g., Roemer 1981: 19). This definition requires economies to produce non-negative physical surpluses of all goods *in each and every period*. As I shall show presently, however, reproducibility actually requires only that non-negative surpluses be produced over some longer time span (and that initial reserve stocks be of sufficient size).

Roemer (1981: 19) first states that reproduction requires that no stock be run down to zero. He notes correctly that one way of "assuring" this—that is, one *sufficient* condition for reproducibility—is to postulate that all physical surpluses are non-negative in every period. Yet immediately thereafter, he pronounces this postulate a "requirement" for reproducibility—that is, a necessary condition. It is easy to show that this is incorrect.

Table 2.1 depicts a two-good economy in which the production of each good requires 0.4 units of both goods. Due to fluctuations in output levels, a negative net product (and thus physical surplus) of good A is produced during the first hour, and a negative net product of B is produced during the second. Over the course of these two periods, however, 25 percent more of each good is produced than is used up. Given an initial reserve stock of A of at least one unit, there is no technological barrier to this economy's expanded reproduction.

Even though some net products are negative, such an economy satisfies the Hawkins-Simon conditions. In essence, these conditions define a self-sustaining economy as one in which all net products would be positive at some levels of output. And all net products would be positive here if, say, fifteen units of each good were produced during each period.

Since fifteen units of each good are indeed produced over two hours, it is possible to include this case among those in which all physical surpluses are non-negative in every period. One needs only to redefine the length of a period as two hours instead of one. Yet once one does so, simultaneist theorems that surplus labor is necessary and sufficient for positive profit will become false. Market prices may change during the lengthened period in such a way that, for instance, surplus labor is extracted in both subperiods, but profit is negative in each of them and therefore over the lengthened period as a whole.[7] (In the present example, this would occur if the relative price of good A were sufficiently high during the first hour and sufficiently low during the second.)

The simultaneist theorems are therefore true only if a non-negative surplus of each good is produced in each and every period, *no matter how short the period*. A period in this context can be no longer than the length of time during which prices remain constant; but they can change from one instant to the next. The shorter the period, however, the less likely it is that all physical surpluses will be positive. Over very short periods, it is almost inconceivable that this is the case. Many factories and offices shut down overnight, but night in one part of the world is midday in another. Some business is

Table 2.1

	First Hour			*Second Hour*			*Two-Hour Period*		
Sector	*Input of A*	*Input of B*	*Output*	*Input of A*	*Input of B*	*Output*	*Input of A*	*Input of B*	*Output*
A	2	2	5	4	4	10	6	6	15
B	4	4	10	2	2	5	6	6	15
Total	6	6		6	6		12	12	

therefore always using up some input that its supplier is not reproducing at that moment. Hence, if the theorems in question are formally true, they fail to apply to the real world, because one of their crucial premises never holds, while if they do apply to it, they are false.

IV. THE TEMPORAL SINGLE-SYSTEM INTERPRETATION

I have shown that surplus labor is not the sole source of profit when inputs and outputs are valued simultaneously. Yet it is also obvious that, under non-simultaneous (temporal) valuation, *nominal* profit can be positive when surplus labor is negative, and vice versa. A sufficiently large rise in the price level during the production period, for instance, can make nominal profit positive although surplus labor is negative. Thus, if there is to be some sense in which surplus labor can be said to be the sole source of profit, it is necessary both that surplus labor and profit be defined in temporal terms and that the definition of "profit" refer to *real* profit.

Yet different methods of adjustment for inflation will yield different measures of real profit. It is therefore impossible to prove or disprove analytically that surplus labor is the sole source of profit, even real profit. The answer will depend upon one's concept of inflation. If the exploitation theory of profit holds under a particular definition of inflation, and one accepts that definition, then one must conclude that surplus labor is the sole source of (real) profit. If one rejects the definition, one must draw the opposite conclusion.

Of the existing interpretations of Marx's value theory, only the temporal single-system interpretation (see, e.g., Ernst 1982; Kliman and McGlone 1988; Giussani 1991–1992; Freeman and Carchedi [eds.] 1996; Maldonado-Filho 1997; Ramos 1997) implies that surplus labor is both necessary and sufficient for real profit to exist, *under completely general conditions*. To demonstrate that the exploitation theory of profit holds under this interpretation, in other words, absolutely *no* restrictive postulates are required. For instance, negative net products can exist and profit rates can be unequal. Production can be a continuous flow, or it can take place with discrete lags between input and output. It is also unnecessary to invoke any of the unrealistic postulates (constant returns to scale, no fixed capital, no joint production, no input substitution or choice of technique, etc.) commonly invoked in input-output literature.

To emphasize this last point, I will discontinue the use of input-output notation and instead define the following economy-wide monetary aggregates. During the period from time t to time $t + 1$, $C(t)$ stands for expenditures on used-up constant capital (materials and depreciation of fixed capital), $V(t)$ is variable capital (the wage bill), and $P(t + 1)$ is the total price of output. In addition, living labor is denoted as $L(t)$ and the "temporalist monetary expression of labor-time" is $\tau(t)$ at time t and $\tau(t+1)$ at $t+1$. This notation implies that production takes one period, yet all of the following relations could be restated in terms of continuous time ($P(t+1)$ would become $P(t) + \mathrm{d}P/\mathrm{d}t$ and $\tau(t+1)$ would become $\tau(t) + \mathrm{d}\tau/\mathrm{d}t$), without affecting any of the results.

Like the newer simultaneist interpretations, the temporal single-system interpretation construes surplus labor as living labor minus the labor-time equivalent of money wages:

$$s = L - \left[\frac{1}{\tau(t)}\right]V \tag{2.7}$$

As measured in labor-time, value added during production is conceived as the difference between the labor-time equivalents of total price and constant capital expenditures, $[1/\tau(t+1)]P$ and $[1/\tau(t)]C$, and this difference is equal to the living labor extracted, since the latter generates all new value. Hence

$$\left[\frac{1}{\tau(t+1)}\right]P - \left[\frac{1}{\tau(t)}\right]C = L \tag{2.8}$$

Nominal profit is $\pi^N = P - C - V$. According to any definition of real profit, however, P must be deflated in order to adjust for changes between times t and $t+1$ in the amount of money that represents one unit of value. Thus

$$\pi^R = \left(\frac{1}{1+i}\right)P - C - V \tag{2.9}$$

According to the temporal single-system interpretation, the rate of inflation is $i = [\tau(t+1) - \tau(t)] / \tau(t)$ (or, in continuous time, $\mathrm{d}\tau/\mathrm{d}t / \tau$), the rate of change in the monetary expression of labor-time. This means that inflation occurs if the same amount of value, as measured in labor-time, is expressed as a greater monetary sum. As I will now show, this is the definition of inflation that the exploitation theory of profit requires.

Multiplying (2.8) by $\tau(t)$ and using this definition, one obtains

$$\left(\frac{\tau(t)}{\tau(t+1)}\right)P = \left(\frac{1}{1+i}\right)P = C + \tau(t)\cdot L$$

Using the last expression in place of the middle one, (2.9) becomes

$$\pi^R = C + \tau(t)\cdot L - \mathrm{C} - \mathrm{V} = \tau(t)\cdot L - V \tag{2.10}$$

or simply

$$\pi^R = \tau(t)s \tag{2.11}$$

This looks very similar to the proportionality between surplus labor and profit that was derived from the newer simultaneist interpretations. Yet whereas σ, the simultaneist monetary expression of labor-time, need not be positive, examination of (2.8) shows that, if C, L, P, and the initial condition $\tau(0)$ are positive and finite, then all subsequent terms of the τ-series must also be positive and finite. The proportionality between surplus labor and real profit, *together* with this result on τ, imply that surplus labor is both necessary and sufficient for real profit to be positive. (According to (2.10), real profit will be zero in Dmitriev's case of fully automated production, since L and V will both be zero. This resolves his paradox.)

I have noted that this result requires that surplus labor and profit be conceived in temporal terms. An anonymous referee disagrees, arguing that τ must be positive, not because it is determined within historical time, but because it is defined in terms of *total* price and value. If τ were instead defined as σ is, in terms of value *added*, it too could be negative. Real profit could thus be negative although surplus labor is positive. Yet this alternative τ would still be determined temporally, so "the introduction of time is irrelevant."

Since it follows from (2.8) that

$$\tau(t+1)=\frac{P}{\left[\frac{1}{\tau(t)}\right]C+L} \tag{2.8'}$$

the referee is correct in noting that τ is the ratio of total money price to total (dead and living) labor. In contrast, her or his alternative τ (converted into my notation) is

$$\tau^{*}(t+1)=\frac{P-(1+i)C}{L} \tag{2.8''}$$

where i is defined in the same way as above. I fully agree that τ^* is the appropriate temporalist counterpart to σ. Both σ and τ^* are ratios of value added in money terms to value added in labor-time terms. Yet here the unit prices of inputs and outputs need not be equal, and nominal value added is adjusted for inflation.

Contrary to the referee's claim, however, τ^* simply *cannot* be negative. The simplest way to show this is to prove that τ, which we already know must be positive, is *identical* to τ^*. Multiplying (2.8') by the denominator of its right-hand side, and recalling that $\tau(t+1)/\tau(t)=1+i$, one obtains $(1 + i)C + \tau(t + 1)\cdot L = P$.

Hence

$$\tau(t+1)=\frac{P-(1+i)C}{L}=\tau^{*}(t+1)$$

The simultaneist monetary expression of labor-time can likewise be written in a manner analogous to (2.8′):

$$\sigma = \frac{p(I-A)x}{\ell x} = \frac{px}{\left(\frac{1}{\sigma}\right)pAx + \ell x}$$

Proponents of the simultaneous single-system interpretations consider the last expression to be the ratio of total money price to total value as measured in terms of labor-time. Whether the monetary expression of labor-time is written as a ratio of totals or as a ratio of values added is therefore irrelevant. Both τ and σ can be written in either form, yet the temporalist interpretation nonetheless implies that surplus labor is the sole source of profit, while its simultaneist counterparts imply the opposite. What *is* relevant is precisely the introduction of time. Since the only difference between τ and σ is that the former is determined temporally and the latter is determined simultaneously, it is this difference that accounts for their contrary implications. For the exploitation theory of profit to hold, temporality is indeed necessary.[8]

V. CONCLUSION

Due to their static character, simultaneist interpretations of Marx's value theory grant value no role in explaining the dynamics of capitalism. Although some proponents of simultaneist interpretations have acknowledged this, they seem untroubled by it. They contend that the "core of the explanatory power of the labor theory of value lies in the analysis of exploitation" rather than in dynamic analysis (Duménil and Lévy 2000: 142). And, invoking the FMT and similar theorems, they have argued that their interpretations do imply that exploitation of workers is the sole source of profit.

This paper has demonstrated, to the contrary, that simultaneism and the exploitation theory of profit are incompatible. The FMT holds only when all physical surpluses are positive (or profit rates are equal) in every period, and similar theorems pertaining to more recent simultaneist interpretations hold only when all net products are positive in every period—*no matter how brief the period.* These conditions have been shown to be implausible and completely unnecessary for reproduction. A choice between simultaneous valuation and the exploitation theory of profit must therefore be made.

Marx's value theory thus seems to be far more of a "package deal" than has hitherto been recognized. The attempts to fragment it into dynamic and static aspects, and to reject the former while embracing the latter, have not succeeded. When his value theory is given a static interpretation, not only do

Marx's explanations of dynamic issues, such as the tendency of the profit rate, seem to be false, so does his explanation of the origin of profit, a putatively static issue. Conversely, the temporal single-system interpretation, which vindicates the internal consistency of his value theory in other respects, also vindicates the logical coherence of the exploitation theory of profit. One may now in good conscience turn directly to *Capital*, unencumbered by others' "corrections" of its alleged errors, in order to help analyze and understand the world in which we live.

NOTES

1. Because it refrains from asserting any relationship between surplus labor and profit (measured in terms of money or a numéraire), the interpretation of Wolff, Callari, and Roberts (1984) is an exception.

2. $A = [a_{ij}]$ is a square matrix of input-output coefficients; a_{ij} is the amount of good i used to produce one unit of good j. b is a column vector of wage goods per unit of living labor, ℓ is a row vector of living labor requirements per unit of output, and x is a column vector of outputs. I is the identity matrix.

3. When no physical surpluses are negative, but some are zero, and some prices and/or values are zero, the aggregate worth of the physical surplus vector can be zero when valued at prices and positive when valued at values, or vice versa.

4. See Kliman (1997) for other criticisms of this concept.

5. I am indebted to Alan Freeman for emphasizing this crucial point.

6. An anonymous referee has noted that the case of 386 computers concerns "technological change over time creating obsolescence in durables, and not . . . valuation in a timeless world where there are negative net products." The point is presumably that the models used to deduce the FMT and similar theorems disregard this case. I agree. It is precisely for this reason that the theorems do not apply to the real world. This is true whether or not it is legitimate to abstract from this phenomenon and whether or not the theorems are interesting and useful.

7. This could occur even if prices fluctuate only slightly and the economy is in equilibrium in all other respects—growth rates and profit rates are equalized over the course of the lengthened period, technology is not changing, wage rates are equalized, and so forth. Numerical examples demonstrating this possibility are available from the author.

8. Of course, it is not sufficient. The exploitation theory of profit would not hold under a different definition of inflation, or under different temporal conceptions of value added and the monetary expression of labor-time.

Chapter 3

On the TSSI and the Exploitation Theory of Profit

Simon Mohun[1]

In a recent article in this journal, Kliman (2001 {chapter 2 of this book}) has argued that only a temporal single system interpretation (TSSI) of Marxian value theory preserves the fundamental Marxian theorem (FMT) and hence finds the origin of profit solely in exploitation. This paper first outlines the TSSI in order to emphasize the particular and controversial definition of value on which it depends. Kliman's logical demonstration of the FMT is then shown to fail on exactly the same grounds for which he indicts rival interpretations.

1. INTRODUCTION

The Marxian account of exploitation is a theory of how surplus labor is extracted, and the form that this takes as profit. In formalizations of Marxian theory, the relationship between surplus labor and profit is expressed by the "fundamental Marxian theorem" (FMT) that the existence of surplus labor is necessary and sufficient for the existence of profit. In a recent article in this journal, Kliman (2001) has argued that in any interpretation of Marx's value theory in which prices and values of inputs and outputs are determined simultaneously, the extraction of surplus labor is insufficient, and in general unnecessary, for the existence of positive profit. He calls such interpretations "simultaneist" and argues that because in such interpretations the FMT fails, they are all incompatible with Marx's theory. By contrast, a "temporalist single system interpretation" (TSSI) does indeed imply that surplus labor is both necessary and sufficient for positive profit. Elsewhere, for example in Kliman and McGlone (1999), it is argued that all of the major propositions of *Capital* can be replicated by the formalism of the TSSI, and that this is not true of any other interpretation in the modern literature. Consequently, the claim is that of all modern interpretations only the TSSI adequately represents the theory presented in the three volumes of *Capital*.

It is important to be clear about what is being asserted. Kliman is not assessing the *adequacy* of any theory, whether this theory be his own, Marx's, or some other. While *desiderata* of a theory might include meaningfulness of assumptions, logical coherence, elegance, insight, and testable implications, none of these is at issue here. Kliman is only presenting an *interpretation* of the theory of *Capital*. In order to decide between rival interpretations, the criterion he employs is whether an account can derive the major propositions of *Capital* (the "replication criterion"), and he sees this as a straightforward test that can decide between rival interpretations.

This paper focuses on Kliman's claim that the TSSI can support a logically robust FMT, that is, one that is valid "*under completely general conditions*" (Kliman 2001: 106, emphasis in original). For convenience, the paper identifies the TSSI with Kliman's writings (as both single and joint author), but further references can be consulted in Kliman (ibid.). Section 2 recalls Kliman's argument, using his notation and terminology. The next section emphasizes that his argument depends upon two assumptions. These are stated (ibid.: 106, immediately before and after equation (3.7)), but it is easy to miss their significance. Adherents to what Kliman calls the "standard interpretation" reject both of these assumptions; adherents to what he calls the "new interpretation" reject one of them. Without both of them, Kliman's demonstration of the FMT fails. The fourth section focuses on his definition of the "monetary expression of labor-time" and shows that this definition requires the two particular assumptions. Section 5 outlines the TSSI method. The following two sections consider whether a non-TSSI FMT is possible, and whether the TSSI proof of the FMT is valid according to the TSSI method. The answers are first, that Kliman has not conclusively shown that the demonstration of the non-TSSI FMT is flawed, and second, that if the non-TSSI FMT is flawed, then so too is the TSSI FMT, and for exactly the same reason. A short conclusion summarizes, and suggests that issues of rival interpretation are not perhaps the best focus for the construction of a coherent theory of today's world.

2. THE TSSI FMT

Consider the TSSI as outlined by Kliman. Time is considered discretely in the following manner. Time t is a period in which inputs are purchased at the outset and then used continuously during the period. The period ends immediately prior to the appearance of output, and the appearance of output denotes the start of period $t + 1$. Output is instantaneously sold, providing profit to the seller and enabling the instantaneous purchase of inputs. A second period of production then ensues. Thus in the present context, temporality refers solely to an insistence that it takes time to *produce* commodities, so that the price of a commodity as input may be different from the price of that same commodity as an output.

The following notation is used.

- $C(t)$ is the total expenditure on used-up means of production at the start of period t, measured in money.
- $V(t)$ is the total wage bill advanced at the start of period t, measured in money.
- $P(t + 1)$ is total revenue received from the sale of output (called "total price" in the Marxian tradition), measured in money.
- π^N is nominal profit, measured in money, and defined as

$$\pi^N = P(t + 1) - C(t) - V(t) \tag{3.1}$$

π^R is real profit, measured in money, and defined as

$$\pi^R = \frac{P(t+1)}{1+i} - C(t) - V(t) \tag{3.2}$$

where i is the discount factor which commensurates monetary magnitudes through time.

- $\tau(t)$ is the monetary expression of labor-time at time t, or the amount of money that represents one hour of socially necessary labor-time at time t. Its inverse is the value of money, the number of hours of socially necessary labor-time represented by one unit of money at time t.
- $L(t)$ is total labor purchased at the start of period t. While he is not explicit, Kliman assumes that this is also the labor-time performed in production during period t. It is therefore measured in hours of socially necessary labor-time. This assumption is not at issue for the argument of this paper.
- $S(t)$ is surplus labor-time, measured in hours of socially necessary labor-time.

Kliman's argument is as follows. Surplus labor-time is the difference between total labor-time and the labor-time equivalent of the wages paid:

$$S(t) = L(t) - \frac{V(t)}{\tau(t)} \tag{3.3}$$

Kliman wants to show that this surplus labor-time is necessary and sufficient for the real profit of equation (3.2) to be positive. Now in the present specification, the only reason why a discount factor is necessary in equation (3.2) is that the monetary expression of labor-time might change. So define the discount factor as the period by period rate of change of the monetary expression of labor-time:

$$i = \frac{\tau(t+1) - \tau(t)}{\tau(t)} \tag{3.4}$$

so that

$$1 + i = \frac{\tau(t+1)}{\tau(t)} \tag{3.5}$$

Substituting for 1 + *i* in equation (3.2),

$$\pi^R = \frac{P(t+1)\tau(t)}{\tau(t+1)} - C(t) - V(t) \tag{3.6}$$

and substituting for *V*(*t*) from equation (3.3),

$$\pi^R = \frac{P(t+1)\tau(t)}{\tau(t+1)} - C(t) - [L(t) - S(t)]\tau(t) \tag{3.7}$$

or

$$\pi^R = \left[\frac{P(t+1)}{\tau(t+1)} - \frac{C(t)}{\tau(t)} - L(t)\right]\tau(t) + S(t)\tau(t) \tag{3.8}$$

Kliman then asserts that value added in terms of labor-time is the difference between the labor-time equivalents of total revenue (total price) $P(t+1)/\tau(t+1)$ and expenditure on the means of production $C(t)/\tau(t)$, and this difference is equal to the living labor extracted *L*(*t*), since the latter generates all new value (ibid.: 107). Hence the expression in the large brackets in equation (3.8) is identically zero, whence

$$\pi^R = S(t)\tau(t) \tag{3.9}$$

Now consider again the large bracket of equation (3.8). Since for Kliman this is zero, it can be written as

$$\frac{P(t+1)}{\tau(t+1)} - \frac{C(t)}{\tau(t)} = L(t) \tag{3.10}$$

and hence in time 1,

$$\frac{P(1)}{\tau(1)} - \frac{C(0)}{\tau(0)} = L(0) \tag{3.11}$$

Assuming that *P*, *C* and *L* are each positive and finite in all time periods, then as long as $\tau(0)$ is positive and finite, so must $\tau(1)$ be positive and finite. Hence so is every member of the τ series. Therefore $\tau(t)$ in equation (3.9) is positive and hence positive surplus labor is both necessary and sufficient for real profit to be positive.

3. TSSI DEFINITIONS

However, in addition to the assumptions stated, this demonstration depends upon two definitions that Kliman treats as unproblematic. Both are contested by what Kliman calls "the standard interpretation of Marx's value theory" (ibid.: 99), and one is contested by what Kliman calls the "new interpretation" (ibid.: 100). Consider each in turn.

3.1. First Definition: Labor-Power and Wages

The first assumption underpins equation (3.3). Kliman presumes that aggregate variable capital in value terms is equal to aggregate wages divided by the monetary expression of labor-time. Now aggregate variable capital in value terms could be one of two products. It could be the value of an individual labor-power multiplied by the number of workers hired, or it could be the value of labor-power per hour of labor hired multiplied by the total number of hours hired. The "standard interpretation" generally uses the first product, in which the value of labor-power is a number of hours, and the "new interpretation" generally uses the second product, in which the value of labor-power is a fraction between 0 and 1. I will consider each in turn.

3.1.1. The "Standard Interpretation" Objection

The "standard interpretation" treats the value of labor-power as the value embodied in the commodities purchased by the wage, or, in shorthand, the value of wage-goods. If $\boldsymbol{\lambda}$ is the vector of unit values, and $\mathbf{b}$ the vector of wage-goods purchased per hour of labor performed, then this means that at any time *t*, total variable capital in labor value terms is $\boldsymbol{\lambda}\mathbf{b}L$. Since *V* is total wages, then its labor-time equivalent for Kliman is V/τ. Hence a "standard interpretation" position can only interpret Kliman as saying

$$\boldsymbol{\lambda}\mathbf{b}L = \frac{V}{\tau} \tag{3.12}$$

which means that, at each t, τ has to satisfy

$$\tau = \frac{V}{\boldsymbol{\lambda} \mathbf{b} L} \tag{3.13}$$

As long as the assumption of "equal exchange" or "exchange of equivalents" is made, then equation (3.13) will hold, for all money prices will be proportional to their corresponding labor values. But as soon as different compositions of capital are combined with the equalization of the rate of profit, then "unequal exchange" will be the norm, and the ensuing prices of production will not relate in any simple way to the "prices proportional to values" of volume 1 of *Capital*. In such circumstances, equation (3.12) only holds in certain rather special cases, and in general does not hold. Hence anyone holding to the "standard interpretation" of Marxian value theory will not find convincing Kliman's demonstration of the FMT. For outside of an equal exchange world, equation (3.3) is mis-specified. In the standard interpretation, Kliman's demonstration of the FMT depends upon an equal exchange assumption in circumstances in which equal exchange in general will not occur.

3.1.2. The "New Interpretation" Agreement and Justification

The "new interpretation" argues that the "standard interpretation" of the value of labor-power is incoherent outside of a volume 1 world. This can be shown as follows. First, labor-power is an attribute of human beings, and human beings are not (in capitalism) produced as commodities. So the value of labor-power cannot be measured by the socially necessary labor embodied in human beings, because there is none. The reason labor-power is a peculiar commodity is that it has no relative form of value. But it does have an equivalent form. There are only two possible choices for that equivalent form: either the wage (divided by the monetary expression of labor-time) for which labor-power is sold, or the value of the bundle of commodities which the worker uses the wage to buy. If the assumption is made that value equivalents are exchanged, then either of these possibilities can indifferently be used (as long as the entire wage is spent). But as soon as explicit account is taken of the different compositions of capital involved in the production of the various wage-goods, no wage-good will in general sell at its value, and hence the money wage (divided by the monetary expression of labor-time) will not be equal to the labor value of the wage-bundle of commodities.

However, the unequal exchange forced by differing compositions of capital combined with the competitive equalization of the rate of profit does not apply to the exchange of labor-power for a wage, because neither composition of capital nor rate of profit is involved in the "production" of people.

Hence in general the value of labor-power is the money wage (divided by the monetary expression of labor-time), and only in the special (volume 1) world of equivalent exchange will this also be the value of the wage-bundle of commodities per hour. In general, the value of labor-power per hour of labor hired is the hourly wage rate (divided by the monetary expression of labor-time); multiplying up by the total number of hours of labor hired gives the variable capital $V(t)/\tau(t)$ of equation (3.3).

This means that proponents of the "new interpretation" accept equation (3.3) as a correct specification, and indeed, have an analytical argument in favor of it, rather than treating it just as a definition.[2] Hence there is no difficulty in deriving equations (3.7) and (3.8).

3.2. Second Definition: Value and Price of Means of Production

However, in deriving his FMT as equation (3.9) from equation (3.8), Kliman assumes that

$$\frac{P(t+1)}{\tau(t+1)} = \frac{C(t)}{\tau(t)} + L(t) \tag{3.14}$$

and this is his second definition. For equation (3.14) to hold, one has to accept the assertions following equation (3.8) above, that total gross value is the labor-time equivalent of total gross revenue (or total price) $P(t+1)/\tau(t+1)$, and that the total value of the means of production is the labor-time equivalent of total expenditure on the means of production $C(t)/\tau(t)$.

3.2.1. The "Standard Interpretation" Objection

Proponents of the interpretation that value and price systems are distinct and different will not be able to attribute any meaning to these aggregate proportionalities. It is true that proportionality might be explicitly assumed for total value and total price (as a normalization condition of the transformation problem). But outside of special cases, that same proportionality *cannot* hold for the subaggregates of total wages and total variable capital in value terms (as already discussed), and total expenditure on means of production and total constant capital in value terms. Exactly as for the relation between total wages and the value of the wage-good bundle, it cannot be the case in an unequal exchange world that the total value of the means of production is in general the labor-time equivalent of total expenditure on the means of production. For "standard interpretation" Marxists, Kliman's demonstration of the FMT only holds in the equal exchange world of volume 1 of *Capital*, and cannot hold in the unequal exchange world of volume 3 of *Capital*.

3.2.2. The "New Interpretation" Objection

Consider further the two proportionalities assumed by Kliman, that total gross value is the labor-time equivalent of total gross revenue (or total price) and that the total value of the means of production is the labor-time equivalent of total expenditure on the means of production. First, these are not independent conditions: either must imply the other if there are proportionalities between price and value of total variable capital, and between profit and total unpaid labor-time. Since in the "new interpretation" both of these latter conditions hold, it suffices to concentrate on just one of the proportionalities assumed by Kliman.

Consider then the proposition that the total value of the means of production is the labor-time equivalent of total expenditure on the means of production. Kliman presents no justification for this assumption. But the assumption is not a trivial one, because it implies that additivity cannot be maintained. The labor value of each individual means of production when added together will not in general equal in the aggregate Kliman's labor-time equivalent of total expenditure on the means of production. The reason is the same as that already outlined. Since the production of each means of production has in general a different composition of capital, the competitive tendency toward equalization of the rate of profit will force price-value deviations across all means of production, and the sum of all prices of production of these means of production will not therefore stand in a proportionality relation with the sum of their values.

3.3. The TSSI Definition of Value

This in turn means that if aggregate proportionality is to be maintained as Kliman asserts, *then value is being defined differently from how it is conventionally understood.* The conventional understanding interprets Marx to say that value is the sum of the abstract labor directly and indirectly embodied in the production of a commodity, so that at unit level,

$$\lambda_i = \sum_j a_{ji}\lambda_j + l_i \tag{3.15}$$

where a_{ji} is the quantity of good j required to produce one unit of good i, and l_i is the number of hours of labor required to produce one unit of good i. Multiplying by the gross output x_i and summing,

$$\boldsymbol{\lambda}\mathbf{x} = \boldsymbol{\lambda}\mathbf{A}\mathbf{x} + L \tag{3.16}$$

where $\mathbf{A}$ is the matrix of input-output coefficients.

But for Kliman, value at unit level is the sum of the living labor performed and the value equivalent of the money laid out on means of production. Moreover, since production takes time, output appears one period after inputs are employed, and hence two periods and two monetary expressions of labor-time are involved. Finally, there are transfers of value in the exchange process. At unit level, a monetary sum g_i is transferred to sector i, and this must be accounted for in the price of the next period. The value (positive, zero, or negative) that is transferred is then $g_i(t)/\tau(t)$. Hence at unit level for inputs of time t and outputs of time $t + 1$, market prices are given by

$$p_i(t+1) = \frac{\tau(t+1)}{\tau(t)}\left[\sum_j a_{ji}p_j(t) + g_i(t)\right] + \tau(t+1)l_i(t) \tag{3.17}$$

and values are given by

$$\lambda_i(t+1) = \frac{1}{\tau(t)}\left[\sum_j a_{ji}p_j(t)\right] + l_i(t) \tag{3.18}$$

In the aggregate, all value transfers must sum to zero, so that multiplying both equations (3.17) and (3.18) by gross output levels and summing yields

$$\frac{P(t+1)}{\tau(t+1)} = \frac{1}{\tau(t)}\mathbf{p}(t)\mathbf{Ax} + L(t) = \frac{C(t)}{\tau(t)} + L(t) \tag{3.19}$$

which is of course equation (3.14) again. Clearly, Kliman's definitions are different from what would be accepted by either the "standard interpretation" or the "new interpretation."

4. ON THE MONETARY EXPRESSION OF LABOR-TIME

Kliman considers the monetary expression of labor-time in terms of equation (3.10), as the ratio of total price to total value,

$$\tau(t+1) = \frac{P(t+1)}{C(t)/\tau(t) + L(t)} \tag{3.20}$$

and he compares this with the analogous expression defined not in terms of the ratio of gross price to gross value, but in terms of the ratio of value added in money terms to value added in labor-time terms. He then correctly shows that the ratio is the same whether defined in gross or net terms (Kliman 2001: 109). But again his argument is premised on his identification of the total value of the means of production with the labor-time equivalent of total expenditure on the means of production, that is, on his specification of price and value by equations (3.17), (3.18), and (3.19). If one were to specify the value equations more conventionally as equation (3.15) and hence (3.16), then a "temporalist" definition of the monetary expression of labor-time becomes

$$\tau(t+1)=\frac{P(t+1)}{\boldsymbol{\lambda}(t)\mathbf{A}\mathbf{x}+L(t)} \tag{3.21}$$

Hence, cross-multiplying and subtracting $C(t)(1 + i)$ from both sides,

$$\tau(t+1)\boldsymbol{\lambda}(t)\mathbf{A}\mathbf{x}-C(t)(1+i)+\tau(t+1)L(t)=P(t+1)-C(t)(1+i) \tag{3.22}$$

Rearranging, and using equation (3.5),

$$\tau(t+1)=\frac{P(t+1)-C(t)(1+i)}{L(t)}-\frac{\tau(t)\boldsymbol{\lambda}(t)\mathbf{A}\mathbf{x}-C(t)}{L(t)}(1+i) \tag{3.23}$$

For Kliman the second fraction on the right-hand side in equation (3.23) is *defined* to be zero, because its first term $\tau(t)\boldsymbol{\lambda}(t)\mathbf{A}\mathbf{x}$ is $\mathbf{p}(t)\mathbf{A}\mathbf{x}$, which is $C(t)$. This will not in general be the case for a more conventional definition of Marxian value. And under a more conventional definition of value, equation (3.23) cannot be signed.

This emphasizes how different Kliman's specification of value and price is. Indeed, assume the amounts of direct labor time worked and the input-output coefficients are given data. Then the n value equations, of which equation (3.18) is one, have to determine n prices (of period t), n values (of period $t + 1$) and the monetary expression of labor time (of period t). And the n price equations, of which equation (3.17) is one, have to determine $2n$ prices (of periods $t + 1$ and t), n transfer coefficients (of period t) and 2 monetary expressions of labor time (of periods $t + 1$ and t). This is hardly a satisfactory specification. It might of course be argued that prices of period t are given data too. Then, *provided the monetary expression of labor-time of period t is known*, each value is determined solely by adding up the given data in each production process, and there is no interdependence at all. And further, *provided the monetary expression of labor-times of periods t + 1 and t are known,* the n transfer coefficients suffice to determine the n prices. A definition of the monetary expression of labor-time is therefore important.

But Kliman does not give one. All that he gives is equation (3.10). That is, he specifies the time path of the monetary expression of labor-time, and he also defines the monetary expression of labor-time in time 0 to be positive and finite. But that is all.[3]

5. THE TSSI METHOD

Thus far, this paper has concentrated on Kliman's assumptions and definitions to show that what is at issue is the definition of value. This section looks at the TSSI justification for its definition of value.

Kliman argues that only the TSSI definition can be used to replicate the Marxian account of exploitation and profit. He concludes:

> Of the existing interpretations of Marx's value theory, only the temporal single-system interpretation . . . implies that surplus labor is both necessary and sufficient for real profit to exist, *under completely general conditions*. [Ibid.: 106. Italics in original]

Kliman and McGlone (1999) argue for the TSSI on two grounds. First, they present textual evidence which "strongly suggests" that it is "at least plausible" that the TSSI faithfully reflects Marx's categories of value and price. Secondly, something that is "even more compelling," they argue that the TSSI replicates Marx's major propositions (concerning value, price and profit), and hence can "make sense out of crucial aspects of his value theory that the standard interpretation (and others) have always found to be incoherent" (Kliman and McGlone 1999: 38, 55). Consider each in turn.

Precise textual evidence confirming the TSSI definition of value as reflecting Marx's category of value does not exist. Instead, passages from *Capital* have to be interrogated with questions such as "could this plausibly be interpreted as meaning that value is the labor-time equivalent of price?" for the various aggregates with which the TSSI is concerned. Such interpretative issues are notoriously difficult to resolve. This is compounded by the difficulty that only volume 1 of *Capital* was prepared by Marx for publication. The remainder of what became volumes 2 and 3, and the three volumes of *Theories of Surplus Value*, were put together out of Marx's notebooks (some written before, and some after, volume 1) after Marx's death. Hence textual evidence is at best ambiguous and inconclusive. Kliman therefore argues for the more hermeneutic approach that quotations are not decisive: a textual interpretation should not depend upon this or that quotation, but should rather be able to understand the text as a coherent, unified whole.

Understanding the text as a whole requires a broader understanding of context, focusing on replication of the theoretical results of the text. An accurate textual interpretation is one which can, on the basis of (an interpretation of) the text's premises, derive (and hence replicate) its theoretical conclusions. This, for Kliman, is the criterion of decidability between rival interpretations. Consequently, while a critic of the TSSI might struggle with the apparent contrast between the TSSI definition of constant capital and Marx's account

(Marx 1991a: 317–19), this is less significant than the criterion of replication, for only the latter addresses the issue of overall coherence.

Two counterarguments to the TSSI are then possible: first, if it could be shown that a satisfactory non-TSSI FMT goes through, and second, if it could be shown that the TSSI FMT does not go through on the basis of Kliman's assumptions. Either would mean that (at least as regards the FMT) the "replicability criterion" would not be able to distinguish rival interpretations and hence rival definitions of value.

6. IS A NON-TSSI FMT POSSIBLE?

Define the "simultaneist monetary expression of labor-time" σ as the ratio, in net rather than gross terms, of the money value of output to its labor value (the first term on the right hand side of equation (3.23) if the time argument is dropped):

$$\sigma = \frac{P - C}{L} = \frac{\mathbf{p}[\mathbf{I} - \mathbf{A}]\mathbf{x}}{\mathbf{lx}} = \frac{\mathbf{py}}{\mathbf{lx}} \tag{3.24}$$

Then if profit is defined as the difference between net output in money terms and total wages, and using the argument of section 3.2.2 above that variable capital in labor value terms is total wages divided by the monetary expression of labor-time, it follows that

$$\pi = \sigma S \tag{3.25}$$

This summarizes Kliman's equations (3.3)–(3.6) (Kliman 2001: 101). Kliman's objection is as follows.

1. Negative net products are a feature of the real world.
2. Hence it is possible to find prices such that net output in money terms $\mathbf{py}$ is negative.

This makes $\sigma < 0$, and hence profit and surplus value have different signs, in which case the non-TSSI FMT fails.

3. The non-TSSI FMT only goes through if net output in money terms is guaranteed to be positive. But this assumption renders the non-TSSI FMT inapplicable in any study of the real world.

That there are some negative net products is undeniable. Whether there are prices such that aggregate net output in money terms is negative is more doubtful. Kliman insists that prices can be chosen arbitrarily, because a general FMT has to hold under all possible prices, and any arbitrary choice of price (yielding a negative net product in money terms) is one such possible set. But this is a misconception. Kliman does not explain how his numerical examples (ibid.: 100, 104–5) could emerge in any economically meaningful way out of the valorization process of competing capitals each of which is attempting to maximize profit. Indeed, no economic structure is specified at all. It is true, but trivial, that combinations of numbers, interpreted as output and price vectors, can be found such that (for some choice of length of time period) a non-TSSI FMT cannot be proved. But economies in disequilibrium still have some structure; if they are technologically and economically viable they can reproduce themselves, prices are not random, and behavior is not arbitrary. A disequilibrium state is not one in which absolutely anything can happen. Kliman's numerical examples give no indication as to whether their outcomes are economically possible in the sense of arising out of economic behavior. To be convincing, a numerical example has to display an economic structure capable of physical reproduction, in which net products are the outcome of profit maximizing choices, and in which a price path is determined by some rule other than imagination. Then at some particular time, multiplying the vectors of net product and price together to determine the money value of aggregate net product has to result in a negative number. The best that can be said about Kliman's numerical examples in these terms is that they are seriously incomplete. He has not therefore shown conclusively that a negative aggregate net product in money terms is economically possible.

7. IS THE PROOF OF THE TSSI FMT A VALID ONE?

In order to prove the FMT, the TSSI makes the following assumptions:

1. temporality as defined by equation (3.4);
2. an understanding of value as defined by equation (3.18) and hence equation (3.19); or, equivalently, the labor value of the bundle of wage-goods is the labor-time equivalent of total wages, and the labor value of the total means of production is the labor-time equivalent of the value in money terms of that total;
3. P, C and L are positive and finite in all time periods;
4. a period 0 in which $\tau(0)$ is positive and finite.

These are all necessary conditions underpinning Kliman's assertion of the superiority of the TSSI approach in replicating Marx's account of the relation between exploitation and profits. Note in passing that it is not only temporality that distinguishes Kliman's approach from that of rival approaches; temporality as defined by equation (3.4) is indeed a part of the story and a necessary one, but no more so than the other definitions and assumptions. Whereas the non-TSSI FMT requires the positivity of aggregate net output in money terms in order that its monetary expression of labor-time σ be positive, the TSSI FMT requires assumptions 3 and 4 above in order to ensure that its monetary expression of labor-time τ be positive in any period. Call these the TSSI sign restrictions.

As a deductive logic the TSSI FMT is not convincing. For consider again equation (3.10), which can be written as

$$P(t+1) - \frac{\tau(t+1)}{\tau(t)}C(t) = \tau(t+1)L(t) \tag{3.26}$$

or aggregate gross output in money terms less the used up means of production (in money terms, adjusted for any change in the monetary expression of labor-time) is equal to aggregate net output in money terms. But the TSSI sign restrictions are that τ and L are always positive and finite, and hence so is their product. That is, *the TSSI sign restrictions ensure that aggregate net output in money terms is always positive*. Hence if net output in money terms can be negative in the real world, the TSSI FMT is formally true but does not apply to the real world, and if it is insisted that the TSSI FMT does apply to the real world, the TSSI sign restrictions must be abandoned, in which case the TSSI FMT fails.

In sum, Kliman asserts that the non-TSSI approach has to assume the positivity of aggregate net product in money terms for the FMT to go through, and this renders it irrelevant. His account of the TSSI FMT is subject to exactly the same strictures.

8. CONCLUSION

The TSSI stresses that it is only an interpretation of Marx, and it stands or falls on interpretative issues. The claim is that only the TSSI definition of value, its notion of temporality, and the TSSI sign restrictions enable a replication of Marx's account of exploitation, so that the TSSI must be the correct interpretation. How should this claim be assessed?

1. Kliman is correct that an aggregate negative net product in money terms invalidates the non-TSSI FMT.
2. Kliman has not convincingly demonstrated that an aggregate negative net product in money terms is a real possibility.

3. The TSSI assumptions rule out any possibility that an aggregate net product in money terms could be negative.
4. It is not therefore possible to decide between TSSI and non-TSSI approaches through an examination of the FMT.

This does not mean that it is not possible to discriminate between TSSI and non-TSSI approaches. But the criterion is not replication. An alternative criterion of demarcation might consider the assumptions required to construct a contemporary theory of capitalism within the Marxian tradition, and might consider how the resulting theory fares in terms of empirical explanation of today's world. The recovery of Marxism as an analytical tool does partially depend on answers to the question "what really did Marx say and mean?" But only partially; it also depends upon what a Marxist understanding can tell us about the world in which we live. What is required is not an assessment of rival interpretations, but a theory for today's world and its use in empirical analysis. The construction of such a theory might well seek inspiration from Marx's own writings, but it is a coherent theory for today's world that is the goal.

On coherence, the TSSI is problematic. One reason that the TSSI excites controversy is that its definition of value and its temporality together amount to a proportionality between prices and values, whether or not equivalent exchange is assumed. Values are fully specified by a knowledge of current labor, prices, and the time path of the monetary expression of labor-time. Hence the TSSI value of the means of production, for example, bears no necessary relation to the labor-time that was expended in the production of those means of production, nor to the labor-time that would have to be expended were those means of production all to be replaced today. This notion of value as independent of labor directly and indirectly expended, save through the (undefined) monetary expression of labor-time, is not obviously compatible with any understanding of a labor theory of value. And as soon as fixed capital and technical change are allowed, then careful distinction must be made between changes in the quality and quantity of labor employed on one hand, and changes in the money value of inventories and fixed capital due to price changes on the other. With the TSSI insistence on historic cost accounting, and its definition of values by prices and the (undefined) monetary expression of labor-time, the careful distinctions necessary between changes that are due to changes in labor expended, and those that are due to changes in prices, are all too easily confused. And on empirical analysis, it is doubtful that historic cost accounting can be of much analytical help.

Many variants of Marxism have the potential to say interesting things about today's world. Whether this includes the TSSI remains an open question, because the TSSI restricts itself to "interpretation of the text." TSSI adherents have yet to demonstrate that they have a theory that theoretically and empirically engages with the world. In this regard, the TSSI framework is unconvincing.

NOTES

1. An earlier version of this paper was presented in July 2001 at a session of the International Working Group on Value Theory seminar at the University of Greenwich. I am grateful to Andrew Kliman for a subsequent email discussion, and to Alfredo Saad-Filho, Roberto Veneziani, and referees of *Capital & Class* for helpful comments. None of them is responsible for errors that remain.

2. Kliman first asserts the assumption in his brief outline of the "new interpretation" (ibid.: 101), but he does not explain it.

3. This point is emphasized in Veneziani (2004). One way to proceed is to investigate what is implied if the monetary expression of labor-time remains constant through time. This makes no sense unless prices and labor-times are also constant through time. In these (equilibrium) circumstances, equation (3.20) shows that the monetary expression of labor-time is well-defined, as the ratio of aggregate money value added to aggregate labor value added. But then equations (3.17) and (3.18) show that prices and values are identical but for the transfer coefficients. None of this is very satisfactory. In addition to Veneziani (2004), see also Mongiovi (2002) for a critique of the role played in the TSSI by the transfer coefficients. {Mohun's original text cites a 2003 mimeographed version of Veneziani (2004).}

Chapter 4

Deriving a Negative PNP

Andrew Kliman

Simon Mohun (2003: 98 {chap. 3 of this book}) has argued that Kliman (2001 {chap. 2 of this book}) did not "show[ ] conclusively" that a negative price of the net product (PNP) is "economically possible in the sense of arising out of economic behavior." The following two examples derive a negative PNP in precisely the manner that Mohun insists upon, and thereby demonstrate that a negative PNP is indeed "economically possible" in his sense.

In both examples, there are two sectors (1 and 2) in the economy. Wages are part of advanced capital, and a_{ij} and ℓ_j are the amounts of good i, and of living labor, needed to produce a unit of good j. There is no fixed capital. The price of good 1, the money commodity, equals 1, and P_2 is the price of good 2. The gross output of good j is X_j, and the normal output level of each good exactly satisfies the demand for it.

Example 1

All $a_{ij} = a < 0.5$, and both $\ell_j = \ell$. The money wage rate per unit of living labor is $w < (1-2a)/\ell$. Normally $X_1 = X_2$, and since $a < 0.5$, both goods' net products are positive. Today, however, good 2's net product is negative ($X_2 < a(X_1 + X_2)$), because of a one-day work stoppage in part of sector 2. If profit rates were equalized, then P_2 would equal 1 and the profit rate would be positive, which implies that the PNP would be positive as well. Yet sector 2 is a regulated monopoly. Because of a data entry error, the regulatory authority has set P_2 at a level such that

$$P_2 > \frac{X_1 - a(X_1 + X_2)}{a(X_1 + X_2) - X_2} > 1,$$

and thus the PNP is negative.

At day's end, statisticians at the regulatory authority discover the error and P_2 is lowered to 1. Thus the profit rate will be positive and equal in both sectors, starting tomorrow. Moreover, sector 2's low activity level was only temporary, and sufficient reserve stocks of good 2 exist, so production can resume tomorrow at levels that once again match demands.

Example 2

Workers' consumption in both sectors is 1/202 units of good 1 and 1/202 units of good 2, per unit of living labor, $a_{11} = a_{22} = 0.1$, $a_{12} = a_{21} = 0.89$, and $\ell_1 = \ell_2 = 0.01$. Capitalists maximize internal rates of return (IRR), and the IRRs are continually equalized. During the daytime, $X_1 = 1$ and $X_2 = 99$; during the nighttime, $X_1 = 99$ and $X_2 = 1$. (The alternating output levels result from profit-maximizing choices.) It is expensive and unprofitable to hire workers at night, so both sectors produce during *their* daytime only. But almost all of sector 2 is located twelve hours away from where almost all of sector 1 is located.) Periods are one-half-day long. In period 0 and before, the economy is in a static equilibrium. $P_{20} = 1$, the IRR = 1 percent, and the PNP is positive. (P_{2t}, the output price of good 2 in period t, is its input price in period $t + 1$. P_{2t}, the other data, and the equal-IRR condition suffice to determine P_{2t+1}.)

Yet beginning in period 1 (a daytime), sector 1, an extractive industry, experiences a technical regress; $0.11123 < a_{11}' < 0.11969$. The economy quickly converges to a new static equilibrium in which the IRR and thus the PNP are again positive. Nonetheless, the path of P_2 is such that the PNP is negative at least during period 1 and perhaps through period 18.

Chapter 5

Exploitation, Profits, and Time

Roberto Veneziani

{The material in this chapter originally appeared as section 3 of Veneziani (2004). The remainder of that article consists of criticisms of the temporal single-system interpretation (TSSI) of the relation between value and price and Marx's law of the tendential fall in the rate of profit. Kliman and Freeman's response to Veneziani, published in chapter 9 of this book, addresses these criticisms as well.}

In this section, the TSS theory of exploitation is examined, focusing on Kliman's (2001 {chap. 2 of this book}) formal analysis. According to TSS authors, even setting aside the well-known problems related to joint production (Steedman 1977), all simultaneist interpretations of Marx's value theory, and not only the standard one, are incompatible with Marx's theory of exploitation, because "in those systems in which the prices and values of inputs are determined simultaneously with the prices and values of outputs, the extraction of surplus labor is insufficient and, generally, unnecessary for the existence of positive profit" (Kliman 2001: 97). Instead, claims (c)–(f) prove that the TSS interpretation "implies that surplus labor is both necessary and sufficient for real profit to exist" (ibid., 106), and thus only under TSS does Marx's exploitation theory of profit hold.[1]

In the standard interpretation, the link between surplus labor and profits is given by the fundamental Marxian theorem (FMT; [Okishio 1963]),[2] which in the generalization proved by Roemer (1981)—and used by Kliman (2001) as a benchmark for discussion—might be stated as follows:[3] let $\boldsymbol{\lambda}^e = \boldsymbol{l}(\boldsymbol{I} - \boldsymbol{A})^{-1}$ be the vector of *embodied* labor values, and let $\boldsymbol{\varphi}_t = (\boldsymbol{I} - \boldsymbol{A} - \boldsymbol{b}_w\boldsymbol{l})\boldsymbol{x}_t$ be the vector of net outputs. Let a *reproducible solution* (Roemer 1981: 19) be a steady-state vector $\boldsymbol{p}_t$ such that, in every t, capitalists maximize profits, consumed goods are replaced, workers receive a subsistence wage—which implies

$\phi_{jt} \geq 0$, all j and t—and endowments are sufficient for production plans. Since in the standard interpretation $\Pi_t = \boldsymbol{p}_t\boldsymbol{\phi}_t$ and $S_t = (\boldsymbol{l} - \boldsymbol{\lambda}^e\boldsymbol{b}_w\boldsymbol{l})\boldsymbol{x}_t = \boldsymbol{\lambda}^e\boldsymbol{\phi}_t$, then the FMT (Roemer 1981: 48, theorem 2.11) proves that under stationary expectations, in a reproducible solution, given the requirement of a non-negative $\boldsymbol{\phi}_t$, all t, $\Pi_t > 0$ if and only if $S_t > 0$, all t.

By means of numerical examples, Kliman (2001) claims that if a different definition of reproducibility is adopted which requires, for example, all net outputs to be positive over a sufficiently long time span, but allows for $\phi_{jt} < 0$, some j, t, then there exist reproducible economies in which $\boldsymbol{\lambda}^e$ and $\boldsymbol{p}_t$ are such that $\Pi_t > 0$ while $S_t < 0$, some t, and vice versa. Although this does not refute the FMT, according to Kliman, it shows that the FMT is theoretically unsatisfactory because it holds only under Roemer's restrictive and unrealistic definition of reproducibility.

Similarly, in the "new interpretation," $\Pi_t = \boldsymbol{p}_t(\boldsymbol{I} - \boldsymbol{A} - \boldsymbol{b}_w\boldsymbol{l})\boldsymbol{x}_t$ and $S_t = \boldsymbol{l}\boldsymbol{x}_t - \boldsymbol{p}_t\boldsymbol{b}_w\boldsymbol{l}\boldsymbol{x}_t/\varepsilon_t^{\mathrm{NI}}$, where $\varepsilon_t^{\mathrm{NI}} = \boldsymbol{p}_t(\boldsymbol{I} - \boldsymbol{A})\boldsymbol{x}_t/\boldsymbol{l}\boldsymbol{x}_t$, and therefore $\Pi_t = \varepsilon_t^{\mathrm{NI}} S_t$. However, unless $(\boldsymbol{I} - \boldsymbol{A})\boldsymbol{x}_t$ is a non-negative vector, $\varepsilon_t^{\mathrm{NI}}$ can be negative, depending on $\boldsymbol{p}_t$: according to Kliman, this feature discloses "a serious conceptual flaw in the claim that the monetary expression of the value added by living labor can be measured by the price of the net product" (Kliman [2001, 102]), and it proves that even in the "new interpretation" $S_t > 0$ is not sufficient to have $\Pi_t > 0$.

There are several reasons why these arguments seem rather unconvincing. Consider, for instance, the standard interpretation: although the generalized FMT allows for different production sets available to capitalists, and thus for non-uniform profit rates (Roemer 1981: 47–50), it is untrue that it "examines the relation between profit and surplus labor under all possible market prices" (Kliman 2001: 100).[4] Even if one questions the requirement that $\phi_{jt} \geq 0$, all j and t, the FMT should be "conceived of as applying in a general expectations framework at a stationary state" (Roemer 1981: 40). Instead, Kliman's (2001) examples are arbitrary and his economies, in which $\phi_{jt} < 0$, some j, t, are clearly not in a reproducible solution as defined above, but no alternative definition is provided: their dynamic structure and capitalists' behaviors are simply not discussed. Although they can "reproduce" themselves in a merely physical sense, no argument is provided to show that they are in a "reproducible" (dis)equilibrium *solution*.

Even in a non-stationary path, the price and value vectors in Kliman's examples are unlikely to be the outcome of an economy with profit-maximizing capitalists. For instance, Kliman (2001: 101–2) claims that in the standard approach it is possible to have $\Pi_t < 0$ even if $S_t > 0$. However, given the technology with non-depreciating circulating capital, capitalists would never operate activities with negative profits, that is, $x_{jt} = 0$, for all goods j such that $\pi_{jt} = 0$, and thus $\Pi_t \geq 0$.[5]

In general, due to the lack of a proper dynamic framework with a definition of reproducibility and equilibrium (or, given TSS methodological claims, a model of disequilibrium dynamics), Kliman's critiques of *both* the standard and the "new interpretation" reduce to the trivially true, and rather uninteresting, algebraic statement that there are arbitrary combinations of the variables such that $\Pi_t > 0$ while $S_t < 0$, and vice versa; that is, to the claim that in a disequilibrium, conceived as a state where "anything goes," the variables can take any arbitrary values so that the FMT may not hold, and the "new interpretation's" MELT may be negative. Appealing to the "real world," claiming that the postulate of positive net outputs "is violated in every actual economy, [and] the theorems do not apply to the real world" (Kliman 2001: 103), does not make the argument more compelling.

Most important, even assuming, for the sake of the argument, Kliman's (2001) critiques to be convincing, it is difficult to see how the TSS approach might provide a superior interpretation of Marx's theory of exploitation, as claimed by TSS authors based on claims (c)–(f). Consider the TSS equation describing the dynamics of the temporalist MELT (Kliman 2001: 107), which, in the linear setting adopted in this paper, can be derived by post-multiplying (1) by $\boldsymbol{x}_t$:[6]

$$\frac{\boldsymbol{p}_{t+1}\boldsymbol{x}_t}{\varepsilon_{t+1}} - \frac{\boldsymbol{p}_t\boldsymbol{A}\boldsymbol{x}_t}{\varepsilon_t} = \boldsymbol{l}\boldsymbol{x}_t \qquad (5.1)$$

According to Kliman, "examination of [(8)] shows that if [$\boldsymbol{pAx}$], [$\boldsymbol{lx}$], [$\boldsymbol{px}$], and the initial condition [ε_0] are positive and finite, then all subsequent terms of the [ε] series must also be positive and finite" (ibid., 108). Hence, claims (c)–(f) hold, proving that, of the existing interpretations of Marx's value theory, it is only under the TSS approach that "the exploitation theory of profit holds" (ibid., 106): in particular, since, by (4) and (5), $\Pi_t^R = \varepsilon_t S_t$, then $\Pi_t^R > 0$ if and only if $S_t > 0$.

This algebraically correct conclusion begs the question: why should ε_0 be positive in the first place? At most, (5.1) describes the motion of MELT, but it does not define it, and thus it says nothing about the sign of ε_0, while the TSS model (1)–(7) is inherently underdetermined. (Moreover, (5.1) forcefully shows that the TSS assumption $\varepsilon_t = 1$, *all t*, is totally arbitrary out of a steady state.)[7]

In a dynamic perspective one might argue that, for t large, ε_t converges to some positive finite value, regardless of ε_0. But then a steady-state argument must be adopted, in contradiction with the TSS "disequilibrium" rhetoric, and in any case nothing would guarantee that $\varepsilon_t \geq 0$ far from the steady state. Again, the desired result can only be obtained by arbitrarily assuming $\varepsilon_t \geq 0$, that is, by *assuming* $\varepsilon_t \geq 0$, all t, which is equivalent to *assuming* a priori that claims (c)–(f)—and, indeed, claims (a) and (b) and the solution of the transformation problem—hold.[8] Thus, the emphasis on historical versus simultaneous valuation seems misplaced and the TSS approach does not offer a "superior" interpretation of Marx's theory of exploitation: no new insights are gained with respect to alternative approaches, while much is lost in terms of analytical rigor and conceptual clarity.

NOTES

1. {Veneziani's phrase "claims (c)–(f)," and his phrase "claims (a) and (b)" that appears at the end of this chapter, refer to the following statement by Kliman and McGlone (1999: 55): "we have shown that, under the temporal single-system interpretation: (a) all of Marx's aggregate value-price equalities hold, (b) values cannot be negative, (c) profit cannot be positive unless surplus-value is positive, (d) value production is no longer irrelevant to price and profit determination, (e) the profit rate is invariant to the distribution of profit, [and] (f) productivity in luxury industries affects the general rate of profit."}
2. For a survey see, for example, Desai (1991).
3. {Veneziani's notation is basically the same as that used by Kliman in chapter 2. The major differences are that Veneziani uses ε^{NI} and ε to refer to the monetary expression of labor-time (MELT) in the new interpretation and the TSSI, respectively.}
4. In Kliman (2001) there is no analysis of capitalists' choices: if they can operate all the activities of the linear technology, the only possible equilibrium p is the equal-profit-rate vector (see Roemer 1981: 20, Theorem 1.2), and all Kliman's (2001) "results" are unwarranted.
5. If $\boldsymbol{A}$ is indecomposable, as in Roemer (1981: 48), Kliman's economy is simply not viable.
6. {Here and below, Veneziani refers to his equations (1) through (7), which appear earlier in his paper. These equations pertain to the following aspects of Marx's theory as understood by the TSSI: (1), commodities' prices; (2), commodities' values; (3), the economy-wide sum of price-value differences; (4), real profit, Π^R; (5), surplus-value, S; (6), prices of production; and (7), the general rate of profit.}
7. {In chapter 9, Kliman and Freeman argue that Veneziani is wrong when he claims that "the value of ε is fixed in an arbitrary, ad hoc way. . . . [I]ts value is determined by the *data*" (emphasis in original) and it generally does not equal one.}
8. Similar conclusions are reached by Mohun (2003) {chap. 3 of this book} in his analysis of Kliman (2001).

Chapter 6

Replicating Marx

A Reply to Mohun

Andrew Kliman and Alan Freeman

"Arbitrary" stands in opposition to "Natural" only if one is attempting to designate the manner in which signs have been established.

—Michel Foucault, *The Order of Things**

INTRODUCTION

Kliman (2001 {chap. 2 of this book}) showed that "simultaneist" interpretations—which hold that Marx valued inputs and outputs simultaneously—contradict Marx's exploitation theory of profit, while the temporal single-system interpretation (TSSI) conforms to it. Mohun (2003 {chap. 3 of this book}) calls these demonstrations into question; this note defends them.[1]

Mohun's is the first critique of the TSSI to address the interpretive controversy in a serious, methodical way. He accepts that the relative adequacy of exegetical interpretations, such as the temporalist and simultaneist accounts, can be evaluated only on the basis of a clear "criterion of decidability."[2] He employs what he calls the "criterion of replication": "An accurate textual interpretation is one which can, on the basis of (an interpretation of) the text's premises, derive (and hence replicate) its theoretical conclusions" (pp. 96–97).

This clear, rigorous test of interpretive adequacy follows from the standard hermeneutic tenet that interpretations need to understand the text as a coherent whole. Proposed by George Stigler, the test has been embraced by other leading historians of economic thought and by proponents of the TSSI (see Kliman 2002). Yet the value-theory controversy has remained unresolved for decades because the TSSI's critics refuse to embrace the test. Mohun's contribution shows that there is a way out of this impasse.

MOHUN'S DEFENSE OF SIMULTANEIST INTERPRETATIONS

Kliman (2001) proved that Marx's profit theory is contradicted by all simultaneist interpretations—namely the standard (Bortkiewiczian) interpretation, the "new interpretation" (NI), and the simultaneous single-system interpretations (SSSI). Employing their definitions of surplus labor and profit, he exhibited logically possible cases in which

1. profit is positive though surplus labor is not, which shows that surplus labor is not *necessary* for profit;
2. surplus labor is positive though profit is not, which shows that surplus labor is not *sufficient* for profit.

These results directly contradict three decades of claims that the so-called "fundamental Marxian theorem" (FMT) proved that the standard interpretation implies that surplus labor is both necessary and sufficient for profit.

Mohun's challenge to Kliman's results is fatally incomplete. He merely questions whether the aggregate money price of the net product (PNP) can be negative. This has nothing to do with the question of necessity. Kliman proved—*without assuming a negative PNP*—that all simultaneist interpretations imply that surplus labor is unnecessary for profit. By failing to address these proofs, Mohun concedes point (1): that surplus labor is unnecessary for profit under *all* simultaneist interpretations.

Kliman also proved, again without assuming a negative PNP, that surplus labor is insufficient for profit under the standard interpretation. The negativity of the PNP is therefore relevant only to point (2)—sufficiency—and only with respect to the NI and SSSI. The only thing that Mohun actually defends, then, is the claim that surplus labor is sufficient for profit under the NI and SSSI. We now turn to that claim.[3]

The NI and SSSI imply that surplus labor and profit must have the same sign when the PNP is positive. Assume for the moment that it is indeed always positive. Does this make surplus labor sufficient for profit? No. It is insufficient, because positive profit requires something *more* than surplus labor—namely a positive PNP.

If the net products of all goods were always positive, as most versions of the FMT assume, then the PNP, too, would always be positive. Crucially, Mohun concedes that this assumption is false: "That there are some negative net products is undeniable" (p. 98). But whenever some net products are negative, there exist logically possible sets of prices that result in a negative PNP, and thus negative profit despite positive surplus labor. Hence, *Mohun implicitly concedes that surplus labor is insufficient for profit.*

Since negative net products exist, as we all agree, the sign of the PNP depends upon the sizes of material input-output coefficients and the extent to which prices deviate from a hypothetical equilibrium. If *either* the input-output coefficients *or* the deviations were sufficiently large, then the PNP would be negative. This could occur even if the Hawkins-Simon conditions were satisfied, that is, even if continual physical reproduction and growth of the economy were possible (see Kliman 2001: 103–5). Given sufficiently small input-output coefficients, however, the PNP will remain positive even in the face of sizeable deviations from equilibrium.[4]

Seizing upon this last fact, Mohun rejects Kliman's refutation of the insufficiency theorem. It was not "shown conclusively," he claims, that a negative PNP is "economically possible in the sense of arising out of economic behavior" (p. 98). *This objection is utterly irrelevant.* We repeat: *surplus labor would be insufficient for profit even if the PNP were always positive, because positive profit requires something more than surplus labor.* It requires small input-output coefficients and relatively modest deviations from a hypothetical equilibrium—the factors that make the PNP positive. If the coefficients and deviations were large enough, then profit would be negative despite the existence of surplus labor. Hence the NI and SSSI clearly contradict Marx's (1894 [1981]: 270, emphasis added) conclusion that surplus labor is "the *exclusive* source of profit."

Certain economic behaviors can perhaps ensure that the PNP is positive, but they cannot make surplus labor sufficient for profit. The very fact that profit depends upon something more than surplus labor—"proper" economic behavior—means that surplus labor is insufficient. Mohun's appeal to behavior therefore proves exactly the opposite of what he intended. It is a tacit admission of insufficiency.

He seems to suggest, however, that Kliman's proof of insufficiency was an illegitimate trick, since it employed "arbitrary" prices (p. 98). But those prices were perfectly legitimate. The FMT of Okishio and Morishima considered the relationship between surplus labor and profit under all positive prices. Kliman did the same thing. He found cases in which surplus labor is positive while profit is negative. This disproved sufficiency—full stop.

A crucial matter of logic is at stake here: a sufficiency theorem is true only if it holds universally, that is, only if no *logically possible* exceptions exist. (Whether the exceptions are "economically possible" is irrelevant. After all, most sufficiency theorems have nothing to do with economics.) A single counterexample refutes a theorem that is said to hold universally. The ball is therefore in Mohun's court, not ours. He must either show that Kliman's counterexample is logically impossible, or concede that the sufficiency theorem has been disproved. To suggest that the theorem does hold true once one ignores the inconvenient ("arbitrary") exceptions is to commit a grave offense against logic.[5]

A properly formulated mathematical theorem is not a pair of designer punk jeans. It is not a ragbag of random exceptions and restrictions assembled for display. It is a coherent sequence of deductions from a definite set of premises, stated *before*, not *after*, exceptions have been identified. If Mohun wants to restrict the FMT to "non-arbitrary" and "economically possible" cases, there is a proper way to do so. He first needs to concede that the theorem as currently stated is false. Then he can formulate a revised theorem, beginning with a clear definition of "nonarbitrary" and "economically possible" circumstances, and ending with a proof that the PNP must be positive under those circumstances.

There are strong reasons to doubt that such a theorem is possible. Two examples in Kliman (2003 {chap. 4 of this book}) derive a negative PNP in precisely the manner that Mohun (p. 98) insists upon, and thereby demonstrate that a negative PNP is indeed "economically possible" in his sense. But even if such a theorem were possible, it would not prove sufficiency nor negate the fact that the NI and SSSI contradict Marx's theory. It would simply clarify their implications.

MOHUN'S CRITIQUE OF THE TSSI

Mohun (pp. 98–99) claims that the TSSI fails to replicate Marx's profit theory (and for precisely the same reason that the NI and SSSI fail). This claim is founded on a mathematical error.

Whenever the PNP is negative, he contends, the temporalist monetary expression of labor time (MELT) must also be negative and, consequently, surplus labor and real profit must have opposite signs. This is incorrect. Mohun has simply misinterpreted the left-hand side (LHS) of his own equation (3.26):

$$P(t+1) - \frac{\tau(t+1)}{\tau(t)} C(t) = \tau(t+1) L(t) \qquad (6.1)$$

where P is the aggregate price of output, τ is the temporalist MELT, C denotes monetary expenditures on used-up constant capital, and L is living labor.

Now Mohun claims that the LHS is the PNP. If that were true, then $\tau(t+1)$ would indeed be negative whenever the PNP is negative (since L is positive). However, the LHS and the PNP are not the same. The LHS equals the *temporalist* MELT times L, while the PNP equals the *simultaneist* MELT times L.

The following example shows that the two MELTs differ and, more important, disproves Mohun's claim that the temporalist MELT must be negative whenever the PNP is negative. A single good is produced. Its price p is constant, as are gross output x, the non-labor input a, and L. Assume that $p = x = L = 1$, and that $a > 1$. The PNP is

$$p(x - a)$$

and the simultaneist MELT is

$$p(x - a)/L$$

Both equal $1 - a$; they are always negative. Yet since $P = px = 1$ and $C = pa = a$, for all t, (6.1) becomes

$$1 - \left(\frac{\tau(t+1)}{\tau(t)}\right)a = \tau(t+1) \tag{6.2}$$

Isolating $\tau(t + 1)$ on the LHS, we obtain

$$\tau(t+1) = \left(\frac{\tau(t)}{\tau(t)+a}\right) \tag{6.3}$$

which shows clearly that if the initial condition $\tau(0)$ is positive, then all subsequent values of τ must also be positive. Surplus labor and real profit consequently have the same sign.

This conclusion holds generally. Kliman (2001: 106–8) proved the following theorem: if P, C, L and $\tau(0)$ are positive and finite, then τ *must always* be positive.[6] It follows that surplus labor and real profit, as understood by the TSSI, *must always* have the same sign. Mohun (p. 99) acknowledges that this theorem is true. Because he misinterprets equation (6.1), however, he denies that the theorem applies to negative-PNP cases. The above example shows that it does apply.

Yet Kliman's theorem has also been challenged for another reason. Veneziani (2004: 6, 15) forcefully objects to its premises, claiming that the MELT is "undefined" and therefore that the positivity of $\tau(0)$ is an "arbitrary *assumption*." He even objects to the "assumption" (without which P and C might be negative) that some prices are positive and none are negative. Mohun, too, calls the premises "sign restrictions" and "assumptions" (p. 99) and claims that the MELT is "undefined" (p. 101).

In order to dispose of these objections once and for all, we now prove that the challenged "sign restrictions" must hold true. Note first that the temporalist MELT is *not* "undefined." As Mohun (p. 94) acknowledges (before contradicting himself), it is "the ratio of total price to total value." Thus the MELT exists only when value is produced, that is, only under commodity production. Our first proof therefore presupposes the existence of commodity production.

Proof that $P > 0$, $C \geq 0$ under commodity production

Commodity production is incompatible with cases in which all prices are zero. Negative prices "exist" in economic theory only by virtue of a definitional quirk. The statement that trash has a negative price, for example, really means that its "buyer" is the seller of a positively priced trash collection service.

Thus any price that has wrongly been designated "negative" can be made positive by reinstating the buyer and seller in their correct positions. Hence no prices are negative, and some are positive under commodity production. And since inputs and gross outputs cannot be negative, and some outputs must be positive under commodity production, it follows that $P > 0$ and $C \geq 0$.

Proof that the temporalist MELT is initially positive and finite

By definition, the price of any item—whether commodity or other asset—equals τ times the amount of labor the item commands in exchange. Also by definition, the "price" of a unit of money equals one. On any date arbitrarily selected as the "initial" one, a unit of money commanded a positive and finite amount of labor—one could buy a finite amount of products of labor with it. Hence τ was initially positive and finite as well.

It might be argued that money did not initially command any labor that *counted as value*, since the products in existence at the start of commodity production were not produced as commodities. Under this interpretation of Marx's theory, the inputs employed at the start of commodity production did not transfer value to the products produced. Hence the total value of commodities (in terms of labor time) was at first just the living labor extracted, a positive quantity. As demonstrated above, total price was also positive. Hence the initial MELT, the ratio of total price to total value, was positive as well.

CONCLUSION: ONCE AGAIN ON REPLICATION

In his conclusion, Mohun states that the TSSI is no better than simultaneist interpretations at replicating Marx's theoretical conclusions (p. 100). This note has demonstrated, on the contrary, that the TSSI succeeds in replicating Marx's profit theory while the simultaneist interpretations fail. There are many other cases like this, and none in which a simultaneist interpretation replicates Marx while the TSSI fails.

Two points remain to be addressed, both of which pertain to Mohun's inconsistent application of the criterion of replication. His embrace of the criterion is a crucial step that opens the way to a constructive dialogue. Consistent application of the criterion would clear still more debris from the path thus opened.

First, Mohun seems to suggest that one may legitimately reject the TSSI in favor of other exegetical interpretations, *even though* it replicates Marx's conclusions but they do not. He implies that the TSSI is unacceptable because it understands Marx's concept of value "*differently from how it is conventionally understood*" (p. 93, emphasis in original)—as if conformation to conventional wisdom, not an interpretation's ability to deduce the author's theoretical conclusions, were the test of its adequacy. For instance, when Mohun notes that the TSSI's critics will not be convinced by the proof that it conforms to Marx's profit theory because they would not accept its "definition of value" (p. 98), he seems to see nothing wrong with that attitude.[7] But what would he think of Einstein's critics, who refused to be convinced by the general theory of relativity because they rejected its "definition of time"? Did this constitute a refutation of his theory?

It is unscientific and dogmatic to demand that an interpretation or theory convince its critics. All new interpretations and theories challenge received definitions. The only way to prevent those who control the journals—and, behind them, those who fund the graduate schools—from dictating what is "true" and "false," "natural" and "arbitrary," is to accept *and consistently apply* a clear, evidence-based criterion of decidability.

Secondly, having incorrectly concluded that the criterion of replication yields indecisive results, Mohun argues that the decisive issue is which of the different "variants of Marxism" (p. 101) offer a "coherent theory for today's world" (p. 100). The TSSI is not among them, since "it is only an interpretation," not a theory in its own right (p. 100). But this comparison ignores the most important variant of Marxism—the Marxism of Marx.

When interpreted in accordance with the TSSI, Marx's own theory is logically coherent, and an *alternative* to the simultaneist revisions of his theory. Consequently, "One may now in good conscience turn directly to *Capital*, unencumbered by others' 'corrections' of its alleged errors, in order to help analyze and understand the world in which we live" (Kliman 2001: 110).

This is not, we repeat for the *n*th time, a claim that Marx is necessarily right. It is, however, a disproof of the false allegation that has stymied progress throughout economics for most of the last century—that Marx is necessarily wrong. The real issue, which Mohun simply ignores, is whether the explanatory power of *Capital* is surpassed or even rivaled by any variant of simultaneist Marxism.

Dozens of simultaneist authors have incorrectly claimed that their models replicate Marx's profit theory, and that they have proved his work to be internally inconsistent in other respects. The TSSI has shown that they are simply wrong. The inconsistencies lie not in Marx, but in their own work.

Thus the real issue is, and remains, that economics, including Marxist economics above all, will never evolve a "coherent theory for today's world" as long as it persistently, willfully, and theologically rules out of court, against all the evidence, the most coherent theory so far available to it—that of Karl Marx.

NOTES

We have benefited greatly, in the preparation of this paper, from discussions with Aldo Fabian Balardini, Andy Brown, and Simon Mohun.

1. Space limitations prevent us from responding to all of Mohun's errors, especially his misunderstandings of the TSSI.
2. Mohun (2003: 97). Hereafter, we reference this paper by page number only.
3. In the remainder of this section, "surplus labor" and "profit" refer exclusively to the NI-SSSI definitions of these terms unless otherwise indicated.
4. It is far less likely that the aggregate price of the physical surplus—the PNP minus wages—will be positive. If it is negative, then so is profit as defined by the *standard* interpretation, even when surplus labor is positive.
5. The TSSI's critics used the same tactic when attempting to dismiss our refutations of the Okishio theorem (see Freeman and Kliman, 2000: 245–47).
6. The proof also goes through when $C = 0$. Note also that any time can be chosen as time 0. Thus if the MELT is positive at *any* time, it must be positive forever after.
7. Mohun also complains that Kliman succeeded in proving that the TSSI replicates Marx's profit theory only because he made use of two "assumptions" (p. 2). Yet the "assumptions"—that values and prices are determined temporally and as a single system—*are* the TSSI. The complaint that Kliman proved that the TSSI replicates Marx's profit theory only because he made use of the TSSI is, therefore, tautological.

Chapter 7

The Incoherence of the TSSI

A Reply to Kliman and Freeman

Simon Mohun and Roberto Veneziani

In this paper, we examine the substantive arguments proposed by Kliman and Freeman (2006) {chap. 6 of this book} in their reply to Mohun (2003) {chap. 3 of this book}. We find them seriously deficient.

1. INTRODUCTION

In recent years, considerable attention has been paid to the temporal single-system interpretation (TSSI) of Marx's *Capital*. Its adherents claim that the TSSI "refutes" what they see as false allegations that Marx made logical mistakes—false allegations based on a "simultaneist" interpretation of Marx that the TSSI "shows" is untenable. They claim that, while Marx was not necessarily correct, the TSSI has an explanatory power surpassing that of any other interpretation of *Capital*, and that only the TSSI is consistent with Marx's method and results (Kliman 2001 {chap. 2 of this book}; Kliman and Freeman 2006). This short paper deals with the substantive arguments in Kliman and Freeman.[1]

2. REPRISE OF A DEBATE

Marxism holds that profits exist because labor is exploited. "Exploitation" has a precise meaning: that the worker is paid the full value of the labor power she supplies, but that property relations entail the appropriation by the capitalist of what the worker produces, whose value is greater than the value of labor power. This theoretical proposition is part of the core of Marxism, however else that core is understood.

In contemporary Marxian economics, this theoretical proposition is called the "fundamental Marxian theorem" (FMT). Loosely, it states that the existence of surplus labor is necessary and sufficient for the existence of profits. Roemer (1981) provides a precise statement of the FMT, and goes on to prove it for a reproducible economy. The proof requires seven assumptions plus four conditions underlying a "reproducible solution," and if any of these is violated, then the FMT does not necessarily hold. Roemer himself discusses the role of the assumptions, and provides some counterexamples to the FMT (ibid.: 48, 50).

Kliman (2001: 99) wrote "general versions of the FMT . . . prove that the theorem holds for any set of positive market prices. . . . Yet these versions of the FMT rely on an equally restrictive condition: in every period, a positive physical surplus of each good must be produced." This is misleading. Roemer's FMT does not hold for any set of positive market prices. It holds for prices that support a reproducible solution (Roemer 1981, theorem 2.11: 48), and reproducibility requires a strictly positive vector of net products (ibid., definition 2.5(a): 41). Hence Kliman's numerical example (Kliman 2001: 100), which demonstrates that if one of the conditions for the FMT does not hold, then the FMT does not hold, is quite beside the point. Nobody could disagree.

What Kliman tried to do was to show that:

1. negative net products of some goods exist in the real world;
2. hence theorems that assume that they do not do not apply to the real world—this includes Roemer's FMT and all other variants of Marxism in which inputs and outputs are valued simultaneously;
3. only the TSSI escapes this stricture, because in the TSSI, the FMT holds "*under completely general conditions*" with "absolutely *no* restrictive postulates" (Kliman 2001: 106, emphasis in original).

Hence only the TSSI "vindicates the logical coherence of the exploitation theory of profit" (ibid.: 110).

As regards point 2: can an "unrealistic" theory have explanatory power? No theory is entirely realistic. Because they do more than describe, all theories make assumptions. All theories abstract from empirical reality, and a theory is a good one if it has explanatory power. But all of these terms are loaded and carry a variety of interpretations. Issues concerning precisely what a theory is, how its adequacy should be assessed, what are necessary and what sufficient conditions for propositions within a theory, and what is required to falsify a particular proposition, are always delicate issues. The degree of the lack of realism of the assumptions required for particular propositions, and the extent to which the explanatory power of the theory is thereby affected are matters of judgment, and we leave it to the interested reader to judge the empirical plausibility of Kliman's constructed numerical examples.

Regarding point 3, Mohun (2003) showed that the TSSI FMT required a particular theoretical concept of temporality, a particular understanding of the measurement of value, and some particular sign restrictions (ibid., 98–99; see also Veneziani 2004). These are not "completely general conditions." Unwittingly perhaps, Kliman and Freeman clearly illustrate the difficulties with the TSSI. We offer three examples.

2.1. Example 1

(Kliman and Freeman 2006: 121) A single good is produced. Its price p is constant, as are gross output x, the non-labor input a, and labor input L. Assume that $p = x = L = 1$, and that $a > 1$. The aggregate money price of the net product is $p(x - a)$, and the simultaneist monetary expression of labor time (MELT) is $p(x - a)/L$. Both are $(1 - a)$ and are negative. The TSSI aggregate value equation is[2]

$$P(t+1) - \frac{\tau(t+1)}{\tau(t)}C(t) = \tau(t+1)L(t) \tag{7.1}$$

On substituting the assumed values, this becomes

$$1 - \frac{\tau(t+1)}{\tau(t)}a = \tau(t+1) \tag{7.2}$$

or

$$\tau(t+1) = \frac{\tau(t)}{\tau(t) + \mathrm{a}} \tag{7.3}$$

Kliman and Freeman conclude that equation (7.3) "shows clearly that if the initial condition $\tau(0)$ is positive, then all subsequent values of τ must also be positive. Surplus labor and profit have the same sign."

But if we are interested in "completely general conditions," then consider a steady state in which the temporalist MELT τ does not change from period t to period $t + 1$. (And, after all, *all* variables are assumed to be constant in this example.) Equation (7.2) then becomes

$$1 - a = \tau \tag{7.4}$$

and τ is negative by the assumption that $a > 1$. This is supposed to illustrate that "τ *must always* be positive" (ibid., emphasis in original).

Clearly, as Mohun (2003) emphasized, quite a lot hinges on the definition of the temporalist MELT and its associated "sign restrictions."

Kliman and Freeman are concerned to "prove that the challenged 'sign restrictions' must hold true." Their "proofs" are the subject of the next two examples.

2.2. Example 2: "Proof" that $P > 0$, $C \geq 0$

(Kliman and Freeman 2006: 122) Kliman and Freeman's argument is that, under commodity production, no prices are negative and some are positive; inputs and gross outputs cannot be negative, and some outputs must be positive. Therefore $P > 0$, $C \geq 0$. The conclusion does not follow. That p and x are semi-positive vectors does not imply that their product P is strictly positive.

2.3. Example 3: "Proof" that the Temporalist MELT is Initially Positive and Finite

(Kliman and Freeman 2006: 122–32) Kliman and Freeman are emphatic that the temporalist MELT τ is not undefined, because it is the ratio of total price to total value. Rearranging equation (7.1),

$$\tau(t+1) = \frac{\tau(t)P(t+1)}{C(t) + \tau(t)L(t)} \tag{7.5}$$

This serves to define the MELT of one period in terms of the preceding period's MELT. For this to be a definition, an independent definition of $\tau(0)$ must be given. Kliman and Freeman conspicuously fail to do this. They have no explanation of why $\tau(0)$ is independent of $\tau(-1)$—if it is not, there is an infinite regress; if it is, then there must be some explanation of why $\tau(1)$ is not independent of $\tau(0)$. None is forthcoming, and hence the TSSI MELT is undefined. Nevertheless, it is clear from equation (7.5) why it is so important for Kliman and Freeman to be able to prove that $\tau(0)$ is positive and finite. Consider, then, their "proof," which we spell out step by step.

1. Define the price of any commodity as τ times the amount of labor the commodity commands in exchange.

$$p_i(t) = \tau(t)l_i(t) \tag{7.6}$$

2. Define the price of a unit of money as being unity.

$$p_m = 1 \tag{7.7}$$

3. Select an arbitrary date (period 0). Then

$$p_m(0) = \tau(0)l_m(0) = 1 \tag{7.8}$$

4. Suppose that a unit of money in period 0 commands a positive and finite amount of labor.
5. Then, since

$$\tau(0) = \frac{1}{l_m(0)} \tag{7.9}$$

the temporalist MELT is initially positive and finite.

There is no logical deduction here, just a series of assumptions, with no explanation of what is meant by "the amount of labor the commodity commands in exchange." Why does this reasoning hold at $t = 0$ but not at any other t? If this argument is valid for "any date arbitrarily selected as the 'initial' one," then at any specified date t it is possible to consider $\tau(t)$ as determined by variables at t only (and not at previous dates); but this contradicts equation (7.5). There is also some confusion in determination, since equation (7.6) uses τ to define price, whereas equation (7.9) uses the labor-commanded price of money to determine τ. In sum, this "proof" by assumption merely confirms that the temporalist MELT is undefined.

3. TIME AND THE MELT

Production takes time; inputs are temporarily prior to outputs. How should inputs be valued? The answer given by almost all schools of economics is that they should be valued at current or replacement cost. When prices are changing, we want to know whether the firm is viable and can reproduce itself. With a labor theory of value, there is another reason: we want to be able unambiguously to attribute the value of net output to the labor that produced it.

For Kliman and Freeman, equation (7.1) shows that the value created by labor is equal to total sales revenue less the monetary expenditure on used-up constant capital, each deflated by the appropriate MELT. But

$$C(t) = p(t)c(t) = p(t+1)c(t) - \{p(t+1) - p(t)\}c(t)$$

so that

$$\frac{P(t+1)}{\tau(t+1)} - \frac{p(t+1)c(t)}{\tau(t)} + \frac{\{p(t+1) - p(t)\}c(t)}{\tau(t)} = L(t) \tag{7.10}$$

The third term on the left-hand side is an inventory revaluation because of price changes. Should its (positive or negative) effects be included as part of the value created by living labor? We say "No," whereas Kliman and Freeman say "Yes."

Because Kliman and Freeman include inventory revaluation effects as part of the new value created by labor, value is dissociated from labor performed. Instead, value is determined from observed prices and quantities for some value of the MELT. But the TSSI MELT is undefined, and hence there is no determination of the new value created.

4. CONCLUSION

In their use of logic, their reporting of the views of those with whom they disagree, and in their elaboration of their own fundamental categories, Kliman and Freeman leave something to be desired.

NOTES

1. Space constraints preclude our replying to the more trivial inaccuracies and distortions in Kliman and Freeman.
2. These symbols are defined in Kliman (2001) and repeated in Mohun (2003) and Kliman and Freeman (2006).

Chapter 8

Simultaneous Valuation vs. the Exploitation Theory of Profit

A Summing Up

Alan Freeman and Andrew Kliman

This paper examines the claims made by Simon Mohun and Roberto Veneziani in their article "The incoherence of the TSSI: A reply to Kliman and Freeman," published in *Capital & Class*, no. 92 {chap. 7 of this book}. We show that they have effectively conceded that simultaneist interpretations of Marx's theory contradict his conclusion that exploitation (workers' surplus labor) is the exclusive source of profit in capitalism. We demonstrate the errors of logic in their claim that the temporal single-system (TSS) interpretation is incoherent. Thus the results of this debate serve to confirm that the TSS interpretation—contrary to simultaneist interpretations—reproduces all of Marx's principal disputed conclusions, and therefore constitutes a superior interpretation of his theory of value.

INTRODUCTION: WHAT IS AT STAKE?

The central issue in this debate has been the incompatibility between simultaneist interpretations and Marx's own theory of profit, as is clear from the title of Andrew Kliman's (2001) initial contribution, "Simultaneous valuation vs. the exploitation theory of profit" {chap. 2 of this book}.[1] Overturning the conventional wisdom of a quarter century, our prior contributions have demonstrated that all simultaneist interpretations of Marx's theory contradict his conclusion that exploitation (workers' surplus labor) is the exclusive source of profit in capitalism.

Simon Mohun and Roberto Veneziani (2007) {chap. 7 of this book} simply evade this issue. They do not refute or even attempt to refute our demonstration, and hence they effectively concede that Marx's theory and simultaneous valuation are indeed incompatible. It is time for the wider community to recognize this as well. As we document below, Mohun and Veneziani also fail to respond directly to several other key arguments contained in our response {Kliman and Freeman (2006); chap. 6 of this book} to Mohun's (2003) critique {chap. 3 of this book}. Instead, they change the subject, railing against what they grandly call the "incoherence" of the temporal single-system interpretation (TSSI) of Marx's value theory, and against our "seriously deficient" arguments, logic, and reporting of opponents' views (Mohun and Veneziani 2007: 139, 144).

The grandness of their rhetoric stands in inverse proportion to the effectiveness and relevance of their arguments. What they actually offer is only a collection of technical and tangential quibbles that evade the significant issues in this debate, and which function principally to cast aspersions on us and on the TSSI. Thus they lambast our demonstration that the TSSI conforms to Marx's theory of profit because we supposedly failed to exclude the possibility that all commodities are free, and the possibility that living labor initially creates a negative amount of value in monetary terms. Yet they provide no argument, much less proof, that either of these extreme, hypothetical cases is logically possible. Even if these and others of their quibbles were formally correct—and we will show that they are not—the flimsiness of Mohun and Veneziani's objections would make clear that they are grasping at straws.

Yet why are Mohun and Veneziani trying to discredit the TSSI? We believe that their ultimate target is Marx. The simultaneist interpretations to which they subscribe are defective (as they implicitly concede), since they have been shown to contradict his exploitation theory of profit. But if it can be shown that the TSSI *also* contradicts Marx's theory, then a strong case can be made that Marx, not simultaneism, is at fault: that the reason that no interpretation replicates his theoretical conclusions is that they cannot be replicated, because his theory is logically incoherent.

And if Marx becomes a dead dog, or at best a source of inspiration without logical coherence, two important consequences follow. First, simultaneist Marxists will no longer have to worry about nor explain away the exegetical inadequacies of their interpretations. Mohun's (2003: 100) wish would become reality: "What is required is not an assessment of [the exegetical adequacy of] rival interpretations, but a theory for today's world and its use in empirical analysis." Second, simultaneist Marxists would have the field to themselves. Marx's own value theory, currently a live alternative to their theories, would cease to be so. The essential function of Mohun and Veneziani's contribution, as it is of so much of the corpus of simultaneist Marxist contributions, is suppressive and antipluralist: its function is to rule Marx himself out of court while keeping it free for his Marxist economist critics.

WHAT HAS BEEN ESTABLISHED

Our previous contributions to this debate have demonstrated the following propositions:

1. All simultaneist interpretations of Marx's value theory contradict his conclusion that workers' surplus labor is the exclusive source of capitalists' profit, because they imply the logical possibility of profit without surplus labor and surplus labor without profit (Kliman 2001: 99–103).
2. The Okishio-Morishima "fundamental Marxian theorem" (FMT) and similar theorems do not refute (1). They merely show that, under simultaneist definitions, both profit and surplus labor are necessarily positive in *imaginary* economies in which the net product of every good is positive at every moment (Kliman 2001: 99–103).[2,3]
3. Economies can and do reproduce themselves without satisfying this restriction: negative net products exist (Kliman 2001: 103–5; Mohun 2003: 98; Kliman and Freeman 2006: 118–19).
4. Whenever the aggregate money price of the net product (PNP) is negative, the "New Interpretation" and simultaneous single-system interpretations imply, contrary to Marx's theory, that profit is negative when surplus labor is positive (Kliman 2001: 100–2; Mohun 2003: 100).
5. A negative PNP is logically possible (Kliman 2001: 100–2).
   Mohun (2003) explicitly acknowledged that (3) and (4) were correct. He also implicitly acknowledged that (1), (2), and (5) were correct (Mohun 2003: 98). Mohun and Veneziani (2007) likewise fail to challenge any of these propositions. Thus there is no disagreement about the central claim put forward in Kliman's (2001) original contribution: *that all simultaneist interpretations fail to replicate Marx's theory of profit in a logically robust manner.*

Our previous contributions have also demonstrated that:

6. Mohun's (2003: 99) claim that the temporalist monetary expression of labor-time (MELT) is negative whenever the PNP is negative is not correct (Kliman and Freeman 2006: 120–21).
7. Even if the PNP were always positive, surplus labor would still not be the exclusive source of profit under simultaneism, because something more—a positive PNP—would be needed in order to guarantee that profit is positive (Kliman and Freeman 2006: 118–20).
8. A negative PNP is "economically possible" in Mohun's (2003: 98) sense (Kliman, 2003).[4]

Mohun and Veneziani fail to challenge, and thereby implicitly concede, points (6) and (7).[5] In response to point (8), they "leave it to the interested reader to judge the empirical plausibility of Kliman's constructed numerical examples" demonstrating that a negative PNP is "economically possible" (Mohun and Veneziani 2007: 141). Were they able to disprove these examples, they would surely have done so instead of dumping the problem in the reader's lap. Moreover, their new demand for "empirical plausibility," for which they provide no justification, is a diversion from Mohun's original challenge that Kliman produce "economically possible" examples.

Finally, our previous contributions have demonstrated that:

9. If the temporalist MELT τ is positive, then the TSSI replicates Marx's conclusion that workers' surplus labor is the exclusive source of profit in capitalism. According to TSSI definitions, real profit will always be positive when, but only when, surplus labor is positive (Kliman 2001: 108).
10. If the total price of output *P*, total living labor *L*, and the initial temporalist MELT, $\tau(0)$, are all positive, and if the total price of inputs used up in production, *C*, is positive or zero, then τ must always be positive thereafter (Kliman 2001: 108; Mohun 2003: 99; Kliman and Freeman 2006: 125, n6).
11. Under commodity production, it is indeed the case that $\tau(0) > 0$, and that, at all times, $P > 0$, $L > 0$, and $C \geq 0$ (Kliman and Freeman 2006: 122–23). Thus the TSSI replicates Marx's exploitation theory of profit (Kliman 2001: 108).

Mohun (2003: 98–99) explicitly acknowledged that propositions (9) and (10) are correct, and Mohun and Veneziani (2007) do not challenge them. Thus of the eleven propositions we have demonstrated, only the final one, (11), is still contested.

PROOF THAT THE TSSI REPLICATES MARX'S THEORY

Mohun and Veneziani put forward two objections to (11). First, they deny that we proved that $P > 0$. They concede that we showed that no prices or output levels can be negative and that some must be positive. However, they argue, *P* will nonetheless equal 0 if none of the commodities that have positive prices are produced! (Mohun and Veneziani 2007: 142). This argument relies on a very uncharitable reading of our proof that isn't consonant with our intended meaning. We noted that "commodity production is incompatible with cases in which all prices are zero" (Kliman and Freeman 2006: 122). Here and later in that paragraph, we were referring to prices *of things that actually exist.* This should have been obvious: if something doesn't exist, then neither does its price.[6] But for the benefit of the rigorous Mohun and Veneziani, we shall now "revise" our "incoherent" and "seriously deficient" (Mohun and Veneziani 2007: 139) proof accordingly:

> Under commodity production, as we showed, $P < 0$ is impossible, and $P = 0$ only if all prices *of things that actually exist* are zero. But commodity production is incompatible with cases in which all prices *of things that actually exist* are zero. Hence $P > 0$.

Second, Mohun and Veneziani (2007: 143) claim that we failed to show that $\tau(0) > 0$ by means of "logical deduction," and that we just made a "series of assumptions." In their characterization of our proof, we "[s]uppose that a unit of money in period 0 commands a positive and finite amount of labor," and we fail to explain "what is meant by 'the amount of labor the commodity commands in exchange'" (Mohun and Veneziani 2007: 143).

These claims seriously misrepresent what we wrote. We did not *suppose* that a unit of money in period 0 commands a positive and finite amount of labor. Our proof instead invoked this *historical fact* as a premise: "On any date arbitrarily selected as the initial one, a unit of money in period 0 commanded a positive and finite amount of labor—one could buy a finite amount of products of labor with it" (Kliman and Freeman 2006: 122–23). Contrary to what Mohun and Veneziani assert, moreover, the final clause explains precisely "what is meant by 'the amount of labor the commodity commands in exchange.'" The remaining steps of our proof were a definition of τ, the *fact* that the price of a unit of money equals 1, and results derived from the other steps. Thus Mohun and Veneziani's challenge to the proof fails.[7]

MOHUN AND VENEZIANI'S OTHER QUIBBLES

We shall now briefly respond to Mohun and Veneziani's other quibbles.

A. They take an equation of ours that illustrates that τ, the temporalist MELT, must be positive even when the simultaneist MELT is negative. Then they assume that τ remains constant. Once they have imposed this condition, τ becomes negative. "This is supposed to illustrate that 'τ *must always* be positive'" (Mohun and Veneziani 2007: 142, emphasis in original), they proclaim triumphantly.

But Mohun and Veneziani's "logic" is preposterous. By the same "logic," we can prove that $0 = 1$. Denote Veneziani's age now and in one year as $A(t)$ and $A(t + 1)$, respectively. Thus $A(t + 1) = A(t) + 1$.

Now assume, in Mohun and Veneziani fashion, that A is constant. Thus $A(t+1) = A(t)$. Subtracting this equation from the one above, we find that $0 = 1$. QED.

The point is that, given the conditions specified in the first equation, the second equation (constancy of τ, constancy of A) is impossible. In our example, it is obvious that the labor-time value of the commodity constantly increases, since the production of one unit of the commodity required more than one unit of the commodity as an input, plus living labor. But the example also assumes that the commodity's price is constant. Hence τ, the ratio of price to value, must continually fall. It cannot be constant.

B. Mohun and Veneziani reiterate Mohun's (2003: 95) complaint that τ is "undefined" (Mohun and Veneziani 2007: 142–43). But Mohun (2003: 94) contradicted himself, noting correctly that Kliman "defined" τ in two equivalent ways, and Mohun and Veneziani (2007: 142, emphasis added) likewise acknowledge that one of these definitions "serves to *define* the MELT of one period in terms of the preceding period's MELT." Will they please make up their minds? And will they please define their undefined term, "undefined"?

The real issue seems to be not that the *concept* of the temporalist MELT is "undefined," but that its *numerical value* is supposedly subject to an "infinite regress" (Mohun and Veneziani 2007: 142), since the input MELT of one period is the output MELT of the previous period, which in turn depends upon the input MELT of that period. . . . As Kliman (2007: 155, n10) has recently noted in a similar context, "Anyone who agrees with this objection must, to be consistent, object to the notion that the physical inputs of one period depend upon the physical outputs of the previous period, which in turn depend upon the physical inputs of that period." If Mohun and Veneziani wish to renounce the physical quantities approach they currently embrace because of this "infinite regress" and the fact that inputs and outputs are "undefined" (i.e., their magnitudes are determined temporally), we certainly have no objection.[8]

C. Our proof that $\tau(0) > 0$ makes no reference to prior periods. If this is valid, Mohun and Veneziani (2007: 143) argue, "it is possible to consider [any subsequent] $\tau(t)$ as determined by variables at t only (and not at previous dates); but this contradicts" an equation of ours which states that one period's MELT depends in part on the prior period's MELT. They fail to understand the difference between the way something is expressed and how it is determined. At every moment, the MELT can be *expressed* as the reciprocal of the amount of labor commanded by a unit of money and, equivalently, as the ratio of the money price of output to the labor-time value of output. But the magnitude of the MELT is always *determined* inter-temporally, since the amount of labor commanded, and the price and value of output, depend in part upon prior events.

Mohun and Veneziani (2007: 143) also complain about our supposed "confusion in determination": we "define" a commodity's price as τ times the amount of labor the commodity commands, but then "determine" τ using the "labor commanded price of money." This statement evinces basically the same misunderstanding. We *expressed* a commodity's price as τ times the amount of labor the commodity commands in exchange. And we showed that this implies that the magnitude of τ is *determined* by the amount of labor commanded by a unit of money (which in turn is determined partly by prior events).

D. Kliman (2001: 106, emphasis altered) stated, "To demonstrate that the exploitation theory of profit holds *under this interpretation* [the TSSI], in other words, absolutely no restrictive postulates are required." Mohun and Veneziani (2007: 141) object, claiming that "the TSSI FMT require[s] a particular theoretical concept of temporality, a particular understanding of the measurement of value, and some particular sign restrictions." But we have proved and proved again that the alleged "sign restrictions" ($\tau(0) > 0$, $P > 0$, etc.) always hold true. And as we have already explained (Kliman and Freeman 2006: 125, n7), the rest of this complaint reduces to the tautology that we used the TSSI in order to prove that Marx's theory holds under the TSSI! Thus Kliman's statement that Marx's theory holds without restrictions *under this interpretation* is precise and correct.

E. Mohun and Veneziani (2007: 140) claim that Kliman (2001: 99, emphasis in original) was "misleading" when he stated that "*general versions* of the FMT . . . prove that the theorem holds for any set of positive market prices." They object that Roemer's FMT only "holds for prices that support a reproducible solution" (Mohun and Veneziani, 2007: 140). So what? This simply means that Roemer's FMT is not among the most general ones. Kliman's statement remains correct, because more general versions of the FMT do exist. The FMTs of Okishio and Morishima, cited in our prior contributions, *do* indeed prove that the theorem holds for any set of positive market prices.

F. "Kliman's numerical example . . . which demonstrates that if one of the conditions for the FMT does not hold, then the FMT does not hold, is quite beside the point" (Mohun and Veneziani 2007: 140). The example in question showed that the standard simultaneist FMT does not hold unless the restrictive "conditions for the FMT" are satisfied. It thereby showed that this FMT fails to prove that surplus labor is the exclusive source of profit: if positive profit requires not only surplus labor, but also additional restrictive "conditions for the FMT," then surplus labor is not the exclusive source of profit. This is not beside the point; it *is* the point.

Thus, if Roemer's FMT imposes the restriction that "prices [must] support a reproducible solution," as Mohun and Veneziani acknowledge, so much the worse for it. It cannot and does not prove that surplus labor is the exclusive source of profit. Attempting to escape from a logical contradiction in a *general* theory by restricting oneself to circumstances that wish away the embarrassing problem does not confirm the theory—it simply demonstrates that there are particular circumstances under which it holds. For instance, if the fundamental magic stick theorem (FMST) says that Mohun and Veneziani will always stay dry if they wave their magic stick at the sky, they will indeed avoid getting wet if they restrict themselves to days without precipitation, but this is obviously no proof of the FMST.

G. "Because [the TSSI concept] include[s] inventory revaluation effects as part of the new value created by labor, value is dissociated from labor performed," contrary to the "labor theory of value" (Mohun and Veneziani 2007: 144). However, the equation to which Mohun and Veneziani refer includes no inventories and thus no "inventory revaluation"; *used-up* inputs are not inventories. Moreover, Mohun and Veneziani's (2007: 144) alternative equation is incoherent and seriously deficient, since it uses the MELT of time t to deflate output prices of time $t + 1$. Once that internal inconsistency is corrected, their alternative equation becomes the standard "New Interpretation" definition of value added, returning us to a "labor theory of value" that contradicts Marx's conclusion that exploitation of workers in capitalist production is the exclusive source of profit.

CONCLUSION

The TSSI interpretation of the new value created by living labor, which Mohun and Veneziani reject, is the *only* one in existence that deduces rather than contradicts Marx's exploitation theory of profit. Simultaneist interpretations must therefore be rejected as implausible, as we and Mohun have discussed before (Mohun 2003; Kliman and Freeman 2006). Mohun and Veneziani and other simultaneists are entitled to their own versions of "the" labor theory of value, of course, including versions that contradict the exploitation theory of profit. But Marx is equally entitled to his theory, especially since all efforts to prove it internally inconsistent, including Mohun and Veneziani's latest effort, have failed.

NOTES

1. Simultaneist interpretations—the dual-system interpretations derived from Bortkiewicz, the "new interpretation," and the simultaneous single-system interpretations

(SSSIs)—hold that inputs and outputs in Marx's theory are valued simultaneously, which implies that the per-unit prices and values of inputs and outputs are necessarily equal.

2. In any period, the physical net product of a good is the difference between the amount of it produced and the amount of it used up as an input throughout the economy.

3. Other versions of the FMT apply only when all profit rates are always equal (and positive). These theorems would likewise not refute (1) even if that restriction were satisfied in the real world, which it is not.

4. To be "economically possible" as defined by Mohun (2003: 98), a negative PNP must result from "an economic structure capable of physical reproduction, in which net products are the outcome of profit maximizing choices, and in which a price path is determined by some rule other than imagination."

5. In an apparent response to (2) through (5) as well as (7), Mohun and Veneziani (2007: 140–41) suggest that unrealistic theories may have explanatory power. This argument—to which we have responded twice already (Kliman 2001: 98; Kliman and Freeman 2006: 119–20)—is simply irrelevant here, where the issue is the logical validity of *theorems*, not the explanatory power of *theories*.

6. If one contracts for the future delivery of things that don't currently exist, the contract exists, and therefore so does the price *of the contract*, but that is a different matter.

7. In case Mohun and Veneziani should object that we have provided no algorithm to determine exactly how much labor a unit of money commanded in period 0, we note that our proof requires no such algorithm. We showed that this amount of labor commanded was positive and finite, and that $\tau(0)$ was consequently positive and finite as well, which is all that we needed to show.

8. The whole of Mohun and Veneziani's objection, in fact, reduces to a refusal to accept an exceptionally standard procedure in any science that makes use of difference or differential calculus—namely the introduction of an initial condition. It is a measure of the obscurity and isolation from all other sciences that the simultaneous approach has introduced into economics that our procedure is still treated by some economic writers as questionable.

Chapter 9

The Truthiness of Veneziani's Critique of Marx and the TSSI

Andrew Kliman and Alan Freeman

A 2004 paper by Roberto Veneziani criticized the temporal single-system interpretation (TSSI) of Karl Marx's value theory as well as Marx's own value theory and law of the tendential fall in the rate of profit. This paper responds to Veneziani's critique, showing that it is teeming with falsehoods and logical problems.[1] When assessed in terms of logical rigor, precision, and truthfulness (as distinct from truthiness—"truth that comes from the gut"), none of his criticisms hold water. The topics discussed herein include: the methodology of the TSSI's refutation of the allegations of internal inconsistency leveled against Marx, the difference between prices and values, the origin of profit, the monetary expression of labor-time, and the law of the tendential fall in the rate of profit and Okishio's theorem.

> *truthiness (noun)*
>
> *1*: "truth that comes from the gut, not books" (Stephen Colbert, Comedy Central's "The Colbert Report," October 2005).
>
> *2*: "the quality of preferring concepts or facts one wishes to be true, rather than concepts or facts known to be true" (American Dialect Society, January 2006).[2]

1. USING TRUTHINESS TO PUT THE TSSI IN ITS PLACE

Roberto Veneziani's critique of Marx and the temporal single-system interpretation (TSSI) of Marx's value theory has been hailed, by no less an authority than Ian Steedman, for having put the TSSI in its place. In a paper prepared for a twenty-fifth-anniversary commemoration of his *Marx after Sraffa*, Steedman (2003: 6) wrote, "Then there are the Temporalist-Single-System

[sic] arguments much noised about these days. It seems to me that Veneziani (2002) has adequately put them in their place."[3]

Like Sraffians generally, Steedman has long been portrayed as a champion of truth, precision, and logical rigor. The paper in which he hails Veneziani's critique opens on this note as well:

> In the 1970s there was a great flurry of writings on "Marxist economics" but much of it (not all) was, unfortunately, of a careless and uncritical kind, showing more signs of ideological fervour than of any determination to ensure that what was said was at least internally coherent and logical. In complete contrast, the 1960s/early 1970s "capital theory" literature . . . had by-and-large been a model of precision, à la Sraffa. . . . The purpose of *Marx after Sraffa* was to show . . . beyond any reasonable dispute, the fallacious nature of many traditional Marxist arguments and claims. (Steedman 2003: 2–3)

Readers are thus led to infer that when Steedman praises Veneziani for having put the TSSI in its place, this judgment is based on considerations of logical rigor, precision, and truthfulness. And since this judgment comes from no less an authority than Ian Steedman, must it not be true? Surely he checked Veneziani's math, verified the accuracy of his citations and attributions, and scrutinized the cogency of his arguments?

Actually, as we document below, Veneziani (2004) is teeming with falsehoods and logical problems. When assessed in terms of logical rigor, precision, and truthfulness, none of his criticisms hold water.

The most striking feature of the collection of erroneous allegations which Veneziani offers, and on which Steedman confers the accolade of his authority, is that—apart from the fact that they are all intended to "put the TSSI in its place"—in other respects they have nothing in common. No single misunderstanding or mistake lies at their root. Veneziani's allegations are just a wide-ranging assortment of mathematical errors, unsubstantiated claims that misrepresent TSSI writings, and arguments that do not make sense.

But how can one paper be filled with so many unrelated mistakes? And how can so many errors have escaped the attention of the referees and editors of *Metroeconomica*, and of such a champion of truthfulness, precision, and logical rigor as Ian Steedman? We find it extremely improbable that so many unrelated errors could have survived if Veneziani et al.'s primary concerns were truthfulness, precision, and logical rigor rather than putting the TSSI in its place. On the other hand, we are unwilling to believe that Veneziani set out to do a hatchet job on Marx and the TSSI, or that *Metroeconomica* or Steedman intended to promote one.

Our conjecture is instead that they all employed *truthiness,* rather than *truthfulness*, as their standard of evaluation. In other words, we suspect that for many critics of the TSSI, the notion that "something is wrong" with this interpretation is a "truth that comes from the gut." They wish it to be true; therefore it is true. The TSSI seems to eliminate the internal inconsistencies in Marx's value theory, but they "know" that Marx was internally inconsistent, and thus they "know" that the contrary findings of the TSSI simply *must* be the result of trickery and/or error. Thus, every new critique is looked to expectantly as finally having provided the proof of what has been intuitively "known" all along to be true. And, in order to decide whether the new critique really is the long-awaited proof, they appeal to their guts.[4]

We believe that the employment of truthiness as a standard of evaluation, especially in order to put theoretical opponents in their place, is what actually deserves to be put in its place. This paper is a contribution to that effort. More broadly, we view this paper as a contribution to the movement for pluralism in economics, as we will discuss in a brief concluding remark.

Before turning to the details of Veneziani's paper, it is important to point out that, although its title suggests that it is only a critique of the TSSI, the ultimate object of the critique is Marx. Veneziani claims that his results "confirm that the adoption of a coherent methodology and a clear distinction between values and prices would imply that not *all* [of] Marx's results hold, as is well known in the literature on Marxian economics. . . . [T]his leads one to question the TSS literal interpretation of Marx's theory" (Veneziani 2004: 98, emphasis in original). Thus, Veneziani claims that not all of Marx's theoretical results hold true. Some cannot be taken literally, but must either be reinterpreted as mere metaphors or rejected outright. Thus, although the TSSI is the immediate target of Veneziani's critique, the ultimate target is Marx. By claiming to refute TSSI findings that vindicate the internal consistency of Marx's theory, Veneziani claims to confirm the charges that Marx himself is internally inconsistent.

2. THE TSSI'S "UNSURPRISING" VINDICATION OF MARX'S CONCLUSIONS

Veneziani (2004: 98) grudgingly concedes that the TSSI undoes the appearance of internal inconsistency in Marx's theory: "the TSS approach . . . 'corresponds to the original [theory of Marx's] in a way that others do not.'"[5] We have purposely quoted Veneziani out of context in order to highlight the fact that he acknowledges this point here. If one does not read his paper with extreme care, it is easy to overlook this very brief acknowledgment.

The remainder of his paper diverts attention from the question of internal inconsistency by making the controversy seem to be about whether Marx's value theory is *true*. But as Veneziani surely knows, the controversy is about whether Marx's theory is internally *inconsistent*. As we will shortly demonstrate, we have made this distinction so clear that an author of Veneziani's competence cannot fail to be aware of it. We thus have to conclude that his diversion from the issue of inconsistency is a deliberate rhetorical device, or that "truth from the gut" imposes such a relaxation of standards that the pursuit of "putting TSSI in its place" has wholly driven out rigor.

Although he admits that the TSSI succeeds in deducing Marx's conclusions, Veneziani (2004: 98, emphasis in original) says that this is "unsurprising"; the conclusions are deduced only because "all [of] Marx's propositions [i.e., premises] are *assumed* to be correct" in TSSI works.

If proponents of the TSSI claimed to prove that Marx's conclusions are true, as Veneziani asserts, his complaint would be legitimate. One cannot prove that conclusions are true simply by showing that they follow from the premises. Yet we have continually stressed that our demonstrations are not efforts to prove that Marx's theory is true, but efforts to prove that the theory can be interpreted in a manner that renders it logically consistent. For instance, *in a paper that Veneziani cites in his text and references*, we stated: "We have never said that Marx's contested insights are necessarily true. . . . We simply say the claims that his value theory is *necessarily wrong*, because it is logically invalid, are false" (Freeman and Kliman 2000: 260, emphasis in original).

Now, the way in which one proves that Marx's theory can be understood to be logically valid is *precisely* by showing that his conclusions follow from his premises (as we interpret them). Once this is understood, Veneziani's revelation that the TSSI arrives at Marx's conclusions by deducing them from (our interpretation of) his premises no longer reads like an exposé of trickery or failure. His statement now seems to be what it actually is—an admission that the TSSI demonstrations have succeeded in refuting the century-old "proofs" of Marx's logical inconsistency.

3. VENEZIANI'S FALSE CLAIM THAT TSSI VALUES = PRICES

According to Veneziani (2004: 102, emphasis in original), the TSSI assumes that

> *in a steady state equilibrium, values are equal to observed market prices, and goods exchange at embodied labour values.* In other words, the TSS approach solves the transformation problem by constructing a "money costs theory of value," where *by assumption* $\boldsymbol{\lambda} = \mathbf{p}$ [i.e., the vector of unit values equal the vector of unit prices], apart possibly from short-run deviations.

This assertion is completely false.

By "steady state equilibrium," Veneziani means that the temporalist monetary expression of labor-time (MELT),[6] all values, and all *market* prices—whether equal to production prices or not—are stationary. Marx's theory as understood by the TSSI holds that, in the hypothetical steady state equilibrium that Veneziani assumes, unit values and unit prices (in terms of labor-time) would be

$$\boldsymbol{\lambda} = \mathbf{pA} + \mathbf{l} = \frac{\mathbf{p}^{\$}\mathbf{A}}{\varepsilon} + \mathbf{l} \qquad (9.1)$$

$$\mathbf{p} = \frac{\mathbf{p}^{\$}}{\varepsilon} = \frac{\mathbf{p}^{\$}\mathbf{A}}{\varepsilon} + \mathbf{l} + \mathbf{g} \qquad (9.2)$$

where $\boldsymbol{\lambda}$ is a vector of unit values in terms of labor-time**,** $\mathbf{p}$ is a vector of unit prices in terms of labor-time; $\mathbf{A}$ is the input-output matrix; $\mathbf{l}$ is a vector of living labor requirements per unit of output; $\mathbf{p}^{\$}$ is a vector of unit money prices; ε, the temporalist MELT, is a scalar; and $\mathbf{g}$ is a vector of per-unit deviations of prices from values.

Now *if* $\mathbf{p}$ were determined ahistorically, within equation system (9.2), the system would be underdetermined. Even if one stipulates that $\varepsilon = 1$, as Veneziani does, (9.2) contains *2n* unknowns (*n* money prices plus *n* elements of $\mathbf{g}$) but only *n* independent equations.

To avoid this indeterminacy, Veneziani claims, it is necessary to impose the "equilibrium condition" $\boldsymbol{\lambda} = \mathbf{p}$. Therefore, he immediately concludes, the TSSI's proponents "construct[ ] a 'money costs theory of value,' where *by assumption* $\boldsymbol{\lambda} = \mathbf{p}$." This inference makes no sense at all. Even if it were true (which it is not) that Veneziani's equilibrium condition is needed for a determinate solution, this would imply only that TSSI authors leave equations (9.1) and (9.2) underdetermined. Yet Veneziani does not make this claim. Instead, he attributes to us a premise which we do not hold and do not need to hold. We *do not* construct any "money costs theory of value." There is no basis for Veneziani's claim that we do. The $\boldsymbol{\lambda} = \mathbf{p}$ condition is his invention, not ours.

This objection is not a mere linguistic quibble. By falsely alleging that proponents of the TSSI construct and assume something that is both ridiculous and at variance with Marx's value theory, Veneziani creates the impression that we either know nothing about Marx's theory or purposely misinterpret it. Each time he claims that we fail to distinguish between values and prices, this impression is reinforced, and the claim is one of his paper's dominant themes. Featured in both his abstract and conclusion, it also appears on pages 98, 102, and 103–4 of his paper.

Veneziani (2004: 102) claims that his $\boldsymbol{\lambda} = \mathbf{p}$ condition is needed, not only in order to obtain a determinate solution, but also "as a matter of logical . . .

consistency." This is simply not true. *Over*determined systems are inconsistent. *Under*determined systems of linearly independent equations never are.

In any case, system (9.2) is neither inconsistent nor underdetermined. It is exactly determined—historically. By assuming that prices are stationary, *Veneziani is tacitly assuming that the input prices that existed at the start of the steady state have prevailed since that time*:

$$\mathbf{p}_0^\$ = \ldots = \mathbf{p}_t^\$ = \mathbf{p}_{t+1}^\$ = \mathbf{p}^\$ \tag{9.3}$$

The key point in this is taken as nearly incontrovertible in calculus and in the theory of differential or difference equations, and must be fully understood by Veneziani: in a temporal formulation, the initial conditions—the elements of $\mathbf{p}_0^\$$—are *data*, not unknowns.[7] They are the input prices of Period 0, that is, the output prices of Period –1, the period immediately prior to the steady state. These prices are *already determined*, through the socioeconomic processes that occurred before and during Period –1.

Since **p** is known, the only *unknown* variables are the n elements of **g**, as well as ε. System (9.2) thus contains n equations in $n + 1$ unknowns. A further equation is provided by fact that, in Marx's theory as interpreted by the TSSI, total price equals total value. Thus the economy-wide sum of price-value deviations is

$$\mathbf{gx} = 0 \tag{9.4}$$

where **x** denotes the vector of gross outputs (see Kliman and McGlone 1999: 38).

Using (9.1), (9.2), (9.3), and (9.4), we can now solve for all the unknowns by means of the following substitutions. Multiplying (9.2) through by ε, we obtain

$$\mathbf{p}^\$ = \mathbf{p}^\$\mathbf{A} + \varepsilon\mathbf{l} + \varepsilon\mathbf{g} \tag{9.5}$$

Post-multiplying by x, and employing (9.3) and (9.4), this becomes

$$\mathbf{p}_0^\$\mathbf{x} = \mathbf{p}_0^\$\mathbf{Ax} + \varepsilon\mathbf{lx} \tag{9.6}$$

or

$$\mathbf{p}_0^\$(\mathbf{I} - \mathbf{A})\mathbf{x} = \varepsilon\mathbf{lx} \tag{9.7}$$

so that

$$\varepsilon = \frac{\mathbf{p}_0^{\$}(\mathbf{I}-\mathbf{A})\mathbf{x}}{\mathbf{lx}} \tag{9.8}$$

Substituting (9.3) and (9.8) into (9.2), and rearranging terms, we then find that

$$\mathbf{g} = \left(\frac{\mathbf{lx}}{\mathbf{p}_0^{\$}(\mathbf{I}-\mathbf{A})\mathbf{x}}\right)\mathbf{p}_0^{\$}(\mathbf{I}-\mathbf{A}) - \mathbf{l} \tag{9.9}$$

while substitution of (9.3) into (9.1) and (9.2) yields

$$\boldsymbol{\lambda} = \frac{\mathbf{p}_0^{\$}\mathbf{A}}{\varepsilon} + \mathbf{l} \tag{9.10}$$

$$\mathbf{p} = \frac{\mathbf{p}_0^{\$}\mathbf{A}}{\varepsilon} + \mathbf{l} + \mathbf{g} \tag{9.11}$$

where the numerical values of ε and $\mathbf{g}$ are those given in (9.8) and (9.9).

These solutions demonstrate that, contrary to what Veneziani asserts, the TSSI neither assumes nor requires the assumption that values equal prices in a steady state. It is clear from Equations (9.10) and (9.11) that values equal prices if and only if $\mathbf{g} = 0$, but (9.9) shows that this is not true in general. Veneziani is also wrong when he states, as he repeatedly does, that the value of ε is fixed in an arbitrary, ad hoc way. Equation (9.8) makes clear that its value is determined by the *data*. It also makes clear that Veneziani (2004: 102) is wrong when he suggests that proponents of the TSSI would have to "assume that the steady state is never reached" in order to avoid indeterminacy without assuming that $\boldsymbol{\lambda} = \mathbf{p}$.

To explain why the money price vector is $\mathbf{p}_0^{\$}$, rather than something else, the above solution appeals to the historical circumstances that gave rise to $\mathbf{p}_0^{\$}$. Veneziani (2004: 102) seems to dislike this kind of explanation, preferring appeals to optimizing behavior and physical data. But we challenge him and anyone else who dislikes this solution to produce a different one, using only the information that he has provided—the input-output data and the stationarity assumption. They will not succeed.[8]

Veneziani also tries to prove that the TSSI requires the $\boldsymbol{\lambda} = \mathbf{p}$ condition when profit rates are equal, that is, when commodities sell at their production prices. "[T]he transformation between [sic] values and production prices is also trivially solved in the TSS framework by *assuming* that they are . . . equal, apart from short-run deviations" (Veneziani 2004: 103–4, emphasis in original). His attempted proof is, if anything, even more feeble than the one above. Veneziani (2004: 103) makes use of the TSSI value, price, and profit-rate equations (his equations (1)–(7)), as well as the following equality:

$$\mathbf{s}_t^* = \mathrm{r}_t\mathbf{p}_t(\mathbf{A} + \mathbf{b}_\mathrm{w}\mathbf{l}) \tag{9.12}$$

which states that, when production prices prevail, the vector of surplus-values equals the vector of profits (both per unit of output).[9]

Now if it were true that surplus-value equaled profit in every industry, then *of course* every commodity's production price would equal its value. Yet no proponent of the TSSI has ever invoked (9.12). It is a ludicrous condition, and entirely Veneziani's own invention. He simply pulls it out of thin air.

It would be simple to prove that values and production prices as understood by the TSSI are generally unequal, but a proof is not worth the effort. Instead, we refer readers to the numerical examples contained in Kliman and McGlone (1988: 72–76)—*which Veneziani cites*—and McGlone and Kliman (1996: 40–44). The examples show how production prices are determined under a variety of assumptions regarding the constancy or variability of prices and the MELT. Individual industries' values and production prices are unequal in all cases.

4. THE ORIGIN OF PROFIT UNDER SIMULTANEISM

Overturning three decades of conventional wisdom, Kliman (2001) proved that all simultaneist interpretations of Marx's value theory (in which outputs' and inputs are priced or valued simultaneously) are incompatible with Marx's theory of the origin of profit. They all contradict his claim that surplus labor is necessary and sufficient for the existence of profit. Veneziani takes issue with this proof, making it seem incorrect. Yet his objections are all diversionary. None of them address whether surplus labor is necessary and sufficient for profit under simultaneism.

Moreover, if one reads Veneziani's critique very carefully, cutting through the disparaging rhetoric, one sees that he *tacitly* concedes that surplus labor is neither necessary nor sufficient for profit under simultaneism. "Kliman's critiques," he writes, "reduce to the trivially true, and rather uninteresting, algebraic statement that there are arbitrary combinations of the variables such that $\Pi_t > 0$ while $S_t < 0$, and vice versa" (Veneziani 2004: 105–06). But this means precisely that it is possible that profit is positive ($\Pi_t > 0$) while surplus labor is negative ($S_t < 0$), and vice versa. Thus, surplus labor is neither necessary nor sufficient for profit under simultaneism. Why does Veneziani fail to acknowledge this in a forthright way, and without obfuscating phrases like "trivially true," "uninteresting," and "arbitrary"? Indeed, these are, precisely, rhetorical rather than logically rigorous assertions. Their function is to distract attention from the substance of the proof under consideration. They have no place in an impartial inquiry after truth and knowledge. What exactly is "uninteresting" about the fact that simultaneist solutions necessarily give rise to circumstances in which profit is positive, while physical surplus is negative? Any mathematically rigorous examination could not but conclude that this "arbitrary" and "uninteresting" result establishes the result that Kliman set out to prove. Why, then, at this *precise* point, abandon logic for rhetoric? The goal of "putting the TSSI in its place" has here, as throughout, driven out the normal criteria of rigor.

Although he tacitly admits that Kliman proved what he claimed to prove, Veneziani (2004: 105) nonetheless holds that Kliman's critique of the Fundamental Marxian Theorem (FMT) "seem[s] rather unconvincing" because, in order to show that surplus labor is neither necessary nor sufficient for profit under simultaneism, Kliman relaxed the restrictions that had heretofore been imposed on the problem by simultaneists—restrictions that cleverly made it *seem* that their interpretations imply that surplus labor is necessary and sufficient for profit. According to Veneziani (2004: 105n7), "all [of] Kliman's (2001) 'results' are unwarranted" because he did not assume that profit rates are equal. His examples were "arbitrary" (Veneziani 2004: 105). His economies were not in a "reproducible solution" (Veneziani 2004: 105).

These objections seem compelling—unless one knows that Kliman's (2001: 97, Abstract) critique of the FMT was precisely that it "rel[ies] crucially on restrictive and implausible conditions." Then Veneziani's objections make no sense at all. He is complaining that Kliman had to relax the FMT's restrictions in order to prove that it relies crucially upon those restrictions! How else could Kliman prove this? Will Veneziani please tell us?

If Kliman had claimed that the FMT was *false*, then Veneziani's complaints would make sense. One cannot disprove a theorem if one violates its premises. But what Kliman claimed, correctly, was something different: the FMT fails to demonstrate that surplus labor is necessary and sufficient for profit. Veneziani is well aware of the difference. He writes, "Although this [demonstration that surplus labor and profit can have opposite signs under simultaneism] does not refute the FMT, according to Kliman, it shows that the FMT is theoretically unsatisfactory because it holds only under Roemer's restrictive and unrealistic definition of reproducibility" (Veneziani 2004: 104–5). Since he understands what Kliman did and did not claim, and tacitly concedes that what he did claim is correct, why has Veneziani responded with "objections" that fail to address the issue?

5. THE NEGATIVE MELT ISSUE

Although Veneziani tacitly concedes that all simultaneist interpretations are incompatible with Marx's theory that surplus labor is the exclusive source of profit, he contends that the TSSI is in no better shape. "[T]he TSS approach does not offer a 'superior' interpretation of Marx's theory of exploitation" (Veneziani 2004: 107) because it, too, fails to imply that surplus labor is necessary and sufficient for positive profit. "[T]he desired result can only be obtained by arbitrarily assuming" that the monetary expression of labor-time (MELT) is never negative (Veneziani 2004: 106).

It is true that *if* the temporalist MELT could be negative, *then* surplus labor would not be necessary or sufficient for positive profit under the TSSI. Given a negative MELT, profit would be negative when surplus labor is positive, and vice versa.

Yet, although Veneziani *alleges* that it is arbitrary to assume that the MELT is non-negative, he gives us absolutely no reason to believe that a negative temporalist MELT is logically possible. A negative MELT would imply that a quantum of labor-time is represented by a negative amount of money. In the absence of any reason why we should believe in such an absurd situation, it is hardly arbitrary to assume that the MELT is positive.

In fact, we do *not* assume that the MELT is positive: we prove it. The proof that the temporalist MELT must always be positive was presented in Kliman (2001) and in Kliman and Freeman (2006). Veneziani's charge that it is "arbitrary" to assume a positive temporalist MELT is false, and had he considered the mathematical implications of his claim in any but the most superficial manner, he himself should have recognized this. And since this false charge is the sole basis for his rejection of the claim that the TSSI succeeds in deducing the conclusions of Marx's exploitation theory of profit, Veneziani's rejection of the claim is unwarranted. Given the importance of this issue, it will be useful to restate the proof of the positivity of the temporalist MELT here.

a. Kliman (2001: 106–8) proved the following theorem: if P (the total price of output, in money terms), C (total expenditures on used-up means of production, in money terms), L (the total amount of living labor expended in production, in labor-time terms), and $\tau(0)$ (the temporalist MELT of time [0]) are all positive and finite, then τ *must always* be positive.[10] (Veneziani (2004: 106) accepts that this result is "algebraically correct.") It follows that surplus labor and real profit, as understood by the TSSI, *must always* have the same sign.
b. The temporalist MELT is the ratio of total price, P, to total value in labor-time terms. Thus the MELT exists only when value is produced, that is,

only under commodity production. The subsequent steps of the proof thus presuppose the existence of commodity production.

c. L is always positive under commodity production (as the latter is defined by Marx).

d. *Proof that $P > 0$, $C > 0$ under commodity production.* Free goods are not commodities. Hence, if commodities are produced, it is not the case that all goods actually produced are free. Hence, $P \neq 0$ under commodity production. Moreover, negative prices "exist" in economic theory only by virtue of a definitional quirk. The statement that trash has a negative price, for example, really means that its "buyer" is the seller of a positively priced trash collection service. Thus any price that has wrongly been designated "negative" can be made positive by reinstating the buyer and seller in their correct positions. Since all prices are therefore non-negative, as are all gross outputs, P is non-negative as well. And since $P \neq 0$ under commodity production, it follows that $P > 0$. Moreover, physical inputs cannot be negative, and this, together with the non-negativity of all prices, implies that $C > 0$.

e. *Proof that the temporalist MELT is initially positive and finite.* By definition, the price of any item—commodity or other asset—equals τ times the amount of labor the item commands in exchange:

$$\text{price} = \tau \times (\text{labor commanded}) \tag{9.13}$$

Also by definition, the "price" of a unit of money equals 1. Thus, on any date arbitrarily selected as "time 0,"

$$1 = \tau(0) \times (\text{labor commanded by a unit of money at time } 0) \tag{9.14}$$

And since a unit of money commanded a positive and finite amount of labor on any such date—since, i.e., one could buy a positive and finite amount of products of labor with it—it follows that τ was initially positive and finite as well.

It might be argued that money did not initially command any labor that *counted as value*, since the products in existence at the start of commodity production were not produced as commodities. Under this interpretation of Marx's theory, the inputs employed at the start of commodity production did not transfer value to the products produced. Hence the total value of commodities (in terms of labor-time) was at first just the living labor extracted, a positive quantity. As demonstrated above, total price was also positive. Hence the initial MELT, the ratio of total price to total value, was positive as well.[11]

f. It follows from paragraphs (c), (d), and (e) that the conditions given in paragraph (a) for the temporalist MELT to always be positive, are satisfied. Hence the temporalist MELT has always been and will always be positive. Hence surplus labor is necessary and sufficient for positive real profit, according to the TSSI. This conclusion replicates Marx's.[12]

6. TSSI DISPROOFS OF THE OKISHIO THEOREM

The Okishio (1961) theorem was long thought to have disproved Marx's law of the tendential fall in the rate of profit, by showing that labor-saving technological changes adopted by profit-maximizing capitalists cannot cause the equilibrium rate of profit to fall. But numerous TSSI works have refuted the theorem (see Kliman 2007, chap. 7).[13]

From a logical point of view, Veneziani's critique of these refutations is an advance over earlier ones. Laibman (1999a, 1999b, 2000), Foley (1999), and others (in unpublished works) had put forward examples which showed, on the basis of the theorem's premises, that labor-saving technological changes *need not always* cause the rate of profit to fall. Yet since the theorem states that such technological changes *cannot ever* cause the rate of profit to fall, the exhibition of even a single falling-rate-of-profit example is sufficient to refute it. Subsequent rising-rate-of-profit examples are irrelevant, as Veneziani (2004: 109) recognizes. Thus, instead of offering such an example, he tries to demonstrate that the temporalist refutations of the Okishio theorem are not "robust": that they depend crucially upon scenarios that are impossible, or almost impossible.

6.1. The Constant-MELT Critique

Two of Veneziani's objections (Veneziani 2004: 110–11, numbers 3 and 4) are criticisms of the assumption in Kliman (1996) that the MELT remains constant. Veneziani suggests that this assumption plays a critical role in the temporalist refutation of the Okishio theorem. Once the constant-MELT assumption is relaxed, the TSSI supposedly produces results that support, rather than contradict, the theorem.

In an attempt to demonstrate this, Veneziani (2004: 110) shows that if the MELT and labor productivity both grow at the same constant percentage rate, then in the long run the temporally determined rate of profit will converge upon Okishio's physicalist rate of profit. So what? Veneziani does not bother to tell us, but his point is evidently that, since Okishio's rate of profit cannot fall as a result of "viable" technical change, the convergence of the temporally determined rate of profit upon Okishio's rate implies that the former also cannot fall if the MELT and labor productivity both grow at the same constant percentage rate.

In fact, however, the convergence result implies the very opposite. Veneziani assumes that the labor-time value of the commodity is initially constant. Thus, if the MELT increases at a constant rate, the money price of the commodity is initially *increasing*. But this implies that the monetary rate of profit is initially *higher* than Okishio's physicalist rate of profit (since the latter is the rate of profit that would exist if the commodity's price were constant). So the fact that the monetary rate of profit converges upon Okishio's rate actually implies that the monetary rate *falls* over time in relation to Okishio's rate. If this fall more than offsets the rise in Okishio's rate that results from technical progress, then the monetary rate of profit will fall over time even though his rate of profit rises.

Anyone can make a mistake, but once again, the question is: why did Veneziani not bother to check his results, and why did *Metroeconomica* and Steedman not catch his error before hurrying to publish and endorse a faulty argument that "put the TSSI in its place"?

Owing to the importance of the issue under discussion here—the possibility of a decline in the monetary rate of profit despite a continuously increasing MELT, under conditions in which the Okishio theorem claims that "the" rate of profit must rise—we shall now consider a simple numerical example in order to check a result that was not checked before publication. Let us examine the simplest case possible: a one-sector ("corn") economy, without fixed capital, in which all of the year's output is invested, planted as seed corn at the start of the next year. (See Table 9.1.) Since all output becomes seed, the farmworkers and farm owners consume none of it.

Because fixed capital and wages are assumed away in this example, the seed corn (*SC*) is the whole of the capital advanced in physical terms, and the physical surplus (*PS*) equals the net product (*NP*)—corn output (*CO*) minus seed corn. Thus Okishio's physical rate of profit (***ROP***) equals the net product divided by the seed corn.

Let us also assume that, between years 1 and 2, the seed corn, the output, and the amount of living labor (*LL*) performed by the farmworkers all increase by 25 percent. The economy is growing, but there is no productivity growth.

Table 9.1 Physical Quantities

Year	*SC*	*NP = PS*	*CO = SC + NP*	***ROP = PS/SC***	*LL*
1	64	16	80	**25.0%**	80
2	80	20	100	**25.0%**	100
3	100	30	130	**30.0%**	100
4	130	45	175	**34.6%**	100

Output per unit of living labor and output per unit of corn input both remain unchanged. Given the physical quantities of year 1 presented in Table 9.1, the figures for year 2 follow from the assumption of 25 percent growth.

In years 3 and 4, technological progress commences. The net product now increases by 50 percent per year, while employment no longer increases—one hundred hours of living labor are performed each year. Output per unit of living labor ("labor productivity"), output per unit of seed corn ("capital productivity"), and the ratio of seed corn to workers (the technical composition of capital) all rise in years 3 and 4. (The seed corn figures for years 3 and 4 are based on our assumption that all output is invested as seed; for instance, $CO = 100$ in Year 2, so $SC = 100$ in year 3.)

Of course, this is an extremely unrealistic set of assumptions. We do not pretend to be modeling the process of accumulation in any actual economy here, but employ these assumptions to establish the logical point at issue: that our disproof of Okishio does not depend on the assumption of a constant MELT.[14]

Let us begin with the constant-MELT case. If we assume that the MELT is $1/hr, the new value added by living labor (*NV*) is always equal to the living labor (*LL*) figures of Table 9.1, and the nominal price of corn, *p*, equals its value, *v*. The resulting flow of value is given in Table 9.2.

The value/price rate of profit is initially equal to the physical rate, and the two rates remain equal as long as productivity is not growing. Once technological progress occurs, however, the value/price rate of profit falls, even though Okishio's physical rate rises.

It is tempting to assume that the nominal (i.e., monetary) rate of profit has declined here only because the MELT is constant, so that the nominal price of corn falls together with its value. Yet this is not the case. Imagine that the price of corn rises by 10 percent year after year. This year's output sells for 10 percent more than it would have sold for last year, but the seed corn advanced at the start of the year also costs 10 percent more than it would have cost last year. The rate of profit—the ratio of sales to costs, minus 1—is consequently

Table 9.2 Temporalist Value/Price Rate of Profit, Given the Law of Value and Constant MELT

Year	$p_{in} = v_{in}$[a]	$C = c = VT = p_{in}\,SC$	$NV = LL = s$	$TV = VT + NV$	**ROP = s/C**	$p_{out} = v_{out} = TV/CO$
1	5.000	320	80	400	**25.0%**	5.000
2	5.000	400	100	500	**25.0%**	5.000
3	5.000	500	100	600	**20.0%**	4.615
4	4.615	600	100	700	**16.7%**	4.000

[a]The input price equals the prior year's output price. Year 1's input price is given.

the same whether we use this year's or last year's prices to value the seed corn and output. In other words, a constant rate of inflation leaves the rate of profit unchanged.

What affects the nominal rate of profit is therefore not inflation per se, but *changes* in the rate of inflation. A rising rate of inflation causes sales revenue to increase by a greater percentage than costs increase, and thus the nominal rate of profit rises. Conversely, when the rate of inflation is falling, sales revenue increases by a smaller percentage than costs, causing the nominal rate of profit to fall. *What matters is not whether prices are rising or falling—that is, whether the rate of inflation is positive or negative—but whether the rate of inflation is rising or falling.*

Hence, productivity growth need not lead to deflation, falling prices, in order to cause the nominal rate of profit to fall. It needs to lead to disinflation, a falling rate of inflation. If this occurs, then the nominal rate of profit, just like the real value rate, must fall in relationship to the physical rate of profit, regardless of whether prices are rising or falling. Unless the physical rate rises by an amount sufficient to offset this effect, both the nominal and the real value rates of profit will decline in absolute terms as well.

The point can also be expressed in the following way. A rising MELT does not cancel out the tendency of the rate of profit to fall. The rate of inflation is approximately equal to the growth rate of the MELT plus the growth rate of values.[15] Thus if the MELT grows at a constant rate, but values fall at an increasing rate as a result of a rising rate of productivity growth, the rate of inflation must decline, and the nominal rate of profit will tend to fall.

It is of course possible, in principle, that the growth rate of the MELT will accelerate, canceling out or more than canceling out this effect. However, there is no inherent reason that it should do so.[16] A rising MELT reflects built-in or exogenous inflation, inflation that arises because of factors other than productivity growth.

To see this more clearly, let us imagine along with Veneziani that the MELT increases at the same rate as labor productivity (net product per unit of living labor) increases beginning in year 3, which is 50 percent per year. Since the MELT equals 1 at the start of year 1, for instance, it equals 1.5 at the end. Instead of the constant-MELT prices of Table 9.2, now have the new prices of Table 9.3 that reflect this 50 percent growth. (The nominal prices equal the values of Table 9.2 times the MELT. To obtain the total value figures, we multiply the corn output figures of Table 9.1 by the output price and, to obtain the nominal value added, we subtract the sum of value transferred from the total value.)

Through year 2, there is no productivity growth, so the value of corn remains constant. Thus the nominal price of corn increases at the same rate as the MELT, 50 percent. This is exogenous inflation, unrelated to productivity

Table 9.3 Temporalist Value/Price Rate of Profit, Given the Law of Value and 50 percent Annual Growth of MELT

Year	p_{in}[a]	$C = c = VT = p_{in} \times SC$	$NV = s = TV - VT$	$TV = p_{out} \times CO$	***ROP* = *s/C***	$MELT_{out}$	$p_{out} = MELT_{out} \times v_{out}$	*Rate of Inflation* $(p_{out} - p_{in})/p_{in}$
1	5.000	320	280	600	**87.5%**	1.500	7.500	50.0%
2	7.500	600	525	1125	**87.5%**	2.250	11.250	50.0%
3	11.250	1125	900	2025	**80.0%**	3.375	15.577	38.5%
4	15.577	2025	1519	3544	**75.0%**	5.063	20.250	30.0%

[a]The input price equals the prior year's output price. Year 1's input price is given.

growth. Once productivity growth commences in year 3, the exogenous 50 percent inflation persists, but the falling value of corn partially offsets this effect, causing the overall rate of inflation to decline. However, the MELT rises more rapidly than the value of corn falls, so the nominal price of corn rises continually; the overall rate of inflation remains positive.

Although the *level* of the nominal rate of profit is significantly greater than the level of the real value rate of profit given in Table 9.2, its *trend* is essentially the same. Both rates are constant through year 2, and both fall once productivity growth begins. The reason why both rates of profit fall is that, as we stressed above, the rate of inflation falls both when the MELT is constant and when it increases at a constant percentage rate. That the price of corn falls in one case and rises in the other is irrelevant.

The exact relationship between the nominal and real rates is

$$1 + r_{nom} = (1 + g_m)(1 + r_{real}) \tag{9.15}$$

where r_{nom} and r_{real} are the nominal and real rates of profit and g_m is the growth rate of the MELT. In year 1, for instance, we have 1.875 = (1.5)(1.25), while in year 4 we have 1.75 = (1.5)(1.167).[17] Thus, if the MELT increases at a more or less constant rate, the nominal price rate of profit will closely track the real value rate. Whether the *level* of the MELT is constant or not makes no difference.

Finally, let us consider what would happen if the above scenario were to persist throughout time, so that the MELT and labor productivity both continue to grow by 50 percent per year, and all corn output continues to be re-invested as seed corn. The answer is that Okishio's physical rate of profit, which started at 25 percent, would converge upon 50 percent by continuing to *rise*, while the nominal rate of profit, which started at 87.5 percent, would converge upon 50 percent by continuing to *fall*. So although Veneziani is correct that the monetary rate of profit eventually converges on Okishio's rate when the MELT rises at the same rate as labor productivity, we see that this result definitely does not mean what he suggests it means. It does not prevent the nominal rate of profit from falling under conditions in which Okishio's rate rises, and thus it does not undermine, but further confirms, the temporalist refutation of Okishio's theorem.

6.2. An Implausible, Singular Case?

Veneziani (2004: 109, emphasis in original) also contends that "Kliman's (1996) conclusions may have some analytical support *only* in the implausible, singular case" that Kliman assumed, the case in which the amount of living labor needed to produce a unit of output approaches zero over time. Actually, any other assumption is implausible, since *any other assumption implies that labor productivity cannot increase beyond a certain point.* The amount of living labor required to produce a unit of output is no more than the inverse of labor productivity. If one unit of labor produces *y* units of some output, then the "amount of living labor required to produce a unit of output" is 1/*y*. To assert that this magnitude, 1/*y*, approaches indefinitely close to zero, is simply to assert that *y* rises without limit. This is a nearly trivial mathematical result and it is astonishing that it has escaped Veneziani's attention. If he wishes to deny this assumption or brand it as "arbitrary," he must in fact assert that there is an absolute upper limit to the productivity of labor, an assertion without theoretical foundation and for which there is no empirical evidence.

Suppose that Veneziani were right, and that, for example, the amount of labor needed to produce a unit of output continually falls over time from one thousand hours to one hour, but cannot decline any further. In that case, an hour of labor can never yield more than one unit of output—not now, and not at any time in the future.

This is precisely what Veneziani (2004: 110) assumes in an attempt to prove that the temporally determined rate of profit approaches the physical "rate of profit" of the Okishio theorem. This *assumption* is what produces his "proof."

In his example, labor productivity is initially equal to $1/(\ell_1 + \ell_2)$, and it asymptotically rises to $1/(\ell_1)$ over time. But it is never, ever allowed to exceed $1/(\ell_1)$. Putting the same point differently, *the rate of growth* of labor productivity in Veneziani's example declines continually over time and asymptotically approaches zero. It is *this case that is implausible and singular*. There is certainly no evidence that the level of aggregate productivity has ever run up against such an insurmountable barrier.

6.3. Capitalist Investment Criteria

Veneziani's (2004: 109) remaining objection (number 1) is that Kliman (1996) assumed that capitalists are "compelled to invest according to a fixed rule, regardless of what happens to the price of output and to the profitability of investment." He does not elaborate further, and his point is unclear. If he is claiming that Kliman assumed that capitalists introduce new technologies regardless of profitability considerations, he is incorrect. Kliman (1995: 219) employed the Okishio theorem's own decision rule: they introduce those new technologies that will boost their rates of profit if prices and the real wage rate remain constant.

Yet Veneziani may be suggesting that if the rate of profit falls, capital accumulation will slow down, which in turn will cause the rate of profit to rise. This is quite possible, but it is difficult to see how it affects "the robustness of TSS results" (Veneziani 2004: 109). Slower accumulation causes a slowdown in productivity growth, and the latter slowdown is what leads to the subsequent rise in the rate of profit. There is nothing here to support the notion that the rate of profit is physically determined; once again, the rate of productivity growth and the rate of profit tend to move in *opposite* directions, contrary to what the physicalist critics of Marx claim to have proved. Moreover, the cyclical behavior of the rate of profit accords with Marx's (1991, Ch. 15, esp. pp. 362–64) law of the tendential fall in the rate of profit.

7. CONCLUSION

This paper has been written as a contribution to the movement for pluralism in economics. By means of a particular case study, we have sought among other things to illustrate the extent to which scholarly standards in economics can break down when the effort of a more entrenched and powerful school to put a less entrenched and powerful one in its place is allowed to go unchecked. We believe this problem is a general one that the movement for pluralism in economics needs to address.

We also believe that this case study indicates the need for greater clarity about what is meant by pluralism. An analogy between "equal rights" and "pluralism" may be helpful here. Some would argue that, if the law treats rich and poor alike, it affords them equal rights. However, we think Anatole France was correct when he suggested that the "majestic equality" of laws which "forbid the rich as well as the poor to sleep under bridges, to beg in the streets, and to steal bread" is actual a parody of equality. By the same token, some would argue that, since Veneziani has had his say, and we have had our say, the present debate has been pluralistic. However, we think that a "pluralism" which allows a more dominant school of thought to level a host of egregiously incorrect criticisms against a less dominant one, and "allows" the latter school to devote much, if not most, of its limited time and resources to defensively replying to this host of unfounded criticisms, is actually a parody of pluralism. For genuine pluralism to exist, its proponents must attend to the need for, and attempt to enforce the use of, proper intellectual standards. This is particularly important in cross-paradigm discourse, especially where the disparities between the contending schools' power and resources are significant. Unless proponents of pluralism are there to actively defend proper intellectual standards, what the members of the more powerful school "know in their guts"—that is, truthiness—is likely to prevail.

NOTES

1. We wish to thank two anonymous referees for their helpful comments on a prior draft of this paper. Any remaining errors are our responsibility.

2. Merriam-Webster Online, www.m-w.com/info/06words.htm. (July 8, 2007). "Truthiness," a term that Colbert takes credit for coining, was voted "Merriam-Webster's #1 Word of the Year for 2006."

3. Steedman is referring to an unpublished draft of Veneziani's work. Veneziani (2004) is a revised version of part of that paper, and Veneziani (2005), which deals with a single paper by Freeman (1996), is a revised version of most of the rest. Owing to space limitations, we shall deal only with Veneziani (2004) here.

4. Other critiques of the TSSI, most of which also suffer from this problem, we believe, are discussed throughout Kliman (2007).

5. The interior quote is from Kliman and McGlone (1999: 43).

6. The MELT is the amount of value, expressed in money terms, that is equivalent to a unit of labor. Thus if an hour of labor creates \$100 of new value, the MELT is \$100/hr.

7. "No unique time path can be determined . . . unless the value of the constant [of integration] *c* can somehow be made definite. To accomplish this, additional information must be built into the model, usually in the form of what is known as an *initial condition* or *boundary condition*" (Chiang 1974: 429, emphases in original). "Solving a differential equation gives rise to a *family* of functions. Specifying an initial condition is a natural way to specialize down to a particular solution" (Krantz 2005: 34, emphasis in original).

8. Recall that $\mathbf{p}^{\$}$ is a vector of *market prices*, not prices of production. Hence uniform profitability cannot be assumed. It is indeed peculiar to assume that a steady state exists even though profit rates may be unequal, but it is Veneziani's assumption, not ours.

9. Since the profit rate, *r*, is the ratio of profit to capital advanced and $\mathbf{p}_t(\mathbf{A} + \mathbf{b}_w\mathbf{l})$ is the vector of capital advances per unit of output, the right-hand side of (3) is the vector of profits per unit of output.

10. The proof also goes through when $C = 0$. Note also that any time can be chosen as time 0. Thus if the MELT is positive at *any* time, it must be positive forever after.

11. Thus the temporalist MELT differs from the simultaneist MELT, which is the total price of the net product divided by the living labor performed, where the net product of any commodity is the gross output of the commodity minus the amount of it that is used up as an input into production. The "total price of the net product" is therefore a simultaneist notion, since it values inputs and outputs at the *same* set of prices, and since it does not recognize that the MELT applicable to the inputs differs from the MELT applicable to the outputs that emerge later. See Kliman (2001) for further discussion of this issue.

12. After this paper was written, Mohun and Veneziani (2007) published a critique of the above proof. See Kliman and Freeman (2008) for our reply.

13. Much of this section of the paper was published, in slightly different form, in Kliman (2007, chap. 7).

14. For a counterexample that disproves Okishio's theorem in a case in which wages are positive and two different products are produced, see Kliman and McGlone (1999). However, even though the present example assumes a zero real wage rate, it too serves to disprove the theorem, since the latter only assumes that the real wage rate remains constant, not that it is positive. Okishio (1961) did acknowledge that viable technical changes can result in a fall in the maximum rate of profit, but only in order to stress that the *actual* rate must nevertheless rise or remain constant. When the real wage rate is zero, the maximum rate of profit equals the actual rate, and the theorem therefore implies that neither can fall. That claim is disproved below.

15. If $A = B \times C$, the growth rate of A is approximately equal to the growth rate of B plus the growth rate of C. Since the level of prices equals the MELT times the level of real values, it follows that the growth rate of prices, that is, the inflation rate, is approximately equal to the growth rate of the MELT plus the growth rate of real values.

16. Even if the growth rate of the MELT does increase enough to cancel out the tendency of the nominal rate of profit to fall, it does not follow that the law of the tendential fall in the rate of profit has been negated. If the accelerating growth of the MELT is caused by rising government debt burdens and overextension of credit, it may well be that the crisis tendencies resulting from productivity growth are displaced, but not negated.

17. It can be shown that this relationship holds true in all cases in which there is no fixed capital, and that a similar relationship obtains when fixed capital is present.

Chapter 10

The Temporal Single-System Interpretation

Underdetermination and Inconsistency

Simon Mohun and Roberto Veneziani

This paper critically evaluates a recent contribution by Kliman and Freeman (2009) {chap. 9 of this book} in this journal. It is argued that none of their arguments dispel previous criticisms of the "temporal single-system interpretation" (TSSI). Indeed the paper confirms the suggestions of many critics that, as the missing parts of the TSSI theoretical constructs are provided, in particular the Monetary Expression of Labor Time, the TSSI rests on inconsistency and arbitrary assumptions.

1. INTRODUCTION

In a recent contribution to this journal, Kliman and Freeman (2009) reconsider some of the criticisms of the Temporal Single-System Interpretation (TSSI) of Marx's theory of value, of which they are two of the most prominent exponents. In particular, they focus on a paper by Veneziani (2004) and argue that all the criticisms contained in the article are either logically incorrect or simply false. They conjecture that this is not apparent to Veneziani because of a psychological a priori commitment to the falsity of the TSSI, in turn founded on a psychological a priori commitment to the demonstration of the internal inconsistency of Marx.

This paper provides a brief response to Kliman and Freeman (2009). We make no conjectures about the psychology of Kliman and Freeman, and seek to remain on the terrain of the logic of their arguments in favor of the TSSI and against their critics. Specifically, we argue that none of their arguments convincingly dispels previous criticisms of the TSSI. Indeed we demonstrate that as soon as the missing parts of the TSSI theoretical constructs are provided, the inconsistencies and arbitrary assumptions of the TSSI are more exposed.

We begin with two preliminary points. First, although we have some differences with Kliman and Freeman (2009) as to what constitutes an accurate representation, and what constitutes distortion, of an argument with which they disagree (particularly here the original arguments in Veneziani, 2004), in what follows we will only engage with the issue of who exactly said what, when it is necessary to the main arguments in the paper. The contributions are publicly available and we encourage interested readers to form their own opinion. Second, although they focus on Veneziani (2004), Kliman and Freeman (2009) present a number of arguments that apply to the wider set of scholars who have criticized the TSSI. Hence we will concentrate on the main theoretical issues thereby raised, because their relevance goes beyond any particularity of their debate with Veneziani (2004). Since we have commented previously on TSSI arguments (Mohun 2003 {chap. 3 of this book}; Veneziani 2004, 2005; Mohun and Veneziani 2007 {chap. 7 of this book}), we will attempt to be brief and to the point. All of our previous criticisms stand and need not be reiterated.

The plan of the paper is as follows. The next section briefly outlines the main TSSI claims as a benchmark for subsequent reference. These claims are divided into those that are primarily "methodological" and those that are primarily "logical." Two sections analyze these in turn. The first takes TSSI "logic" for granted in order to focus on claims such as "to criticize the TSSI is to criticize Marx," and the second explicitly examines TSSI "logic," in particular, whether the TSSI has a well-defined concept of the Monetary Expression of Labor Time (MELT). The paper concludes that none of the TSSI claims (whether "methodological" or "logical") withstand serious scrutiny.

2. THE TSSI

What is the main aim of the TSSI? As repeatedly stated, it is to rescue Marx from the accusation of logical inconsistency. According to TSSI proponents, not only have they provided an interpretation of Marx that is fully coherent, but also the TSSI corresponds to Marx's own theory in a way that all other approaches do not. As Veneziani (2004) noted, TSSI proponents claim to have proved the correctness of the following propositions:

> (a) all of Marx's aggregate value-price equalities hold; (b) values cannot be negative; (c) profit cannot be positive unless surplus-value is positive; (d) value production is no longer irrelevant to price and profit determination; (e) the profit rate is invariant to the distribution of profit; (f) productivity in luxury industries

> affects the general rate of profit; and (g) labor-saving technical change can cause the profit rate to fall. (Kliman and McGlone, 1999: 55)

In what follows we will call these "Claims (a)–(g)". TSSI adherents argue that since the TSSI establishes Claims (a)–(g), then the TSSI fully replicates Marx's original theory and thus, *as an interpretation of Marx*, it is indisputably superior to all alternatives. Furthermore, any criticism of the TSSI is inevitably a criticism of Marx:

> By claiming to refute TSSI findings that vindicate the internal consistency of Marx's theory, Veneziani claims to confirm the charges that Marx himself is internally inconsistent. (Kliman and Freeman 2009: 339)

The structure of the TSSI argument is essentially the following. Following the standard TSSI notation, at any given t, let $\mathbf{p}_t$ denote the price vector, let λ_t denote the vector of values, and let $\mathbf{g}_t$ denote the vector of value-price deviations. Further, let the technology be described by $(\mathbf{A}, \mathbf{l})$ where $\mathbf{A}$ is the input-output matrix and $\mathbf{l}$ is the vector of direct labor inputs, both of which are assumed, for simplicity, to be constant over time. Let $\boldsymbol{x}_t$ be a vector of activity levels at t and let τ_t denote the TSSI Monetary Expression of Labor Time (MELT) at t. Then the TSSI asserts the following.

A1. In its core equations

$$\mathbf{p}_{t+1} = \tau_{t+1}\left(\frac{\mathbf{p}_t\mathbf{A}}{\tau_t} + \mathbf{l} + \mathbf{g}_t\right) \tag{10.1}$$

$$\boldsymbol{\lambda}_{t+1} = \frac{\mathbf{p}_t\mathbf{A}}{\tau_t} + \mathbf{l} \tag{10.2}$$

$$\mathbf{g}_t\mathbf{x}_t = 0 \tag{10.3}$$

the TSSI is an interpretation of Marx's theory of value.[1] Note that the $g_{i,t}$ are the amounts of value gained or lost by individual capitals at unit level because individual prices are not proportional to values; equation (10.3) says that in total such transfers sum to zero.

A2. On the basis of equations (10.1)–(10.3), Claims (a)–(g) are established as a matter of logical deduction.

A3. Because claims (a)–(g) are logically established, this hermeneutically validates the TSSI as an interpretation of Marx. Textual evidence (or lack of it) for equations (10.1)–(10.3), particularly regarding the labor value of constant capital, is not germane. The validity of the TSSI as an interpretation of Marx is hermeneutical, not textual.

A4. The issue of the empirical validity of Claims (a)–(g) is not relevant.[2] The main criterion in adjudicating between alternative theoretical approaches is the ability to replicate Marx's results.

A5. Only the TSSI provides a fully consistent account of Marx's theory.

We have made many criticisms of these assertions elsewhere, in particular concerning A1 and A3, and we shall not repeat our arguments. Here we focus primarily on A2, A4, and A5. There are two different types of issue involved. One concerns whether criticism of the TSSI is ipso facto criticism of Marx, how one should adjudicate between different approaches, and what is the nature and purpose of theory. We call these "methodological issues." The other concerns the logic of the TSSI arguments used to establish claims (a)–(g). We call these "logical issues." We do not suggest that methodological issues involve no logical concerns, and we do not suggest that logical issues involve no methodological concerns. We consider these issues separately, and in turn, purely for the sake of clarity.

3. METHODOLOGICAL ISSUES WITH THE TSSI

In order to focus on methodological issues, and *only for the sake of argument*, in this section we assume that A1, A2, and A3 hold. We first argue that, even if one assumes that A4 and A5 also hold, criticism of the TSSI is not equivalent to criticism of Marx, and TSSI claims to the contrary are just polemical rhetoric. Then we note that A5 is unwarranted, so that the alleged superiority of the TSSI over alternative approaches is not established, *even if* one believed in A1 to A4. Finally, we argue that the TSSI emphasis on A4 is misplaced.

3.1. Are Criticisms of the TSSI Also Criticisms of Marx?

First, even assuming, and *only for the sake of argument*, that A1 to A5 hold, the claim that to reject the TSSI is essentially equivalent to criticizing Marx is dubious, from both a logical and a theoretical viewpoint. For one may legitimately reject the TSSI and search for a different interpretation, which is also logically consistent and "replicates" Marx. One may legitimately argue that the premises from which claims (a)–(g) are derived are not entirely convincing and try to derive the results in a more satisfactory way. Perhaps more important, one may also argue that the relevant propositions to be established are not claims (a)–(g), but some alternative set of results. That all of claims (a)–(g) definitionally incorporate the essential insights of Marx's theory is an implicit assumption of the TSSI, but it has not been convincingly proved and it is certainly not beyond dispute.

Secondly, even assuming, and *only for the sake of argument*, that A1 to A5 hold, one can criticize the TSSI without any implication concerning the logical consistency of Marx's theory. For it is simply false that *all of* claims (a)–(g) must hold in order for Marx's theory to be logically consistent. From a purely logical viewpoint, to argue that one, or even various propositions in a given set of results is/are incorrect is completely different from stating that the propositions in some set are logically inconsistent. Further, from a purely logical viewpoint, to state that one, or even some of claims (a)–(g) are incorrect does not imply that all of them are. TSSI proponents have never proved that claims (a)–(g) are logically equivalent, either in their own system or, more generally, under any plausible interpretation of Marx's theory. From a theoretical viewpoint, it is important to note again that the TSSI *assumes* that claims (a)–(g) jointly define Marx's theory, but there is no reason why anyone else should accept this assumption. But then it follows that one can legitimately drop, say, claim (g) without deriving a contradiction in Marx's value theory.[3] The statement that "not all of Marx's results [as understood by the TSSI] hold" (Veneziani 2004: 339) means exactly that; not all of claims (a)–(g) hold. For this statement to be true, it is sufficient that only *one* of claims (a)–(g) is false, contradicting the TSSI but without implying that Marx is logically inconsistent.

But A5 is false, for the TSSI is not the only approach that provides a consistent interpretation of Marx's theory of value and exploitation, and therefore to reject the TSSI does not entail abandoning the only approach that "makes sense" of Marx. For example, the "New Interpretation" (NI) proposed by Duménil (1980) and Foley (1982) represents a fully coherent account of Marx's theory, although not all of claims (a)–(g) necessarily hold. Indeed, the NI holds that a different set of claims defines what is relevant in Marx's theory. But given that A5 does not hold, the superiority of the TSSI compared to other approaches is far from evident: even if one endorses A4, a comparative evaluation of the TSSI and alternative approaches is not based on logical consistency, but at best on which and how many of Marx's propositions hold in the various perspectives.[4]

From these observations, it follows that assertions such as

> although the TSSI is the immediate target of Veneziani's critique, the ultimate target is Marx. (Kliman and Freeman 2009: 339)

and

> why are Mohun and Veneziani trying to discredit the TSSI? We believe that their ultimate target is Marx. . . . The essential function of Mohun and Veneziani's contribution . . . is suppressive and antipluralist: its function is to rule Marx himself out of court while keeping it free for his Marxist economist critics. (Kliman and Freeman, 2008: 108–9)

are merely polemical tropes with little credibility.

3.2. What Constitutes a Theory and How Should it be Evaluated?

Consider now A4. What makes a theoretical construct—where the latter term is here intended in a rather broad sense—interesting, or relevant? On one hand, there is the issue of the explanatory power of a theory, which turns on empirical relevance. Kliman and Freeman are insistent that this is not an issue for the TSSI, because the TSSI is not a theory at all. It is an interpretation. They are therefore not concerned with whether Marx was correct or incorrect, and are only concerned with whether the TSSI is a correct interpretation of Marx's theory (in the sense of A3 above). Nor is the empirical relevance of claims (a)–(g) addressed. There is some sleight of hand here, since if it were shown that Marxian propositions were indubitably *empirically* false, then A1–A3 would constitute a trivial and uninteresting episode in the history of economic thought. Since for Kliman and Freeman the TSSI stands or falls with Marx, there must be some unstated premise that Marx is interesting and relevant, and some reason why. Indeed, there should also be some unstated premise that what is interesting and relevant in Marx is captured precisely by claims (a)–(g). But Kliman and Freeman will not engage with this.

On the other hand, instead of focusing on the explanatory power of theories, one might emphasize the logical validity of theorems, and this seems the main explicit justification of the TSSI enterprise (see for example Kliman and Freeman 2008 {chap. 8 of this book}: 116, n5). Setting aside A1 and A3, for the sake of argument, this implies that the validity of A2 is essential for the TSSI. To see this, suppose that, as claimed by many critics, equations (10.1)–(10.3) only "prove" claims (a)–(g) by producing a severely underdetermined system in which no variable is determined except *ex post*. Then the TSSI would be theoretically vacuous. For the interpretation that we can observe $\mathbf{p}_{t+1}$, $\mathbf{p}_t$ and $\mathbf{I}$, and then determine $\mathbf{g}_t$ is just a tautology: it is always possible to define $\mathbf{p}_{t+1}$ to be equal to something plus an arbitrary variable $\mathbf{h}_t$ and support it with the data, but this arbitrary $\mathbf{h}_t$ has no meaning.[5]

We now turn directly, and substantively, to the internal logic of the TSSI to show that A2 is untenable.

4. LOGICAL ISSUES WITH THE TSSI

In this section, we focus on A2 and argue that the TSSI core results can only be obtained by assumption within a theoretically underdetermined system. As soon as the system is closed, inconsistencies and arbitrary assumptions emerge, and this is particularly evident in the TSSI treatment of the MELT. We also show that, as suggested in section 3.1 above, even the alleged superiority of the TSSI as compared to alternative approaches can only be established by assumption, as a brief analysis of the falling rate of profit and the Fundamental Marxian Theorem forcefully demonstrates.

4.1. The Monetary Expression of Labor Time

Consider A2. In general, critics of the TSSI face a serious problem in evaluating TSSI substantive claims: the TSSI theoretical system is severely underdetermined, in that some crucial variables are undefined and the meaning of some of the key relations is unclear, so that it is often obscure what determines what. This implies that in any attempt to evaluate claims (a)–(g), critics have either to fill in the relevant gaps with some assumptions that seem coherent with the rest of the approach, and/or to formulate their criticisms in the form of conditional statements, trying to produce an exhaustive list of possibilities. It is not difficult for TSSI proponents then to rebut criticisms by noting that critics are making arbitrary assumptions that are not part of the TSSI system, or even noting that alternative criticisms are inconsistent.

The best example of this is the TSSI treatment of the MELT. As noted by many critics, TSSI proponents "fail to put forward a single, consistent definition" (Foley 2000: 33; see also Mohun 2003; Veneziani 2004; Mohun and Veneziani 2007).

In TSSI contributions, the "simplifying" assumption is often made that $\tau_t = 1$, all t, "without loss of generality" (see, for example, Freeman 1996: 235; Kliman and McGlone 1999: 36), but this is completely arbitrary, given that no formal, explicit definition of the MELT is provided.

Of course TSSI adherents disagree. For the temporalist MELT is "usually defined as the ratio of total money price to total labor-time value" (Kliman 2007: 187).

On the face of it, this claim is straightforward. For multiplying each of equations (10.1) and (10.2) through by the gross output vector $\mathbf{x}_t$, combining them and using equation (10.3) yields

$$\mathbf{p}_{t+1}\mathbf{x}_t = \tau_{t+1}\boldsymbol{\lambda}_{t+1}\mathbf{x}_t \tag{10.4}$$

whence

$$\tau_{t+1} = \frac{\mathbf{p}_{t+1}\mathbf{x}_t}{\boldsymbol{\lambda}_{t+1}\mathbf{x}_t} \tag{10.5}$$

as Kliman asserts. But this is not a definition that is different from equations (10.1)–(10.3)—it merely repeats them in a different guise. For the TSSI MELT is also on the right-hand side of equation (10.5) by virtue of equation (10.2).

Kliman has another definition of the MELT:

> The temporalist MELT, usually defined as the ratio of total money price to total labor-time value, can also be defined, equivalently, as a ratio of a unit of money to the amount of labor commanded by a unit of money. (Kliman 2007: 187. See also Kliman and Freeman 2006 {chap. 6 of this book}: 122)

Formally, this seems to be a simple rewriting of equation (10.5) as follows:

$$\tau_{t+1} = \frac{1}{\dfrac{\boldsymbol{\lambda}_{t+1}\mathbf{x}_t}{\mathbf{p}_{t+1}\mathbf{x}_t}} \tag{10.6}$$

Again, this is obviously not a formal definition that is different from equations (10.1)–(10.3); it is just their repetition. Again the TSSI MELT remains on the right-hand side of equation (10.6) by virtue of equation (10.2). Moreover, the interpretation that equation (10.6) represents the "ratio of a unit of money to the amount of labor commanded by a unit of money" clearly requires the auxiliary assumption that there are no hoards of money. Yet in an economy with metallic circulation, Marx (*Capital*, vol. 1, chap. 3) considered hoarding to be essential (Marx 1990a: 231–32). The Kliman and Freeman interpretation of equation (10.6) therefore does not seem readily compatible with Marx's writings on money.

Finally, yet another definition of the MELT appears to be implied when Kliman and Freeman state "By definition, the price of any item . . . equals τ times the amount of labor the item commands in exchange" (Kliman and Freeman 2009: 351).

That is, for *any* commodity, not just the gross output vector **x**,

$$\text{price} = \tau \times \text{(labor commanded)} \tag{10.7}$$

As is so often the case in the TSSI, in equation (10.7) "labor commanded" is not defined. But we can use the *i*th equation in the matrix equation (10.1) to define it as follows:

$$p_{i,t+1} = \tau_{t+1}\left(\frac{\sum p_{j,t}a_{ji}}{\tau_t} + l_i + g_{i,t}\right) \tag{10.8}$$

"Labor commanded" is then the brackets in equation (10.8). But again this is just a rewriting of equations (10.1) and (10.2), and the MELT is not independently defined.

In all of these "definitions" the words seemingly make sense, but the best that one can do in terms of causal relations of determination is to combine equations (10.1) and (10.3), after multiplying through by $\mathbf{x}_t$, to derive the difference equation

$$\tau_{t+1} = \frac{\tau_t \mathbf{p}_{t+1}\mathbf{x}_t}{\mathbf{p}_t \mathbf{A}\mathbf{x}_t + \tau_t \mathbf{l}\mathbf{x}_t} \tag{10.9}$$

And that is all.

In fact, TSSI adherents do argue that the TSSI MELT should be "determined" dynamically, and equation (10.9) is all that matters in deriving the main conclusions of the TSSI.[6] Kliman and Freeman write "the magnitude of the MELT is always *determined* inter-temporally, since the amount of labour commanded, and the price and value of output, depend in part upon prior events" (Kliman and Freeman 2008: 113, their emphasis).

By contrast, "At every moment, the MELT can be *expressed* as the reciprocal of the amount of labour commanded by a unit of money, and, equivalently, as the ratio of the money-price of output to the labour-time value of output" (Kliman and Freeman 2008: 113, their emphasis).

Is the latter distinction useful in order to provide a clear definition of what the TSSI MELT is, and how it changes over time? It might be useful if the TSSI were able to provide a clear definition of the MELT at the initial period $t = 0$, which is consistent with the rest of their theoretical and formal system, and in particular with equations (10.1)–(10.3). As is obvious from Kliman and Freeman's (2009) own discussion, the MELT is not a physically observable magnitude, one that can be measured without a theory, but a theoretical construct, and thus the determination of the MELT at $t = 0$ requires the specification of the variables that define it and that must be measured at $t = 0$.

The distinction between "determination" and "expression" is of no help in resolving this issue. Kliman and Freeman argue that the MELT can be *expressed* at time $t = 0$ as τ_0 even though its *determination* involves knowledge of what happened before $t = 0$. The difficulty is that the *determination* shown in equation (10.9) and the *expression* shown in equation (10.8) involve the same intertemporality. It is just not true that the MELT at $t = 0$ can be *expressed* without knowledge of what happened prior to $t = 0$. It is not surprising then that no explicit formal definition of τ_0 is provided in TSSI writings, and that the "proof" of the positivity of the MELT in Kliman and Freeman (2009) provides no explicit formula, with clearly specified variables defining τ_0. This is not a minor issue. For suppose that the initial MELT τ_0 can indeed be defined as "the ratio of total price to total value"; then all terms must be defined in terms of variables observable at time $t = 0$, or else a problem of infinite regress arises. According to equation (10.9), the TSSI definition of total value at t involves the MELT at $t - 1$. If infinite regress is to be avoided, this cannot hold at $t = 0$. Yet it is never explained why the TSSI MELT at $t = 0$ is defined in terms of concurrent variables, when it is not so defined at any other t.

The discussion of the MELT in Kliman and Freeman (2009) adds further elements of perplexity. Given the "dynamic determination" of the MELT by equation (10.9), nothing more can be said without a clearly specified initial condition (see, for example, Kliman and Freeman 2009: 343, n. 5). Hence without such a condition, nothing can be said about the sign of τ_t at an arbitrary t. The difficulty of course is not in supplying *some* arbitrary initial condition, but in providing an initial condition that is coherent with the rest of the system. So far, the TSSI has not been able to do this and there exists no explicit formula for τ_0 that could be used, for example, to construct an empirical measurement of the TSSI MELT at $t = 0$. Noting that semi-formal and ill-specified statements like equation (10.7) do not constitute a rigorous formal treatment, Kliman and Freeman (2009) seem to limit themselves to a verbal discussion because an explicit formulation of the MELT would expose the ad hoc nature of their treatment.

Consider in particular the claim that, at $t = 0$, "the total value of commodities (in terms of labor-time) was at first just the living labor extracted, a positive quantity" (Kliman and Freeman 2009: 352) which would seem to imply that the numerator of the TSSI MELT at $t = 0$ is just total labor time $\mathbf{lx}$. Of course, this solves the issue of infinite regress, but it raises more issues than it resolves. We consider two of these.

First, there is no way in which this statement can be made consistent with the rest of the TSSI system, and in particular with equations (10.2) or (10.9), unless $\mathbf{p}_t\mathbf{A}\mathbf{x}_t = 0$ at $t = -1$. Indeed, this is the only way of using equations (10.5) or (10.9) consistently at $t = 0$ without infinite regress. But why does constant capital vanish in the determination of value at $t = 0$, given that the specification of constant capital in value theory is one of the defining features of the TSSI? It is worth stressing that the definition of the MELT at $t = 0$ is not a matter of innocuous simplifying assumptions, because a number of crucial properties of the TSSI depend on the sign of τ_0.[7] Possibly Kliman and Freeman have in mind an actual historical initial period, lost in time, in which pre-capitalist commodity production took place without intermediate inputs. Even were we to accept such a strange assumption, this would render their whole system theoretically undetermined, as it would rest on an initial condition that simply cannot be observed.[8] Or, perhaps they consider their assumption as a simplifying one, but this is not possible because in their own system it is always true that value derives (is transferred from) from constant capital too. In sum, in any dynamic system, the choice of $t = 0$ is in principle arbitrary and if such a simplifying assumption can hold, without loss of generality, at any arbitrarily selected $t = 0$, then for the TSSI an inconsistency arises: it cannot be true at the same time that (i) at any given t, value depends on the constant capital of the previous period, and (ii) at any arbitrary t chosen as the initial period the total value of commodities is just equal to the living labor that was performed.

Second, in their reply to Veneziani (2004), they claim that in a steady state (in which prices and the MELT do not change over time) the following expression[9] holds

$$\tau = \frac{\mathbf{p}_0(\mathbf{I}-\mathbf{A})\mathbf{x}}{\mathbf{l}\mathbf{x}} \tag{10.10}$$

But again the only way in which equation (10.10) is compatible with the claim that the TSSI MELT is "the ratio of *total* price to total value" (Kliman and Freeman 2009: 352, emphasis added) is when production requires no non-labor inputs.[10] This is particularly evident if one notes that for equation (10.10) to hold, it is sufficient for the economy to be stationary in two adjacent periods: equation (10.10) need not describe the limit point of a long dynamic process. Therefore if all variables are stationary across the two periods $t = 0$ and $t = 1$, equation (10.10) holds for the relevant periods. Therefore, it is immediately obvious that if "the total value of commodities (in terms of labor-time) was at first just the living labor extracted" (Kliman and Freeman 2009: 352), in general the right-hand side of equation (10.10) represents *total* price over total value only in an economy without non-labor inputs. It is difficult to imagine that the TSSI was intended to apply as a theory for Adam Smith's world prior to the accumulation of "stock."

Hence despite all claims to the contrary, Kliman and Freeman (2009) have not convincingly shown that the TSSI has a well-defined notion of the MELT. Without it, equations (10.1) and (10.2) are not well-defined, and the only precise claim that can be made about the MELT is that there are an (uncountably) infinite number of time paths of the TSSI MELT consistent with equation (10.9). Given this theoretical underdetermination of the TSSI, any critic who wishes to take TSSI claims seriously (for example, concerning the fundamental difference between the TSSI and the NI, and the possibility that the TSSI MELT can be set equal to unity in every period without loss of generality) is hard put to find a way of rendering the whole system coherent, without making completely ad hoc assumptions.

In sum, TSSI adherents have to provide a definition of the MELT that is coherent with the rest of their theoretical system. The TSSI MELT is defined by, and expressed by, equation (10.9), and functionally there is nothing else. Specificity requires some initial condition τ_0. But TSSI adherents make two mistakes. First, they seek to apply one or another of their verbal definitions to τ_0, but this is not possible without infinite regress. Secondly, they seek to "prove" $\tau_0 > 0$, and this too is not possible, for either equation (10.9) applies to τ_0, or τ_0 is a nonzero arbitrary initial condition of any sign. Kliman and Freeman maintain that critics who object that it is arbitrary to assume that the MELT is non-negative, give us

> absolutely no reason to believe that a negative temporalist MELT is logically possible. A negative MELT would imply that a quantum of labor-time is represented by a negative amount of money. In the absence of any reason why we should believe in such an absurd situation, it is hardly arbitrary to assume that the MELT is positive. (Kliman and Freeman 2009: 349)

This is absurd. The burden of proof is on TSSI adherents. Thus far they have not been able to provide a coherent account of their MELT, and, given the nature of their mathematical framework, it is unlikely that they will ever be able to do so.

4.2. The Falling Rate of Profit and the Fundamental Marxian Theorem (FMT)

All of the TSSI "refutations" of the FMT and the Okishio theorem (Okishio 1963; Roemer 1981) are not refutations in the strict mathematical sense of disproving a result, as acknowledged by Kliman and Freeman (2009). Both the FMT and the Okishio theorem are mathematically true. At best, the TSSI arguments show that, once the assumptions are violated, the results do not hold: positive profits can occur without positive surplus value (and vice versa) and the rate of profit may increase {sic} after the introduction of cost-reducing technical change. This is indisputable and indeed has long been acknowledged, as have the rather restrictive assumptions under which the two results hold. For example, Roemer (1981: 49ff.) notes that it is sufficient to drop a technical assumption (called "Independence of production") to allow for a situation whereby profits are positive in the absence of exploitation. On the other hand, Skillman (1997) has shown that, once the traditional assumption of perfect competition is dropped, cost-reducing technical changes can decrease the rate of profit. Therefore, in general terms, the issues raised by TSSI proponents are far from original. To reiterate, it is well-known that the FMT and the Okishio Theorem hold only under very restrictive assumptions (for example, the general version of the FMT proved by Roemer (1981: 48) is based on no fewer than seven technical hypotheses and the assumption of stationary expectations), and that if the latter are violated the results do not hold.

TSSI adherents can only claim originality for their results by ignoring the existing literature. Consider the following defense of an example with a zero real wage allegedly refuting the Okishio Theorem.

> However, even though the present example assumes a zero real wage rate, it too serves to disprove the theorem, since the latter only assumes that the real wage rate remains constant, not that it is positive. Okishio (1961) did acknowledge that viable technical changes can result in a fall in the maximum rate of profit, but only in order to stress that the actual rate must nevertheless rise or remain

> constant. When the real wage rate is zero, the maximum rate of profit equals the actual rate, and the theorem therefore implies that neither can fall. That claim is disproved below. (Kliman and Freeman 2009: n14)

That the maximum profit rate (corresponding to a zero wage rate) would fall after a cost-reducing innovation has been known for very many years, and it has been admitted even by supporters of the Okishio Theorem (see the discussion in Roemer 1981: 115ff).

In order to provide some original results on these issues, TSSI adherents would need to construct an economically interesting and theoretically relevant setting in which the FMT and the Okishio Theorem do not hold, so that one could derive interesting insights on the reasons why this might be so. None of this can be found in TSSI writings, which simply pick arbitrary combinations of parameters and variables to construct ad hoc examples wherein the FMT and the Okishio theorem do not hold. From an economic viewpoint, little insight is gained from this kind of refutation.[11]

Finally, consider the claim that, unlike the TSSI, no simultaneist approach to value theory can preserve the Marxian relation between exploitation and profits. Since we have analyzed the issue at length elsewhere (Mohun 2003; Veneziani 2004; Mohun and Veneziani 2007), we will not examine all the TSSI arguments here. However, an additional argument can be provided to illustrate a number of problems plaguing the TSSI. The main TSSI proof that in the NI it is possible to have positive profits with negative surplus value (and vice versa) consists in some examples allegedly showing that the NI MELT can be negative (Kliman 2001 {chap. 2 of this book}). Suppose, for the sake of argument, that the type of counterexample constructed by Kliman (2001) is sufficient to establish the desired claim. Then it is easy to show that exactly the same argument proves that the relation between surplus value and profits cannot hold in the TSSI. That is, if Claim (c) does not hold in the NI, then it does not hold in the TSSI either. First, take Kliman and Freeman (2009) at face value and suppose that equation (10.10) does indeed coherently describe the TSSI MELT in the situation in which prices do not change, so that in the special case of a stationary economy equation (10.10) holds. But then, at least in this special case, the TSSI MELT coincides with the NI MELT and therefore whenever the latter is negative, so too is the former. One might argue that, from a TSSI perspective, the TSSI MELT is equal to the NI MELT only in a very special case. Yet, according to TSSI epistemological principles, this objection is irrelevant, because one example—no matter how special, arbitrarily constructed, or far from the original assumptions—is sufficient to disprove the claim of generality.[12] Provided that the TSSI MELT is analyzed in a steady state, all of the examples used by Kliman (2001) against the NI are immediately applicable to the TSSI.

This provides a nice illustration of the inconsistencies of the TSSI and the logical problems in the "derivation" of their results. For either the "proof" in Kliman and Freeman (2009) that the TSSI MELT is always positive is wrong, or equation (10.10) never holds in the TSSI. If the former, one would have to conclude that the claim that the TSSI has proved a general positive relation between surplus value and profits is false. But if the latter, the TSSI MELT is undetermined, which problematizes the determination of the TSSI system both in the steady state, and in general, as noted in the previous section and by Veneziani (2004).

5. CONCLUSIONS

The Temporal Single-System Interpretation of Marx's theory of value does not convincingly prove the claims that it makes. As repeatedly noted by critics, TSSI results hold only by assumption, that is the relevant conclusions are assumed to be definitionally true, thanks to the severe underspecification of the TSSI system. Whenever the TSSI system is closed, inconsistencies and arbitrary assumptions immediately emerge. The paper by Kliman and Freeman (2009) is an excellent illustration of this property.

NOTES

1. Our equation (10.1) is equation (5) in Kliman and McGlone (1999), our equation (10.2) is their equation (4), and our equation (10.3) is stated just before their equation (6). See Kliman and McGlone (1999: 37–38).
2. Kliman and Freeman (2009) state that they have never claimed all of Marx's insights to be true. It is worth clarifying that nobody suggested that they have done so; Veneziani (2004) simply noted that they maintain that all of claims (a)–(g) to be true in the sense of logically valid.
3. Especially if claim (g) is correctly understood as a well-defined claim in a properly constructed theoretical framework, under well-specified assumptions. More on this in section 4 below. Of course, claim (g) may be argued to be extremely relevant from a theoretical viewpoint, but that is a different issue.
4. As argued in the next section (section 3.2), however, A4 is questionable, and hence these types of comparison are reductive and uninteresting. In section 4 below, we argue that even in this more limited sense, TSSI claims of superiority are unwarranted.
5. We thank Jesus Fernandez-Villaverde for this observation.
6. It is worth noting in passing that equation (10.9) forcefully shows that, far from entailing no loss of generality, the assumption that $\tau_t = 1$, all t, is completely arbitrary, given the lack of restrictions on all variables.

7. In particular, in the initial period that their analysis describes, the assumption of commodity production is crucial to the TSSI "proof" that the TSSI MELT is strictly positive.

8. And, as well as theoretically undetermined, empirically useless.

9. Equation (10.8) in Kliman and Freeman (2009).

10. Or when only one good is produced, or when the organic composition of capital is equal in all sectors. That is, unsurprisingly, whenever all other approaches hold.

11. For example, if in order to establish claim (g), namely the result that the profit rate can fall after the introduction of a cost-reducing innovation, it is sufficient to produce an example such as the economy with zero wages analyzed in Kliman and Freeman (2009), then it is easily proved that claim (g) holds in every theoretical approach, Marxian or mainstream.

12. See for example Kliman and Freeman 2006: 120.

Chapter 11

No Longer a Question of Truth?

The Knell of Scientific Bourgeois Marxian Economics and a Positive Alternative

Alan Freeman and Andrew Kliman

This reply to Simon Mohun and Roberto Veneziani (2009 {chap. 10 of this book}) points out that they have not addressed, much less overturned, our refutations of Veneziani's celebrated criticisms of Marx and the temporal single-system interpretation (TSSI) of Marx's value theory. Instead, they have filled their "response" with non-responsive irrelevancies. We argue that they do so in order to try to divert the debate without appearing to do so. Thus, the significance of their failure to respond is that the debate is over: Marx's critics have run out of arguments against the TSSI. The reply criticizes Mohun and Veneziani's lack of concern to arrive at the truth and their resort to methods that do not permit inquiry to arrive at truth, and it proposes, as a positive alternative, some rules to guide scholarly debate.

> It sounded the knell of scientific bourgeois economy. It was thenceforth no longer a question, whether this theorem or that was true, but whether it was useful . . . or harmful, expedient or inexpedient. . . . [D]isinterested enquirers [. . . and] genuine scientific research [were replaced by . . .] apologetic.
>
> —Karl Marx, preface to the second German edition of *Capital*, vol. 1

1. In the last issue of this journal {chap. 9 of this book}, we argued that Veneziani's (2004) arguments against Marx's value theory and the temporal single-system interpretation (TSSI) of the theory "are just a wide-ranging assortment of mathematical errors, unsubstantiated claims that misrepresent TSSI writings and arguments that do not make sense" (Kliman and Freeman 2009: 337). In order to explain as charitably as possible how a noted theorist could produce a paper filled with so many and such a wide range of errors, we argued further that the purpose of Veneziani's critique was not to arrive at the truth, but to put the TSSI in its place.[1] Mohun and Veneziani's

unwillingness and evident inability to respond to our paper's arguments and demonstrations—and thereby cooperate with us in an effort to separate fact from fiction—strikingly confirms these conclusions.

2. Of course, Mohun and Veneziani (2009: 279) give a different explanation for why they refuse to address our paper's arguments and demonstrations: "All of our previous criticisms stand and need not be reiterated." There is no justification for claiming that all of their previous criticisms "stand" simply because they choose to say so, without responding to the detailed refutation of Veneziani that we provided.

Moreover, the claim that all of his criticisms "stand" is outrageous and it reveals a serious lack of interest in arriving at the truth. Consider, for instance, Veneziani's (2004, 103–4, emphasis in original) previous criticism that "the transformation between values and production prices is . . . trivially solved in the TSS framework by *assuming* that they are . . . equal, apart from short-run deviations." As we noted, the charge that "we fail to distinguish between values and prices . . . is one of his paper's dominant themes. Featured in both his abstract and conclusion, it also appears on pages 98, 102, and 103–4 of his paper" (Kliman and Freeman 2009: 342). And the charge is an extremely serious one, because, "[b]y falsely alleging that proponents of the TSSI construct and assume something that is both ridiculous and at variance with Marx's value theory, Veneziani creates the impression that we either know nothing about Marx's theory or purposely misinterpret it. Each time he claims that we fail to distinguish between values and prices, this impression is reinforced" (Kliman and Freeman 2009: 342).

We disproved Veneziani's allegation by citing "the numerical examples contained in Kliman and McGlone (1988: 72–76)—*which Veneziani cites*—and McGlone and Kliman (1996: 40–44). The examples show how production prices are determined under a variety of assumptions regarding the constancy or variability of prices and the MELT [monetary expression of labor-time]. Individual industries' values and production prices are unequal in all cases" (Kliman and Freeman 2009, emphasis in original). One such example, page 73 of Kliman and McGlone (1988), is reproduced here as Table 11.1. Commodities' values appear in the $C + s$ column, and their prices of production appear in the $C'–M'$ column.[2] *It is immediately obvious that the values and prices of production are never equal, not even when short-run deviations are eliminated as the economy approaches a hypothetical stationary state in periods 13 and 14.*

So, to repeat, Mohun and Veneziani's claim that "[a]ll of our previous criticisms stand" is outrageous and false. They are correct that the criticism "need not be reiterated." Actually, it needs to be retracted. We ask readers of this journal and the larger scholarly community to note that a false claim has

Table 11.1

Period	*Department*	*m*	*M–C*	*MP*	*L*	*… P …*	*s*	*C + s*	*C′–M′*	*π*	*General Rates of Profit and Surplus-Value*
1	I	—	150.00	100.00	50.00	150.00	50.00	200.00	214.29	64.29	r = 0.4286
	II	—	200.00	100.00	100.00	200.00	100.00	300.00	285.71	85.71	e = 1.0000
	Total	—	350.00	200.00	150.00	350.00	150.00	500.00	500.00	150.00	
2	I	59.52	154.76	107.14	47.62	154.76	52.38	207.14	222.86	68.10	r = 0.4400
	II	83.33	202.38	107.14	95.24	202.38	104.76	307.14	291.43	89.05	e = 1.1000
	Total	142.86	357.14	214.29	142.86	357.14	157.14	514.29	514.29	157.14	
3	I	62.86	160.00	111.43	48.57	160.00	51.43	211.43	226.98	66.98	r = 0.4186
	II	82.86	208.57	111.43	97.14	208.57	102.86	311.43	295.88	87.31	e = 1.0588
	Total	145.71	368.57	222.86	145.71	368.57	154.29	522.86	522.86	154.29	
13	I	65.14	165.14	115.14	50.00	165.14	50.00	215.14	230.28	65.14	r = 0.3944
	II	84.86	215.14	115.14	100.00	215.14	100.00	315.14	300.00	84.86	e = 1.0000
	Total	150.00	380.28	230.28	150.00	380.28	150.00	530.28	530.28	150.00	
14	I	65.14	165.14	115.14	50.00	165.14	50.00	215.14	230.28	65.14	r = 0.3944
	II	84.86	215.14	115.14	100.00	215.14	100.00	315.14	300.00	84.86	e = 1.0000
	Total	150.00	380.28	230.28	150.00	380.28	150.00	530.28	530.28	150.00	

been perpetuated even after its falsity has been documented, and to respond appropriately to this breach of scholarly norms.

In the abstract and again in the introduction to their paper, Mohun and Veneziani (2009: 277 [Abstract]; cf. p. 278) contend that "none of their [Kliman and Freeman's] arguments dispel previous criticism of the 'temporal single system interpretation.'" This is an equally outrageous falsehood. By documenting that the TSSI does not assume that prices equal values, we have indeed conclusively dispelled the previous criticism that it does assume this.

3. Mohun and Veneziani seriously misrepresent our overriding objection to Veneziani (2004) when they portray it as speculation about his psychological commitments. In fact, our point had to do with his actual conduct as a scholar. Mohun and Veneziani (2009: 278) state that we "conjecture that [his paper's logical and factual errors were] not apparent to Veneziani because of a psychological a priori commitment to the falsity of the TSSI, in turn founded on a psychological a priori commitment to the demonstration of the internal inconsistency of Marx." This is not our conjecture. "Our conjecture is instead that [Veneziani and other critics of Marx] all employed *truthiness* [truth that "comes from the gut"], rather than *truthfulness*, as their standard of evaluation. . . . We believe that the *employment of truthiness as a standard of evaluation* . . . is what actually deserves to be put in its place" (Kliman and Freeman 2009: 338, final emphasis added).

If the "truth" coming from Veneziani's gut told him that his arguments were valid, that is a matter of psychology. Our objection, however, was that he and other critics of Marx evidently chose to employ "truth that comes from the gut" as the standard by which to evaluate the success of his arguments. This is not a matter of psychology, but of failure to abide by proper norms of scholarly conduct.[3] Mohun and Veneziani fail to address this issue, which is a further indication that scholarly debate which aims to arrive at the truth is not among their chief concerns.

4. Although they claim that our arguments fail to dispel previous criticism, Mohun and Veneziani have not refuted *any* of our disproofs of Veneziani's allegations. Our main disproofs are listed below.

Contrary to what Veneziani (2004) claimed:

- The TSSI does not assume that market prices and values are equal in a steady-state equilibrium.
- The TSSI does not assume that prices of production equal values.
- Although assumptions differing from those of the "Fundamental Marxian Theorem" are employed in Kliman's proof that all simultaneist interpretations of Marx's value theory imply that surplus labor is neither

necessary nor sufficient for profit to be positive, this does not make the proof "unwarranted."

- The temporalist MELT was initially positive, which implies surplus labor is both necessary and sufficient for profit to be positive, according to the TSSI.
- The TSSI produces results that contradict the Okishio theorem both when the MELT is held constant and when it is not (e.g., when it rises at a constant percentage rate).
- The TSSI does not produce results that contradict the Okishio theorem only in the "singular" and "implausible" case in which labor productivity can increase without bound over time—because this case is not singular or implausible, but the actual experience of capitalism to date.
- Kliman's (1996) refutation of the Okishio theorem does not rely on the implausible assumption that capitalists "invest according to a fixed rule, regardless of what happens to the price of output and to the profitability of investment."

5. In only one case do Mohun and Veneziani even *try* to refute these disproofs.[4] Instead, they employ a diversionary stratagem. The stratagem has two components. First, they simply ignore our disproofs of Veneziani's allegations against the TSSI and Marx.[5] This allows Mohun and Veneziani to avoid having to concede that the allegations are baseless despite their inability to refute what we demonstrated.

Second, to obscure the fact that our demonstrations are being evaded, they fill their paper with irrelevancies—arguments which address neither the points in Veneziani's (2004) paper nor our criticisms of them, and which thus do not belong in this debate but are properly the subject of a completely new paper. Had Mohun and Veneziani's paper consisted of a title and their names followed by twenty-five blank pages, it would have been all too obvious that they cannot answer our arguments. Yet since these twenty-five pages are not blank, they serve to obscure the fact that our demonstrations have been evaded. Although the material in these pages is "about the TSSI," it is irrelevant to the present debate, and thus a smokescreen. Unsuspecting readers may wrongly conclude that Mohun and Veneziani are engaged in a genuine discussion of the two prior contributions and wrongly regard their "response" as evidence that the debate has not yet ended.

This is not the first time that they have resorted to this stratagem. In Kliman and Freeman (2008 {chap. 8 of this book}: 101–2, emphases added), we noted:

> The central issue in this debate has been the incompatibility between simultaneist interpretations and Marx's own theory of profit, as is clear from the title of Andrew Kliman's (2001) initial contribution, "Simultaneous valuation vs. the

> exploitation theory of profit." Overturning the conventional wisdom of a quarter century, our prior contributions have demonstrated that all simultaneist interpretations of Marx's theory contradict his conclusion that exploitation (workers' surplus labour) is the exclusive source of profit in capitalism.

Simon Mohun and Roberto Veneziani (2007 {chap. 7 of this book}) *simply evade this issue. They do not refute or even attempt to refute our demonstration,* and hence they effectively concede that Marx's theory and simultaneous valuation are indeed incompatible. It is time for the wider community to recognize this as well. As we document below, Mohun and Veneziani also fail to respond directly to several other key arguments contained in our response to Mohun's (2003) critique. *Instead, they change the subject*, railing against what they grandly call the "incoherence" of the temporal single-system interpretation (TSSI) of Marx's value theory, and against our "seriously deficient" arguments, logic and reporting of opponents' views (Mohun and Veneziani, 2007: 139, 144).

6. Since Mohun and Veneziani's paper is filled with non-responsive irrelevancies, its actual significance is not that the debate continues, but the very opposite. The debate is over. Marx's critics have run out of arguments against the TSSI refutations of the claims that Marx's value theory and law of the tendential fall in the rate of profit have been proven internally inconsistent. The time has come to draw a line under the discussion and recognize that the defense of Marx's value theory against inconsistency is proven.

In his famous 1977 work, *Marx after Sraffa*, Ian Steedman (1997: 49 n15) wrote: "The present type of argument [the case for inconsistency in Marx] has been examined, in various forms, by many different writers over the last eighty years. The same conclusions have always been reached and no logical flaw has ever been found in such arguments." This can no longer be defended as a true statement. Over twenty scholars working in the TSSI tradition, from widely different backgrounds, have indeed examined the case for inconsistency, have found the logical flaw in the argument, and reached the different conclusion that Marx's value theory is entirely consistent.

At first, the critics chose to ignore these refutations, then they came forward with responses that proved unequal to the task. Every single one of their attempts to overturn our refutations was responded to, and none was sustained. Finally, however, along came Roberto Veneziani. Even before it appeared in print, his work earned the distinction of being celebrated by Steedman (2003: 6) himself for having "adequately put [the TSSI arguments] in their place." All's well that ends well, the critics were led to believe.

But Veneziani's failure to respond to our counterdemonstrations is quite a different ending. Every single one of his attempts to overturn our refutations has been responded to, and none has been sustained.

No scholar with any pretension to integrity can now fail to recognize that, until significant new evidence or arguments are introduced, the case is settled; Steedman's judgment in *Marx after Sraffa* has been refuted. Thus, from the vantage-point of logic if not of myth, the allegations of inconsistency are past history. There is therefore no logical imperative to correct or reject Marx's theories. Those who accepted the allegations of inconsistency, and constructed alternative theories and approaches in order to circumvent the inconsistencies, should take note of the fact that their projects are founded upon on a premise that is no longer sustainable.

7. The methods that critics of the TSSI are employing are increasingly evolving into a test of integrity. It is simply not serious to propose, as a "response" to a detailed point-by-point refutation, a text that does not respond to these very same refutations. If such conduct continues to evolve and to be accepted as good practice, Marxism—and indeed, economic theory—will be deprived of any criterion of truth and will simply become a slugfest.

Moreover, the correct representation of opposing views is an issue of integrity in its own right. Mohun's and Veneziani's first responses to the TSSI (Mohun 2003; Veneziani 2004) attempted to grapple in good faith with what TSSI authors have actually written. This now no longer appears to be the case. The most serious gaps in their latest response do not concern the substance of TSSI arguments at all, but their refusal to respond to our corrections to their misrepresentations of what the TSSI even *says*, as we documented in point 2 above.

If economic theorists are permitted to place any words they choose in the mouths of opponents whose views they find uncomfortable, then of course anything can be proven. For example, we could refute Keynes at a stroke by simply repeating, insistently and without paying attention to anyone else, that he claimed the economy could be saved by printing money. For that matter, we could refute Mohun and Veneziani by attributing to them any wild claim we cared to think of, for example that they assert the unconditional truth of neoclassical theory. If such methods of debate are accepted, nothing is left of scholarship.

8. The most serious problem with Mohun and Veneziani's reply to us, as far as the larger scholarly community is concerned, is that it employs methods that do not permit inquiry to arrive at truth. It is directed to the single objective of "putting the TSSI in its place." This is not a mere issue of "psychology"; it pertains to their behavior and its pernicious effects.

Rather than simply complain about this, we shall now propose a positive alternative—ground rules for how scholarly debate needs to be conducted in order to allow it to make progress in arriving at the truth. We will immediately conduct ourselves according to these rules, and we urge others in the scholarly community to implement them promptly as well.[6]

a. Critiques need to characterize opponents' arguments and views accurately, and to provide the documentation required to substantiate the characterizations.
b. Papers written in reply to other papers (including rejoinders) must actually reply to them, carefully and thoroughly addressing their major arguments and/or evidence.
c. Since papers that consist wholly or mainly of newly introduced matters do not constitute replies, they should instead be submitted as new, self-standing papers.
d. Claims that have been shown to be false need to be retracted in a clear and forthright manner, without trying to divert readers' attention or change the subject.[7]
e. Replies must not ignore the issues already under discussion and introduce new ones *instead*, since this diversionary tactic has several pernicious effects.[8]
f. Parties whose arguments have been answered with diversions must not respond to those who have resorted to diversion.
g. However, they are obliged to respond *privately* about the new issues that have been raised when approached by disinterested persons who wish to arrive at the truth.
h. If a paper addresses the issues already under discussion in accordance with point (b), above, it is acceptable and non-diversionary for it to *also* introduce new ones.
i. If some of the original issues remain unresolved, the parties should first try to resolve them before new points are engaged.

The rationale behind many of these rules is self-evident. With regard to others, we offer the following comments.

The pernicious effects of the diversionary tactic discussed in point (e) include the following: (1) it prevents debates from being resolved; (2) it impedes recognition of truths, since baseless claims and invalid arguments do not get retracted; (3) it wastes the scarce time, energy, and resources of parties whose refutations of such claims and arguments are ignored and rendered pointless; and (4) it lets the weaker argument appear to be the stronger one. When new baseless claims and invalid arguments replace old ones without the latter first having been retracted, a party that repeatedly puts forward such claims and arguments appears to be on the intellectual offensive, while the party that repeatedly demolishes them appears to be on the defensive.

If diversion does take place, point (f) is intended to prevent a cycle of diversion-refutation-new diversion from developing. Point (g) is based on the recognition that even diversionary claims and arguments are not necessarily false, and that the scholarly community is entitled and obliged to separate fact from fiction. Also, if responses to disinterested parties are kept private, this will help prevent a cycle of diversion-refutation-new diversion from developing. Original issues take precedence over the new ones in point (i) in order to facilitate the resolution of debates and the recognition of truths.

9. We look forward to a genuine reply by Mohun and Veneziani to our counterarguments against Veneziani's (2004) paper. In the meantime, it should not be assumed that we accept any of their new characterizations or criticisms of our work or the TSSI.

NOTES

1. "Then there are the Temporalist-Single-System [sic] arguments much noised about these days. It seems to me that Veneziani (2002) has adequately put them in their place" (Steedman 2003: 6). Steedman is the author of *Marx after Sraffa*.

2. If the two departments' products sold at their prices of production, each would obtain the same ratio of profit (given in the π column) to capital advanced (**M–C**).

3. So is the other possibility (which we remain unwilling to believe), namely that Veneziani et al. wrote, published, and celebrated a paper that they knew to be riddled with illogic and error.

4. The exception is that they try to overturn our proof that the "initial value" of the temporalist MELT, τ_0, was positive. Mohun and Veneziani (2009: 295) claim that this cannot be proved, because there are only two possibilities; either the value of the MELT is indeterminate because of an infinite regress, or "τ_0 is a nonzero arbitrary initial condition of any sign." Confirming that truth is no longer the primary objective of their response, they offer no support for their claim that these are the only possibilities, and the claim is incorrect. We proved that a third possibility exists when we proved that τ_0 is a historically determined (and therefore non-arbitrary) initial condition that necessarily has a positive sign (Kliman and Freeman 2009: 352–53).

Mohun and Veneziani (2009: 292) also egregiously misrepresent our proof by alleging that we "claim that, at [time] $t = 0$, 'the total value of commodities (in terms of labor-time) was at first just the living labor extracted.'" We made no such claim. We offered two different *possible interpretations* of Marx's theory—the first being that the total value of commodities at $t = 0$ included a constant-capital component, the other being the interpretation that Mohun and Veneziani misrepresent as a claim—and we proved that τ_0 was positive according to *both* interpretations. So our proof goes through whether or not the "claim" is true.

5. Our reply to Veneziani noted that Marx was the ultimate target of his critique. Mohun and Veneziani (2009: 285) claim that this statement of ours is a "merely

polemical trope[ ] with little credibility." But Veneziani's (2004: 98; 1st emphasis in original, 2nd emphasis added) own words substantiate our statement: "in this paper it is confirmed that the adoption of a coherent methodology and a clear distinction between values and prices would imply that not *all* Marx's results hold, as is well known in the literature on Marxian economics. . . . *[T]his leads one to question the TSS literal interpretation of Marx's theory.*" In other words, Veneziani claimed some of Marx's theoretical results "cannot be taken literally, but must either be reinterpreted as mere metaphors or rejected outright" (Kliman and Freeman 2009: 339). It was for this reason, and not because "TSSI adherents argue that . . . any criticism of the TSSI is inevitably a criticism of Marx" (Mohun and Veneziani 2009), that we concluded that Marx was the ultimate target of Veneziani's critique.

6. These rules are intended as a supplement to the Scholarship Guidelines of the International Working Group on Value Theory (see Freeman, Kliman, and Wells (eds.) 2004: 287–89) that we worked out earlier.

7. "One need not accept that Marx's disputed conclusions are true in order to acknowledge that they are logically valid. One need not accept that they are logically valid in order to acknowledge that there exists an interpretation according to which they are valid. One can even continue to believe that Marx's conclusions are logically invalid while acknowledging that the proofs of inconsistency have been decisively refuted. And one can do all this clearly and forthrightly, without trying to divert readers' attention or change the subject" (Kliman 2007: 209).

8. "In recent years, Marx's critics have found it increasingly difficult to defend the allegations of inconsistency [in his value theory] against the TSSI [temporal single-system interpretation] critique. Thus they generally try to avoid this issue altogether. Instead, they now prefer to debate the pros and cons of Marx's work and of alternative approaches to Marxian economic analysis. In other contexts, these are of course important and interesting topics, but to discuss them here and now is to fall into a diversionary trap, at the very moment when correction of the record has become a real possibility. I will be glad to discuss these topics with Marx's critics once the record has been set straight and they have done their part to help set it straight. This book, however, purposely refrains from offering a positive case for Marx's ideas or for Marxian economic analysis informed by the TSSI" (Kliman 2007: xiii–xiv).

Part II

EXCHANGE BETWEEN ROBERT PAUL WOLFF AND PROPONENTS OF THE TSSI

Chapter 12

Once More unto the Breach, Dear Friends, Once More

Robert Paul Wolff

MAY 4, 2014

All right. I am going to have one more go at this, and then, as they say in the soaps, I am going to move on with my life. Chris {Byron} says that as of now he has never heard a good reason why people reject Marx's value theory. Of course, that is a bit vague. "Marx's value theory" may mean "Marx's version of the Labor Theory of Value," which is how I interpret the remark. But it may also mean, more generally, Marx's claim that capital rests on the exploitation of the working class. Chris and I agree about the latter. I am pretty sure he means the former.

Now, I have written a whole book and a serious mathematical article about this subject, so I could simply refer to them (as I do periodically on this blog), but I am unaware of anyone who has actually answered my critique and analysis (except John Roemer, a brilliant Marxist mathematical economist, but that is a somewhat different story), so I am going to tell that story again right here, without the math, and wait for a serious direct engagement with my argument. Settle down and get a cup of coffee. This is going to take a while, but hey, this is my blog, and I really care about this stuff. Those who find it boring may wish to spend the time reading economic statistics on the website of the Bureau of Labor Statistics, always a fun site to visit. Here we go.

Adam Smith in 1776 argued that in the primitive state of things, before the accumulation of stock or the appropriation of land, commodities would exchange in proportion to the amount of labor it took to produce them (I told you this was going to take a while). But he understood that once you took account of the fact that some commodities require a good deal of capital to produce, in the form of tools, factories, etc., whereas others require much less capital and a lot more labor ("labor intensive" rather than "capital intensive," as later economists learned to say), this simple "Labor Theory of Value" would not be correct. Forty-one years later, David Ricardo came up with brilliant solutions to the problems both of accumulated stock and of land. Never mind land—that is a great story but beside the point here. Ricardo noted that tools and raw materials and buildings and such, which are needed for the production of commodities, are all the products of labor expended in earlier production cycles. Today's tool, needed as input into the making of a car, is last year's output of the toolmaker. So we can view the tool as embodying a certain amount of the toolmaker's labor, which is then carried forward and bestowed on, or embodied in, the car that is made with its aid. Indeed, *everything* that we use in this cycle of production to make commodities, save for the new fresh labor expended now by workers, can be thought of as simply so much embodied labor carried forward from previous cycles. Now, of course, last year, when the toolmaker made the tool now being used to make the car, he or she used tools and materials that were themselves the products of even earlier cycles of production, and so forth backward ad infinitum. But this does not pose a problem, Ricardo correctly intuited (without any actual mathematics to back him up), because the infinite number of bits of fresh labor expended at various times in the past form a series that *converges* to a finite sum! (This is all easy enough to prove mathematically. You can look it up in the appendix to my book, *Understanding Marx* {Wolff (1984)}.)

So Ricardo said, commodities will not exchange in proportion to the amounts of new, fresh, direct labor that their production require. But they *will* exchange in proportion to the amounts of labor *directly or indirectly* required for their production. In short, commodities will exchange in proportion to the amounts of labor *embodied* in them.

As soon as had he made this genuinely brilliant breakthrough, Ricardo realized that it was not quite correct. To be sure, if the ratio of new, fresh labor to old embodied labor is the same in each line of production [if, to use Marx's language, the *organic composition of capital* is the same in all lines of production], then commodities will indeed exchange in proportion to the amounts of dead and living labor required for their production—they will exchange at their *labor values*. *But*, if some industries are capital intensive, using lots of dead labor embodied in machines, such as semi-automated oil refineries, and others are labor intensive, using relatively little embodied labor and lots of living labor, such as sweatshop-style clothing production, then competition in the free market will make prices diverge from their labor values, and the Labor Theory of Value will be wrong.

Ricardo never solved this problem and was still puzzling over it when he died. Fast-forward a half century to Marx. Marx believed he had a solution to Ricardo's problem, but he also thought there was an ever deeper problem that neither Ricardo nor Smith before him had even seen. What is more,

Marx thought he had a very deep and important solution to this unrecognized problem, a solution that would demonstrate the fundamental fact that capitalism rests on the exploitation of the working class. Therefore, he wrote all of volume 1 of *Capital* without even discussing Ricardo's problem, leaving that for volume 3.

The problem, to put it as simply as possible, is this: Why is there any profit at all in a capitalist system? How do capitalists turn a profit? Look, Marx said. Let us suppose we have a dead simple capitalist system in which each line of production exhibits the same ratio of living to dead labor. In other words, assume a system in which there is equal organic composition of capital in all lines, so that commodities exchange at their labor values, as Ricardo correctly said. In this system, capitalists, like everyone else, buy their inputs into production at their labor value [by hypothesis] and sell their output also at its labor value. How on earth do they make any profit?

There were some economists, so-called, in Marx's day who had been puzzled by this, and had come up with some really dumb answers, which Marx has a lot of innocent fun ridiculing. Some said the solution was that the capitalists total up their costs and tack on 10 percent for profit. But, Marx noted, since the capitalists from whom they buy their inputs do the same thing, that doesn't really explain the origin of profit. One hapless chap with the implausible name "Nassau Senior" (there was no Nassau Junior) suggested that all the profit came from the last hour of production, all the previous hours being required just to pay for the costs of the inputs. Hence, he concluded triumphantly, if the then current proposal to reduce the work day from twelve hours to ten hours was put into effect, capitalists would make no profit at all.

In a famous passage in *Capital*, from which I took the title of one of my books, Marx put the problem in this deliciously ironic fashion: "Our friend, Moneybags, must be so lucky as to find, within the sphere of circulation, in the market, a commodity, whose use-value possesses the peculiar property of being a source of value, whose actual consumption, therefore, is itself an embodiment of labour, and consequently, a creation of value. The possessor of money does find on the market such a special commodity in capacity for labour or labour-power." (Opening paragraph of chapter VI of volume 1 of *Capital*.)

The solution to the puzzle of the origin of profit, Marx says, lies in the distinction between labor-power, or the capacity to labor, and labor itself, the effort and time expended by workers in the production process. In a capitalist system, workers are treated in the marketplace like any other producers of a commodity that they offer for sale. And like all other commodity producers, they are compelled by the workings of competition to sell their commodity at its labor-value. But what is the labor value of any commodity? It is simply the amount of living and dead labor required to produce it. So the labor-value of labor-power is just the amount of living and dead labor embodied in it.

How much is that? Well, it is however much labor it takes to produce the food, clothing, and shelter that the worker needs to stay alive and go to work the next day. Like any prudent commodity producer, the worker must set aside a little for depreciation. In his or her case, that means raising children. who will. {sic} When the adult worker is worn out and dies, the children can step into the production process as labor-power sellers as soon as they are able, say at age twelve.

How much embodied labor is actually required by the worker in the form of food and clothing and necessaries? Well, Marx says quite correctly, *less than the number of hours of new living labor that worker can perform.* And here is the solution to the mystery of profit. The capitalist (let us suppose just to out some numbers on it) pays the worker an amount of money equal to six hours of labor—which is to say, the capitalist pays the worker a wage with which they worker can buy the necessary food and clothing and such, which stuff embodies six hours of labor The capitalist has paid the worker a fair wage—he has paid the worker a wage equal to the cost of production of the worker's product, labor power, just as the capitalist has paid the tool manufacturer and the iron ore salesman and all the other input providers a price equal to the labor value of their goods. *But the worker is required to labor for twelve hours (assuming Nassau Senior has his way).* And those extra six hours of labor are embodied in the capitalist's output, which of course he owns since he has paid for all the inputs at their fair market value. So when the capitalist comes to sell his output, he pockets the money equivalent of those extra six hours of labor, *and there is his profit.* The capitalist has found a commodity, in Marx's words, "whose actual consumption, therefore, is itself an embodiment of labour, and consequently, a creation of value."

Problem solved.

Let us call the extra six hours of labor performed by the worker *surplus labor*. The first six hours of labor is *necessary labor*, because it is required to reproduce the labor consumed in the production process—in other words, it is required to keep the worker alive for another day of work. What relation does this surplus labor bear to the profit that the capitalist makes in each cycle of production and sale of what is produced? Well, it will come as no surprise, I would imagine, to learn that the profit appropriated by the capitalist *just exactly equals the surplus labor performed by the workers*. In short, *profit is nothing but surplus labor-value*.

This, in essence, is Marx's Labor Theory of Value. The key, Marx tells us, is the distinction between labor-power and labor. So what is wrong with it? (Never mind the problem of unequal organic composition of capital—that is a complication that must await the settling of the status of the basic theory.) Remember, please, I am not disagreeing with Marx that profits come out of the hides of the workers. Not at all. I am simply saying that his theoretical analysis of this fundamental fact is wrong, that a different theoretical analysis is required. The new analysis does not let the capitalists off the hook. Not a bit of it.

Now we come to my contribution to this debate. When I published it, in the article "A Critique and Reevaluation of Marx's Labor Theory of Value" {Wolff 1981}, I was unaware that anyone had ever put forward these arguments before. The aforementioned John Roemer pointed out that a year earlier, a Spanish economist, Josip Vegara, had published a book in which he proved something similar. Sigh. So much for my Nobel Prize in Economics. Anyway.

Let us ask a question that it never occurred to anyone to ask: How much iron does it take, directly or indirectly, to produce a bushel of corn or a car or a shirt? In short, what is the *iron value* of a bushel of corn or a car or a shirt? We might equally ask, How much corn does it take to make a ton of iron, a car, or a shirt? In short, what is the *corn value* of each of these commodities? And, while we are at it, let us ask what the iron value or corn value is of a day's labor.

Now, this sounds crazy, right? Smith did not talk like this, Ricardo did not talk like this. And Marx certainly did not talk like this. Well, maybe so, but if we ask this peculiar question, here is what we find:

1. So long as the system as a whole produces some sort of physical surplus in each cycle over and above what is required to run the system for another year, it is mathematically necessary that the iron value of a unit of iron will be less than one unit of iron, that the corn value of one unit of corn will be less than one unit of corn, that the X-value of one unit of X will be less than one unit of X for any X that is a required input in to all lines of production, directly or indirectly. In order for this to be true, it is not necessary that there be a surplus of X in the system each year. If we are calculating iron values, it is certain that the iron value of a unit of iron will be less than 1 even if there is no surplus of iron itself produced in the system.
2. No matter which commodity we choose as the "substance of value"—be it labor, iron, corn, or whatever—all the propositions that Marx states about labor value will be true for that commodity as well—for iron values, corn values, and so forth. Because it takes less than one unit of iron to produce one unit of iron, whenever the capitalist uses a unit of iron there will be some "surplus iron value" embodied in the product being produced. The sum total of all that surplus iron value will exactly equal the profit appropriated by the capitalist, measured in units of iron value. The same is true for corn or any other factor of production. If an economic system exhibits equal iron-organic composition of capital—which means that in each line of production there is the same ratio of direct to indirect iron inputs—then

the prices of commodities will be strictly proportional in that system to the iron-values of the commodities.

3. *AND ALL OF THIS IS TRUE, EVEN THOUGH THERE IS NO PLAUSIBLE DISTINCTION BETWEEN IRON AND IRON POWER OR CORN AND CORN POWER. THEREFORE, MARX IS WRONG WHEN HE SAYS THAT THE DISTINCTION BETWEEN LABOR AND LABOR POWER IS THE KEY TO THE EXPLANATION OF THE ORIGIN OF PROFIT IN A CAPITALIST SYSTEM.*

So if Marx's Labor Theory of Value is wrong, what is the correct analysis? In my article, I offered an answer which I think has some merit, but I do not want to summarize that here because this has gone on long enough.

One final word, before, as I promised, I move on with my life. Marxism is not a religion. There is no catechism, no official teaching of the Marxist Church to which one must subscribe in order to be allowed to call oneself a Marxist. Marx was a great social scientist, a great philosopher, and also, as it happens, a great writer. But he was not the Second Coming (or even the First). So let us once for all time set aside debates about who is and who is not a true Marxist. There is more important work to be done.

Chapter 13

Physicalism and the Exploitation Theory of Profit are Incompatible

A Response to Robert Paul Wolff

Chris Byron, Alan Freeman, and Andrew Kliman

MAY 9, 2014

The Sraffian-influenced philosopher Robert Paul Wolff published a blog piece on May 4 {chap. 12 of this book} in which he claimed that, if one wishes to show that "capital rests on the exploitation of the working class," it is possible (and necessary) to do so without Marx's own exploitation theory of profit. Noting that he has "written a whole book and a serious mathematical article about this subject," Wolff says that "I am unaware of anyone who has actually answered my critique and analysis (except John Roemer . . .)."

What follows is that answer.

In essence, two of the authors of this response (Freeman and Kliman) have disproved Wolff's claim in various publications during the last decade and a half. They have shown that, contrary to what the so-called "Fundamental Marxian Theorem" seems to imply, the physical quantities approach of Sraffian (and physicalist Marxist) economists is incompatible with Marx's exploitation theory of profit. Physicalist models actually imply that profit can be negative although workers perform surplus labor, and that profit can be positive even if workers don't perform surplus labor. Hence, surplus labor is neither a sufficient condition nor a necessary condition for the existence of profit. In other words, physicalist models imply that, contrary to what Marx argued, surplus labor is not the exclusive source of profit.[1]

Wolff's commentary suggests that he considers his book and mathematical article to be a new or distinct contribution, even within the Sraffian literature. We assume that this is why he believes that nobody has "actually answered" his critique and analysis. However, Freeman and Kliman's previous proofs demonstrate that *any* physical quantities approach is incompatible with Marx's exploitation theory of profit. Although Wolff's specific argument may differ from other physical quantities arguments, it is in fact simply another variant of a generic approach whose claims Freeman and Kliman have refuted. To re-establish this point, we will provide here a variant of our general refutation that refutes Wolff's specific claims.

Wolff's argument doesn't run in terms of surplus labor and profit. He claims instead that there will be positive profit whenever less than one unit of each commodity is needed, directly and indirectly, to produce a unit of that commodity. (This condition ensures that a surplus of every produced commodity is possible.) In fact, he claims, total profit will be exactly equal to the physical surplus "value." For instance, if we choose to make iron the "substance of value," "[t]he sum total of all that surplus iron value will exactly equal the profit appropriated by the capitalist, measured in units of iron value."

Although Wolff's conclusion is not about surplus labor specifically, Freeman and Kliman's prior demonstrations have disproved it precisely because, as Wolff himself states and indeed emphasizes, labor has no privileged status in physicalist models. It is just one input among many. Thus, what the prior demonstrations have shown regarding surplus labor actually applies to every possible "'substance of value'—be it labor, iron, corn, or whatever" (Wolff): physicalist models imply that profit can be negative even though a surplus of every produced commodity is possible, and they imply that profit can be positive even when a surplus of every produced commodity is impossible.

We trust that this last comment, together with the previous demonstrations by Freeman and Kliman, suffices as a proof for Wolff and for anyone else who is familiar with physicalist models. That the demonstrations carry over from labor to "iron, corn, or whatever" is obvious. But since this is undoubtedly not obvious to everyone, we here provide a *direct* disproof of Wolff's conclusion.

Consider an economy in which there are just two produced commodities, Gummi Bears and Botox. Gummi Bears, Botox, and labor are needed to produce Gummi Bears, and these same three inputs are needed to produce Botox. The amounts of each input that are needed to produce one unit of each commodity are given in Table 13.1.

These input-output coefficients satisfy the Hawkins-Simon conditions (to which Wolff refers implicitly in point 1 near the end of his blog post). In

Table 13.1 Input-Output Coefficients

	Input per Unit of Output		
Industry	*Gummi Bears*	*Botox*	*Labor*
Gummi Bears	0.49	0.49	0.02
Botox	0.49	0.49	0.02

other words, an input of less than one Gummi Bear is needed, directly and indirectly, in order to produce one Gummi Bear, and an input of less than one dose of Botox is needed, directly and indirectly, in order to produce one dose of Botox. Another way of saying the same thing is that a physical surplus of Gummi Bears and a physical surplus of Botox are both possible at the same time. For instance, if both industries produce one thousand units of output, it would be possible to have a surplus of up to twenty Gummi Bears and up to twenty doses of Botox. Multiplying all of the figures in Table 13.1 by one thousand, we obtain Table 13.2.

The maximum potential surplus of Gummi Bears is the output minus the economy-wide input, 1,000 – 980 = 20, and similarly for Botox. (The size of the actual physical surpluses will depend on how many Gummi Bears and doses of Botox the workers receive. If they receive fewer than twenty units of each good, physical surpluses of both goods would be positive.)

To measure the economy's *total* surplus and profit, we need to add up the Gummi Bear surplus and the Botox surplus, and thus we need a measure of value (which is what Wolff means by "substance of value"). One can't add up Gummi Bears and Botox because they are heterogeneous goods with no common measure, but one can add up the value of Gummi Bears and the value of Botox.

Recall that labor has no privileged status in the physicalist models. It is just one input among many. So instead of choosing labor, we make Botox the "substance" (i.e., measure) of value.

To compute the Botox-Values, let us use λ_g to denote the per-unit value of Gummi Bear and λ_l to denote the per-unit value of labor. (Since Botox is the measure of value, its per-unit value equals one.) Using the input-output coefficients in Table 13.1, the Botox-Values of Gummi Bears and labor are the solutions to the following two equations:

$$0.49\lambda_g + 0.49 + 0.02\lambda_\ell = \lambda_g$$

$$0.49\lambda_g + 0.49 + 0.02\lambda_\ell = 1$$

and the solution is $\lambda_g = \lambda_l = 1$.

The maximum potential surplus Botox-Value of Gummi Bears in the above system is therefore $1{,}000\,\lambda_g - 980\,\lambda_g = 20\,\lambda_g = 20$, and the maximum potential

Table 13.2 A Gummi Bear–Botox Economy for Which Wolff's Conclusions Hold

	Inputs			
Industry	*Gummi Bears*	*Botox*	*Labor*	*Output*
Gummi Bears	490	490	20	1,000
Botox	490	490	20	1,000
Total	980	980	40	

surplus Botox-Value of Botox is (1,000 × 1) – (980 × 1) = (20 × 1) = 20. So the total, economy-wide, maximum potential surplus Botox-Value is positive.

What about profit? Well, in the physicalist models, profit is just the total price of the physical surpluses. So, given only that Gummi Bears and Botox have positive per-unit prices, the maximum potential profit—the total price of the twenty potentially surplus Gummi Bears plus the total price of the twenty potentially surplus doses of Botox—must be positive.

This *seems* to confirm at least part of Wolff's conclusion. There is, potentially, positive total profit and positive total surplus Botox-Value. And thus, if one doesn't think too hard about the matter, it's possible to argue that the positive total surplus Botox-Value is the exclusive *source* of the positive total profit. (Actually, in this physicalist model, the sources of the profit, and of the surplus Botox-Value, are the physical surpluses of the two goods, but no matter.)

But the above example is just one particular case. Does Wolff's conclusion hold true in all cases? As we will now show, it does not.

In point 1 near the end of his blog post, he tells us that it holds true "[s]o long as the system as a whole produces some sort of physical surplus in each cycle over and above what is required to run the system for another year. . . . In order for this to be true, it is not necessary that there be a surplus of X in the system each year."

Let us suppose that a physical surplus of Botox is produced—this is "some sort of physical surplus"—but there is a physical deficit of Gummi Bears. More Gummi Bears are used up as inputs into the production of Gummi Bears and Botox than are produced as outputs at year's end. Specifically, imagine that nine hundred Gummi Bears and 1,100 doses of Botox are produced. Multiplying the input-output coefficients in the first row of Table 13.1 by nine hundred and those in the second row by 1,100, we obtain the input-output system shown in Table 13.3.

The maximum potential surplus of Gummi Bears is, again, the output minus the economy-wide input, which is now 900 – 980 = –80. The maximum potential surplus of Botox is 1,100 – 980 = 120. Thus, the total (economy-wide) maximum potential surplus Botox-Value is $-80\ \lambda_g$ + (120 × 1) = (–80 × 1) + (120 × 1) = 40.

Table 13.3 A Gummi Bear–Botox Economy for Which Wolff's Conclusions Do Not Hold

	Inputs			
Industry	*Gummi Bears*	*Botox*	*Labor*	*Output*
Gummi Bears	441	441	18	900
Botox	539	539	22	1100
Total	980	980	40	

The actual total surplus Botox-Value depends also on the Botox-value of the workers' wages (BVWW). If they are paid in kind, BVWW is the Botox-Value of the Gummi Bears they receive, plus the number of doses of Botox they receive, from their employers. (If they are paid money wages, BVWW is the Botox-Value of the Gummi Bears they buy, plus the number of doses of Botox that the remainder of their wages enables them to buy.) Thus,

$$\text{actual total surplus Botox-Value} = 40 - \text{BVWW} \tag{13.1}$$

What about profit? Let us denote the per-unit price of Gummi Bears as P_g and let the per-unit price of Botox equal 1. In this physicalist model, total profit is the total price of the physical surpluses minus BVWW, that is

$$\text{actual total profit} = -80\,P_g + (120 \times 1) - \text{BVWW} \tag{13.2}$$

Now recall that all conditions that Wolff stipulated hold true here. Less than one Gummi Bear is needed, directly and indirectly, to produce a Gummi Bear. Less than one dose of Botox is needed, directly and indirectly, to produce a dose of Botox. And there is "some sort of physical surplus" in the system as a whole. Given these conditions, he contends, total profit must be positive if total surplus Botox-Value is positive.

It is trivial to show that this claim is incorrect. Assume that $P_g = 1.05$ and BVWW = 38. Plugging these number into equations (13.1) and (13.2), we obtain

$$\text{actual total surplus-Botox-value} = 40 - 38 = 2$$

$$\text{actual total profit} = (-80 \times 1.05) + (120 \times 1) - 38 = -84 + 120 - 38 = -2$$

Q.E.D.

It is also trivial to show that total profit can be positive even if total surplus Botox-Value is negative. Assume that $P_g = 0.95$ and BVWW = 42. Plugging these number into equations (13.1) and (13.2), we obtain

$$\text{actual total surplus-Botox-value} = 40 - 42 = -2$$

$$\text{actual total profit} = (-80 \times 0.95) + (120 \times 1) - 42 = -76 + 120 - 42 = 2$$

The first demonstration shows that positive surplus Botox-value is not a sufficient condition for the existence of profit. The second demonstration shows that it is not a necessary condition, either. Hence, surplus Botox-value is not the exclusive source of profit.

As we noted above, Freeman and Kliman have produced several analogous demonstrations which show that physicalist models imply that surplus labor is not the exclusive source of profit. Physicalist economists have continually tried to dismiss these demonstrations on the grounds that they use "arbitrary" prices (see Mohun 2003 {Chap. 3 of this book}: 98; Veneziani 2004 {Chap. 5 of this book}: 105–6; and *Reclaiming Marx's "Capital": The Movie* {Anti-christ Productions 2012}). We trust that Wolff, as a competent philosopher who understand and respects logic, will not employ such a stratagem.

He undoubtedly understands that one counterexample is enough to disprove a claim such as his if it satisfies the stipulated conditions but not the conclusion, as our counterexample does. And he undoubtedly understands that no deductive argument is valid if its premises include certain restrictions while the conclusion it purports to derive pertains to circumstances in which those restrictions do not hold true.

Thus, he undoubtedly understands that if he were to try to rescue his argument by imposing additional restrictions that prevent the price of Gummi Bears from being 1.05 or 0.95, he could not validly conclude that positive surplus Botox-Value is a sufficient condition or a necessary condition for the existence of profit. He could, at best, conclude that a set of conditions that includes restrictions which prevent the price of Gummi Bears from being 1.05 or 0.95 is necessary and sufficient. Such a demonstration would tell us nothing about the origin of profit *in the real world* unless Wolff could also prove that the additional restrictions hold true in the real world.

The above argument has demonstrated that, if one wishes to argue that "capital rests on the exploitation of the working class," it is not possible to do so validly by means of Wolff's version of the physicalist model. Freeman and Kliman's previous demonstrations have shown that it is also not possible to do so validly by means of physicalist versions of "the labor theory of value." Yet there is a valid way to make such an argument—Marx's way.

But Marx's argument is logically valid *only* if it is interpreted properly, not misinterpreted in the physicalist manner. On the basis of the non-physicalist interpretation of which we are proponents, the temporal single-system interpretation of Marx's value theory (TSSI), it does indeed follow validly that surplus labor is the exclusive source of (real) profit.[2] A decade of debate confirmed this result beyond reasonable doubt.[3]

Let us now turn to two other issues. One is Wolff's complaint, in the article to which he refers us {Wolff 1981}, against Marx's conclusion that labor is the substance of value, and that commodities' values are therefore determined by the amount of labor socially necessary to produce them. Wolff objects that "Marx's argument for [this], at the beginning of chapter I of *Capital*, is extremely weak—so weak as not to constitute any argument at all." He says nothing more; we have quoted the objection *in its entirety*. Clearly, it is extremely weak—so weak as not to constitute any argument at all.

Secondly, we wish to comment on the following remark that Wolff makes at the end of his blog post:

> Marxism is not a religion. There is no catechism, no official teaching of the Marxist Church to which one must subscribe in order to be allowed to call oneself a Marxist. Marx was a great social scientist, a great philosopher, and also, as it happens, a great writer. But he was not the Second Coming [or even the First]. So let us once for all time set aside debates about who is and who is not a true Marxist.

For far too long, proponents of the TSSI have been victims of Sraffian boilerplate invective about critics' supposed religious attitudes, fundamentalism, and obscurantism. It is illogical—ad hominem and straw man argumentation—and it is uncalled for, especially because TSSI arguments are more rigorous and respectful of logic than their own arguments, as has been shown consistently. We hope that this is not what Wolff had in mind.

NOTES

1. See chapter 10 of Kliman (2007) for a relatively non-technical discussion and numerical examples. Also see Kliman (2001), Kliman and Freeman (2006, 2008, 2009), and Freeman and Kliman (2009) {chaps. 2, 6, 8, 9 and 11 of this book, respectively}.
2. See Kliman (2001), chap. 10 of Kliman (2007), and Kliman and Freeman (2006, 2008, 2009).
3. See Kliman and Freeman (2008) and Freeman and Kliman (2009).

Chapter 14

Response to Professors Freeman and Kliman and Mr. Byron

Robert Paul Wolff

MAY 10, 2014

Mr. Chris Byron and Professors Alan Freeman and Andrew Kliman have written a seven-page critique {chap. 13 of this book} of my critique of Marx's Labor Theory of Value entitled "Physicalism and the Exploitation Theory of Profit are Incompatible: A Response to Robert Paul Wolff." In what follows, I shall comment on their essay and do my best to reply specifically to the example they construct as a demonstration that my statements are false. I am going to proceed as follows: First, I shall make some general remarks about the dispute; second, I shall address myself in detail to their counterexample; and third, I shall close with a final remark.

I. SOME INTRODUCTORY REMARKS

Let me begin by thanking the three authors for taking the time and putting in the effort to write their response to me. Professors Freeman and Kliman are senior distinguished professional economists, and Chris Byron is a very bright young graduate philosophy student. All three of them obviously have better things to do than rebut the claims of an aging amateur, and I am grateful to them.

It should be obvious to anyone reading their essay that I have managed to irritate Byron, Freeman, and Kliman, and I am really sorry about that. I have not read either the six articles or the book authored by them and listed in their bibliography, but here is my impression of the situation. Kliman, Freeman, and others have been engaged for some years in an ongoing argument with a number of economists whom they identify as backing the "physical quantities approach of Sraffa." They have, they believe, decisively refuted the claims of those authors a number of times, and they are just a little ticked off when I wander onto the scene like Pierre at the Battle of Borodino and announce that I have written a book and an article that no one has refuted. Freeman and Kliman, they tell us, embrace a "temporal single-system interpretation of Marx's value theory" which shows, as I understand it, that Marx did **not** contradict himself.

Now, this is a hunt in which I do not have a dog, as they say down here in North Carolina. First of all, I do not think Marx contradicted himself. I think many of Marx's claims are true. I just don't think his way of expounding and demonstrating them succeeds, for the reason I give in my essay, and I therefore try to find *in Marx's own writings* an alternative way of capturing what I take to be his foundational claim, that capitalism rests on the exploitation of the working class. I may be all wet, but if so, I am so in a manner different from that of the Sraffian physicalists (from whom, let me be clear, I have learned a great deal).

In particular, I have no fixed opinion on Marx's claim that there is a tendency, as capitalism develops, for the rate of profit to fall. This, unless I am mistaken, is a question of great importance to Kliman and Freeman, one on which they have written extensively (or so I gather). For all I know, they are right in this debate and Okishio is wrong. But that is something I have not written about, and it really is not a part of what I was trying to get at in my essay.

I know that Professors Freeman and Kliman have read my essay, because they list it in their bibliography, but to my great regret they have chosen not to address any of the arguments in the second part of it, which I have always thought of, rather proudly, as my one stab at saying anything original about economics. John Roemer did address that part of the essay in a response he wrote right after it was published. I had presented a little mathematics to show that exploitation takes place because the workers, divorced from the means of production, have no choice but to sell their labor to capitalists. John, whose command of mathematics is to mine as Pinchas Zuckerman's playing of the viola is to mine, offered a lengthy, detailed, and very deep critique and analysis of my argument, which in my opinion takes things a great deal farther than I was able to. With his agreement, I have reproduced John's essay in volume II of my collected papers, available as an e-book from Amazon.com.

Finally, let me withdraw the remarks I made about religion at the end of my blog post, remarks that captured the attention of Kliman and Freeman. I most certainly was not referring to them, and however relaxed the standards of discourse may be on blogs, I had no business saying something that might even conceivably be construed as directed at them or their position. So, let us just say that I apologize and withdraw them. My bad.

II. BOTOX AND GUMMI BEARS

Now let us get down to the meat of the essay by Professors Freeman and Kliman [Chris Byron tells me that he did not have a hand in the mathematics]. Following a long and honorable tradition in economic theory, they have constructed a counterexample that bears no conceivable relation to the real world. But that is in no way an objection to their counterexample. As they quite correctly point out, when someone has advanced a universal proposition, any genuine counterexample, no matter how outré, is sufficient to refute the proposition.

Since some of you may be unfamiliar with this habit of economists, it might help you [though it adds nothing to the argument] to tell a little story with the example. So, let us suppose that workers eat nothing but Gummi Bears, hence their rotting teeth, and periodically give themselves Botox shots, which explains why they all have fixed smiles on their faces even though they are being screwed by the capitalists.

Take a look at Tables 13.1 and 13.2 in the Kliman/Freeman/Byron paper. This is a little model they have constructed for which my claims hold. But the existence of a case in which my claims are correct proves nothing about the truth of my claims, as they point out, because I made a universal claim. They accurately quote me as asserting that my claims are true "so long as the system as a whole produces some sort of physical surplus in each cycle over and above what is required to run the system for another year. . . . In order for this to be true, it is not necessary that there be a surplus of X in the system each year" where X is the input arbitrarily chosen to serve as "substance of value" in my value calculations.

So now comes the crusher, Table 13.3. Professors Kliman and Freeman carry out the Botox-Value calculations for this new model (Botox here having been chosen as the X), and discover that in this system, the total profit is actually *negative*! Good grief, as Charlie Brown would say. Is that the end of the story? Professors Kliman and Freeman certainly think so. On the very next line after they have demonstrated a negative profit in the system described by Table 13.3, they write Q.E.D. After that, there is nothing more to be done but what a Special Forces unit might call mopping up.

But wait. Let us take a closer look at Table 13.3. After all, the prospect of a hanging does concentrate the attention. If you examine the numbers carefully, you will notice that in the economy described in Table 13.3, 980 units of Gummi Bears are required as inputs, but only nine hundred units of Gummi Bears are produced as output. This is very definitely not a system which produces "what is required to run the system for another year," as Kliman and Freeman accurately quote me as stipulating. Even if the workers just live on Botox injections, there are not enough Gummi Bears to operate the system at the same level in the next cycle. So the entire system will have to be contracted. But there will still not be enough Gummi Bears in the next cycle after that so the system will shrink even more. It will, in fact, be in a death spiral. It will not be a self-reproducing system. That is why I added the standard proviso that the system produce "what is required to run the system for another year."

All right, so they made a little mistake. It is not as though they were trying to capture some feature of the real world in their example. I mean, who has ever seen an economy of nothing but Gummi Bears and Botox? Surely they can just tweak their numbers a bit so that the system is capable of reproducing itself, and then go on to prove the same crushing counterexample, right?

Well, um, no. As a matter of fact [or, to be more precise, as a matter of mathematics], they cannot do that, because it is impossible. So long as the system "as a whole produces some sort of physical surplus in each cycle over and above what is required to run the system for another year," all the prices will be positive, the amount and rate of profit will be positive, the surplus value will be positive, and all the values calculated, be they labor values, Gummi Bear values, or Botox values, will be positive. Those who have a stomach for this sort of thing will find the formal mathematical proofs in my book, *Understanding Marx* {Wolff 1984}, in appendix A, section IV (pages 187–91) and section V, pages 205–6.

Does this show that I am right and Kliman and Freeman are wrong? Good heavens, no! It just shows that they have [as yet] failed to refute the claims I actually made in my book and essay. Mind you, they may very well have refuted the people they have been arguing against for years. About that much more important matter, I haven't a clue.

III. FINAL REMARK

To be honest, the truth of the claims I made thirty-three years ago is not the most important thing in the world to me. I care a great deal more about the misery and poverty in the midst of obscene wealth that is the defining mark of capitalism. I suspect the same could be said for Chris Byron, Andrew Kliman, and Alan Freeman. Chris Byron is a young man, and he may yet get a chance to break a lance for the rectification of that injustice. I am an old man, and Kliman and Freeman are no spring chickens, so we have probably seen our last hurrah, but if by some happenstance I should find myself at the barricades, I have no doubt that I will find them there as well, on the same side of the cobblestones, facing our common enemies. They are my comrades in a world where there are all too few of us, so let us agree to continue our debates with good cheer, and hope for the day when we will have something better to do.

Chapter 15

Subsequent Dialogue between Kliman and Wolff

Andrew Kliman and Robert Paul Wolff

A REJOINDER TO ROBERT PAUL WOLFF

ANDREW KLIMAN

MAY 10, 2014

In the interests of quick communication, I am writing this rejoinder alone, and speaking for myself alone. What follows does not necessarily reflect the views of Chris Byron or Alan Freeman, co-authors of the piece published yesterday to which Robert Paul Wolff has now (already!) responded {chaps. 13 and 14 of this book, respectively}.

First, I want to thank him for the graciousness and the seriousness of his rejoinder. This is not something we are accustomed to, not by a long shot. In particular, his rejoinder stands in marked contrast to the way in which Sraffian and physicalist-Marxist economists have engaged (and failed to engage) with contributions by proponents of the temporal single-system interpretation of Marx's value theory.

Wolff claims that we "made a little mistake" in our counterexample, that this mistake causes the counterexample to violate a premise of his argument, and that we have therefore "failed to refute the claims I actually made in my book and essay."

It definitely was *not* a mistake. We discussed at great length how exactly to interpret the premise in question. This was the main factor that delayed our response to Wolff's blog post. In the end, we decided to interpret the premise strictly and literally. Wolff now says that this was a mistake. My response is that his alternative reading is self-contradictory.

The premise is contained in point 1 of his original blog post {chap. 12 of this book}, which reads as follows:

> 1. So long as the system as a whole produces some sort of physical surplus in each cycle over and above what is required to run the system for another year, it is mathematically necessary that the iron value of a unit of iron will be less than one unit of iron, that the corn value of one unit of corn will be less than one unit of corn, that the X-value of one unit of X will be less than one unit of X for any X that is a required input in to all lines of production, directly or indirectly. In order for this to be true, it is not necessary that there be a surplus of X in the system each year. If we are calculating iron values, it is certain that the iron value of a unit of iron will be less than 1 even if there is no surplus of iron itself produced in the system.

We interpreted "So long as the system as a whole produces *some sort* of physical surplus in each cycle over and above what is required to run the system for another year" (emphasis added) to mean that "there is a physical surplus of *at least one* produced commodity." Wolff now tells us that his phrase "over and above what is required to run the system for another year" means that there must be a physical surplus of *every* produced commodity in *every* cycle of production. Why? He says that if there is not a physical surplus of *every* produced commodity in *every* cycle of production, then the economy hasn't produced "what is required to run the system for another year." The economy "will, in fact, be in a death spiral. It will not be a self-reproducing system."

Below, I will deal with this last claim, which isn't correct. But here my point is that Wolff's interpretation of his premise is self-contradictory. On one hand, the premise requires that there be a physical surplus of every produced commodity in every cycle of production. On the other hand, Wolff's original statement of the premise says explicitly that this is *not* a requirement: "In order for this to be true, it is not necessary that there be a surplus of X in the system each year." X is one of the produced commodities, and "it is not necessary that there be a surplus of" it each year.[1] So it is both necessary and unnecessary that there be a physical surplus of X in every cycle of production. This is self-contradictory.

Thus, given Wolff's *actual, original premises, interpreted in a manner that makes them internally consistent,* our counterexample disproves his claim that his physicalist model shows that total profit must be positive if total surplus X-Value is positive.[2] The larger claim in which this is embedded—the claim that, if one wishes to show that "capital rests on the exploitation of the working class," it is possible (and necessary) to do so without Marx's own exploitation theory of profit—fails as well.

But now we are being made to disprove a moving target. Wolff originally stipulated that there be some sort of physical surplus over and above "what is required to run the system for another year." Now he objects to our counterexample on the grounds that "[e]ven if the workers just live on

Botox injections, there are not enough Gummi Bears to operate the system *at the same level* in the next cycle" (emphasis added). The requirement that the system operate next year (and the year after, and the year after that, . . .) at the same level it operated this year is *indescribably more stringent* than the simple requirement that the system be able to operate for another year. After all, real-world capitalism has continued to operate from year to year, despite the Great Depression, the Great Recession, and other events that have kept it from operating *at the same level* year in and year out. It has never, ever, produced the exact same amounts of each and every thing in successive years.

Economic crises are not the only reason it has not done so. As Alan Freeman has continually stressed for two decades, reproduction of an economy, even in normal times, doesn't take place by producing the exact same amounts of each and every thing each year. For example, as the economy shifted from one that produced documents on typewriter to one that produces them with computers and printers, what we had for a considerable time was a physical deficit of typewriters. More typewriters were being used as inputs (i.e., to produce documents) than were being produced as outputs. *Yet capitalism was not "in a death spiral" on that account.*

The following simple physicalist model, adapted from pp. 181–82 of my book, *Reclaiming Marx's "Capital": A Refutation of the Myth of Inconsistency* {Kliman 2007}, is an example of an economy that is clearly not in a death spiral. Over every two-day period, there is a physical surplus of *both* produced commodities. Yet total profit is never positive even though total surplus X-Value is always positive.

Apples (good A) and broccoli (good B) grow on their own. Workers are needed to harvest the output, but no other inputs are needed. The physical data of Table 15.1 are based on the following assumptions. The daily real wage (physical wage) is 0.4999 lbs. of apples and 0.4999 lbs. of broccoli per

Table 15.1

	Industry	*Labor*	*Output*	*Real Wages*	*Physical Surpluses*
Day 1	A	4	4A, 0B	1.9996A, 1.9996B	2.0004A, –1.9996B
	B	2	0A, 2B	0.9998A, 0.9998B	–0.9998A, 1.0002B
	Total	6	4A, 2B	2.9994A, 2.9994B	1.0006A, –0.9994B
Day 2	A	2	2A, 0B	0.9998A, 0.9998B	1.0002A, –0.9998B
	B	4	0A, 4B	1.9996A, 1.9996B	–1.9996A, 2.0004B
	Total	6	2A, 4B	2.9994A, 2.9994B	–0.9994A, 1.0006B
Days 1 + 2	A	6	6A, 0B	2.9994A, 2.9994B	3.0006A, –2.9994B
	B	6	0A, 6B	2.9994A, 2.9994B	–2.9994A, 3.0006B
	Total	12	6A, 6B	5.9988A, 5.9988B	0.0012A, 0.0012B

worker. Workers are paid at the end of the day. One day of labor is needed to harvest one pound of each product. On Day 1, four workers pick apples and two workers harvest broccoli, while on Day 2 the figures are reversed. The capitalists, who own the land, have an initial stock of at least one lb of broccoli (acquired through their own labor); given this assumption, the necessary exchanges can take place.

Even though there is a negative surplus of one good in the economy as a whole on both days, the economy reproduces itself over the two-day period. More than enough apples are produced *and* more than enough broccoli is produced, to pay the workers the apple-and-broccoli wages they need in order to return to work on Day 3, and so on.

Let apples be the measure of value. The per-unit value of apples is therefore one. Since one labor-day is needed to produce a pound of apples, the per-unit apple-value of labor is therefore one as well. Thus the per-unit apple-value of the labor need to produce a pound of broccoli is also one, so the per-unit value of broccoli also equals one.

Total surplus apple-value, the total apple-value of the two total-economy physical surpluses, is therefore (1 × 1.0006) + (1 × –0.9994) = 0.0012 on Day 1 and (1 × –0.9994) + (1 × 1.0006) = 0.0012 on Day 2.

Total physicalist profit is the total price of the physical surpluses. Since apples are the measure of value, their per-unit price is one on both days.

Assume that the price of broccoli is 1.0013 on Day 1. Then total physicalist profit is (1 × 1.0006) + (1.0013 × –0.9994) = –0.00009922 . . . on Day 1. Assume that the price of broccoli falls to 0.9987 on Day 2. Then total physicalist profit is (1 × –0.9994) + (0.9987 × 1.0006) = –0.00010078 . . . on Day 2.

So there is negative physical profit each day, even though total surplus apple-value is positive each day *and* even though this economy is not in a death spiral.

This example shows, once again, that physicalist models are incompatible with the exploitation theory of profit. We see that such models imply that positive surplus X-value ("labor-value" or "apple-value" or "broccoli-value," etc.) *does not* guarantee that profit exists. Hence, they imply that positive surplus X-value, exploitation, is not the exclusive source of profit.

But what about Wolff's case, in which there is a positive physical surplus of every produced commodity in *every* cycle of production (every day, every hour, every minute, . . .)? In that case, physicalism implies that positive surplus X-value and positive physicalist profit *happen to coexist*. But even in this case, physicalism continues to imply that positive surplus X-value does not guarantee that profit exists, so that exploitation is therefore not the exclusive source of profit. What guarantees that profit exists is not positive surplus X-value alone, but positive surplus X-value *in conjunction with* the barely imaginable, exceptionally stringent, and wholly unrealistic restriction that there is a positive physical surplus of every produced commodity in every cycle of production. It is clearly this latter restriction, not the positive surplus X-value, which does all the work.

If this is not 100 percent clear, imagine that I said that I can always kill a flock of sheep just by putting a curse on them (provided that I also feed them all arsenic). And lo and behold, every time I put a curse on a flock of sheep (and feed them arsenic), the whole flock dies. The curse and the death of the flock *happen to coexist* in every case. But this does not mean that my cursing the sheep guarantees that the sheep will die. What does guarantee that they will die is not the curse alone, but the curse *in conjunction with* the arsenic. And it is clearly the arsenic that does all the work.

ONE MORE GO-ROUND
ROBERT PAUL WOLFF
MAY 11, 2014

By now, probably, most of you have decamped for a more interesting blog, but since at least one person—Matt D—seems to be enjoying the back-and-forth between Professor Kliman and myself, I am going to continue for one more go-round. As Chris has pointed out, Professor Kliman has posted a reply {the preceding entry in this chapter} to my reply {chap. 14 of this book} here, and I am simply going to assume that Matt D and anyone else still with us has taken the time to follow the link and read it. Please do. It is not fair to Professor Kliman for you to rely on my redaction of what he has said.

The first thing I must do is definitively clear up a confusion. I am afraid that I have managed to completely mislead Professor Kliman, although I confess that when I reread what I wrote it seemed clear to me. [Isn't that always the way? I am perpetually telling students that what matters is not whether what you have written is clear to you! What matters is whether it is clear to your readers.] So let me say it again: I have intended all along to be talking about single product linear reproduction systems in which *at least as much* is produced of each commodity in each cycle of production as is required by the inputs into the system as a whole, and *in addition* in *at least one line of production an actual excess is produced over what is required by the inputs into the system as a whole*. To put the same thing another way, the vector of outputs net of required inputs is semi-positive [i.e., each element of the vector is either zero or greater than zero and at least one element is greater than zero].

Now, I would have thought that Professor Kliman would be familiar with this stipulation, since it is the standard stipulation made by all the "Sraffians" against whom he has been arguing for many years, and with whom he conflates me. But if I failed to make myself clear before, I apologize. I hope I have done so now.

So we come to the real meat of Professor Kliman's reply, his apples and broccoli example. (I do wish he had made it an apples and oranges example. Then I could have made some jokes about how he is talking about apples and oranges. Oh well. Another time.)

I must confess that when my eye caught Table 15.1 on page 3, I skipped the intervening text and went straight for the numbers, which puzzled me considerably, because I could not see that any apples or broccoli inputs were specified. But then I went back and read what Professor Kliman had written [always a good idea, by the way], and there it was in black and white. "Apples (good A) and broccoli (good B) grow on their own." Whoa! I said to myself. This is very strange indeed.

Let me break into my response to explain something to my readers. Professor Kliman knows all about what I am going to say, being a professional economist, but my readership [such of it as is still with me] consists of philosophers and artists and Lord knows whom else, so this may be news to them.

The discipline of economics as we now know it got its start in the eighteenth century with the work of several Frenchmen who came to be known in the trade as Physiocrats. The central idea they gave to posterity was that an economy is actually an organized process of cyclical *reproduction*, in which what is produced as output in one cycle of production serves as input into production in the next cycle of production. They had in mind agriculture, in which some of the crop is set aside as seed for the next planting, but their idea has quite general application. Both Adam Smith and David Ricardo adopted this way of thinking about the economy, and Ricardo especially made it central to his analysis. Ricardo was of course well aware that one can find some things for sale in the market that are not *reproducible* in the way imagined by the Physiocrats. His examples were old master paintings and fine wines grown on a particular side of the hill (you gotta love Ricardo!). The prices of these things, no doubt, he said, were determined by the intersection of supply and demand—by their scarcity and by how much buyers wanted them. But Ricardo brushed these aside as of no interest, because, he thought, they were not typical of the commodities being poured out of the factories or grown on the entrepreneurial farms in nineteenth-century England. The prices of those commodities, Ricardo said, were determined by the amount of labor required, either directly or indirectly, for their production.

There was of course one input into production that it was absolutely impossible to brush aside in the way that Ricardo had dealt with old masters and fine wine, namely **land**. The entrepreneurs who rented land in order to run profit-making agricultural enterprises paid rent on that land to the aristocratic hereditary landowners. So how could the price of their corn be determined solely by the labor directly or indirectly required for its production when in addition to the cost of wages and other inputs, they were forced to pay rent? In a brilliant *tour de raison*, Ricardo succeeded in demonstrating that those rental payments are in fact a diversion of profits from the capitalists to the landowners, *not* part of the cost of production, and hence play no role in the determination of price.

Marx, who was thoroughly familiar with the entire history of economic theory up to his own day, embraced this conception of reproduction, and made it the foundation of his new version of the Labor Theory of Value. Like Ricardo before him, Marx concentrated his attention on *reproducible* commodities whose inputs into their production were the output of previous cycles of production. Everything in his Labor Theory of Value depends on this assumption.

Consequently, when I read Professor Kliman's statement that apples and broccoli "grow on their own," I was puzzled. What sort of economy could it be in which the goods consumed by the workers are not *produced* but rather *grow on their own*? A feudal economy? Certainly not. In a feudal economy, the peasants use tools and seed and other produced goods as inputs into their productive activities? A slave economy? No, for the same reason.

And then it struck me. Professor Kliman must be talking about a *hunting and gathering* economy, like those that anthropologists tell us characterized the lives of our forebears prior to the Neolithic Revolution ten thousand years ago or so. In the apples and broccoli world that Professor Kliman has conjured up for us, men and women range across the savannah collecting apples from wild apple trees and gathering wild broccoli. (Wikipedia tells me that there is no such thing as wild broccoli, the plant having been developed by selective breeding in the Northern Mediterranean in the sixth century B.C., but that is neither here nor there.) They do this for wages, we may suppose, because, as always seems to happen, a few men have used force of arms (and the ideological rationalizations of philosophy and religion) to exclude the rest of the population from access to the wild apple and broccoli groves.

Well, I must admit, Professor Kliman has stumped me. In all the years that I have been turning this subject over in my mind, albeit as an amateur, it simply has never occurred to me to wonder whether Marx's Labor Theory of Value is valid for hunter-gatherer economies. If he says it is, I will take his word for it, so long as he will agree with me that it does not do the trick for economies of produced commodities.

There is another point that needs to be discussed, and I have a suspicion that Professor Kliman may consider it a good deal more important than all of our quibblings about corn/iron or Gummi Bear/Botox or apple/broccoli hypothetical examples. On page 3, Professor Kliman alludes to things his colleague, Professor Freeman, has been saying for many years now about how *real* capitalist economies actually function. What he cites Professor Freeman as saying is of course true, but it also raises an important methodological question that I ought to address.

In trying to get a handle on the real inner workings of something as complex as a capitalist economy, there are, it seems to me, two quite different ways in which we may proceed. The first way is to seize the actual economy in all of its confusion and try to wrestle it to the ground, as it were, gathering facts and attempting to impose some order on what is, at first sight, hopelessly complex. That approach can be frustrating and extremely difficult, but it has the great virtue of keeping one in touch with the reality of the world. The second way is to start with a deliberately simple case and analyze it, formulating general propositions about it that one can demonstrate to be true precisely because one has bracketed out all the complications. Then, step by step, one starts to add in those complications, at each stage checking to see whether one's original propositions can still be defended. Economists have a nice term for this. The more complexity one can introduce into one's explanation while still managing to defend the explanation, the more *robust* it is [by analogy with a person who is described as physically robust if she can withstand heat or cold or hunger or attacks by bacteria].

As I have several times indicated, I interpret Marx as having adopted this second line of attack, but Marx never says that, so far as I am aware, and so it is obviously open to another reader of Marx to insist that he adopted some other method. I don't think it makes much sense to argue about this. The proof is in the pudding. All that matters is which approach proves more fruitful. *And of course, in matters of fruitfulness as in matters of pudding, taste plays a large role.*

Well, that concludes my response, but I cannot stop without at least taking note of the business about arsenic and sheep. Professor Kliman does me the great courtesy of simply assuming that I will recognize the reference, but since my readers may be unfamiliar with it, let me explicate. Voltaire, ever the enemy of the Catholic Church, observed sardonically "Incantations will destroy a flock of sheep if administered with a certain quantity of arsenic." Joan Robinson {(1967)}, the *doyenne* of the English Sraffians, invoked Voltaire's remark in her book, *An Essay on Marxian Economics*:

"No point of substance in Marx's argument depends upon the labour theory of value. Voltaire remarked that it is possible to kill a flock of sheep by witchcraft if you give them plenty of arsenic at the same time. The sheep, in the figure, may well stand for the complacent apologists of capitalism; Marx's penetrating insight and bitter hatred of oppression supply the arsenic, while the labour theory of value provides the incantations." [Quoted in my *Moneybags Must Be So Lucky* {(Wolff 1988)}, page 15.]

Professor Kliman, in a lovely concluding paragraph, takes this condescending [and utterly wrongheaded] jest by Robinson and turns it on me. Touché, Professor Kliman. I tip my hat to you.

E-MAIL MESSAGE TO ROBERT PAUL WOLFF
ANDREW KLIMAN
MAY 11, 2014

Dear Professor Wolff,

Thank you for another quick reply (to my reply to your reply to the co-authored reply to your initial blog post).

Last night, I finally guessed that you had a semi-positive vector of physical surpluses (or net outputs) in mind, so that when you specified that the surplus of X didn't have to be positive, you didn't mean that it could be negative. You meant only that it could be either positive or zero. That eliminates the apparent self-contradiction in your premises; I was wrong about that.

But this restriction of yours, which prevents there from being a deficit (negative surplus) of anything, doesn't help you to prove what I think you want to prove, that exploitation of workers (positive surplus X-value) is the exclusive source of profit. In fact, the restriction makes it impossible to prove that, as I said.

You can at best claim to have proved that if there is exploitation of workers *and* there is never a negative surplus of anything, then positive surplus X-value and positive profit will happen to coexist. But what you need to prove is that they coexist *because* there is positive surplus X-value, and to try to prove that, you would need to remove the additional restriction. And then you'd find that you still couldn't prove what I think you want to prove, because (as we've shown) profit can then be negative even though surplus X-value is positive.

This was the point of my concluding comment about sheep and arsenic, of course. You appreciated the comment, but as far as I can see, you haven't yet addressed the crucial logical point at issue. I say it's the crucial logical issue because the validity of your main conclusion is at stake. So permit me to ask you directly: do you accept that one has not proven that positive surplus X-value is either a necessary condition or a sufficient condition for positive profit if the only thing that one has actually proven to be necessary and sufficient is positive surplus X-value *in conjunction with* the restriction that there's never a negative physical surplus of any produced commodity? If you don't accept this, why not?

I trust that you understand that this is a point about logical validity of arguments, not a point about realism of premises.

My apple-broccoli example is definitely about capitalism. It refers explicitly to wage-labor and capital ("Workers are paid at the end of the day. . . . The capitalists, who own the land . . ."). Of course, real-world capitalist production requires non-labor inputs. I excluded them in order to make the example easy to follow and the computations simple. But it's easy to include them, and I will be happy to provide an example that does so, if you wish.

However, if you insist on rejecting any counterexample unless it's one in which there is never a negative physical surplus of any produced commodity, not even for a moment, there is obviously no point in working up a version of my apple-broccoli demonstration that includes non-labor inputs. It will still be the case that there is a negative physical surplus of something on every day (or hour, or minute, etc.) even though there is a positive physical surplus of everything over each two-day (or -hour, or -minute, etc.) period.

But the apple-broccoli demonstration does more than show that physicalist profit can be negative even though physicalist surplus X-value is positive and all physical surpluses are positive over every two-day (or -hour, or -minute, etc.) period. It also removes your justification for the restriction that there is never, ever, a negative physical surplus of any produced commodity.

In your blog post of yesterday, you justified this restriction on the grounds that, if there is a negative physical surplus of anything (even in one period), then the economy is incapable of reproducing itself physically. It's in a "death spiral." The apple-broccoli demonstration removes this justification because it shows that the economy can indeed reproduce itself physically, even if there is *always* a negative physical surplus of one of the two goods.

As far as I can see, you haven't yet addressed this aspect of the demonstration. So permit me to ask you directly: do you accept that it removes the stated justification for the restriction you wish to impose? If not, why not? (If necessary, I can provide a similar, but more cumbersome, example that includes non-labor inputs.) Let me emphasize that here, too, realism of premises is not the issue. The issue is simply whether the existence of some negative physical surplus implies that the economy is in a death spiral.

Best wishes,
Andrew Kliman

FINAL EXCHANGE BETWEEN MYSELF AND ANDREW KLIMAN
ROBERT PAUL WOLFF
MAY 12, 2014

What follows is an email exchange between Andrew Kliman and myself. Andrew tried to post it as a comment and Google would not let him [corporate America strikes again!].

{Here, Wolff reproduced Kliman's preceding e-mail message and responded as follows.}

Dear Andrew,

Thank you again for your message, and my apologies for the Google problems, which are far above my level of competence to do anything about.

I think our exchanges are producing clarity about the issues that separate us, if not agreement on them, and that is good. After reading and reflecting on your e-mail message, it occurs to me that we are arguing somewhat at cross purposes.

You focus in your message very much on the "restriction" I have imposed that there cannot be a negative output in any line of production relative to the quantity of that input required in the system as a whole, but I do not think that is what separates us. Let me try to explain.

I start from Marx's claim that capitalism rests on the exploitation of the working class and that the ever-increasing wealth of the capitalist class is the direct consequence of that exploitation. I think Marx is correct about that, and I think he has correctly explained this ongoing exploitation as the historical result of the separation of the great majority of men and women from access to or command over the land, the forests, the mines, the oceans, and even the knowledge and craft skill needed to wrest a living from nature. Marx thought that capitalism is mystified, in that it presents the appearance of equal uncoerced exchange in the marketplace between workers and employers, so that it is puzzling how capitalists can keep accumulating more and more capital while the workers who actually create that capital by their labor remain propertyless. Marx's solution to this puzzle is the distinction between labor and labor-power and the concomitant introduction of the concept of surplus labor value. Thus far, I would imagine, although I do not know, that we would agree.

When I began to study this subject more closely, I found that one can set up labor value equations that demonstrate that the labor value of the physical surplus in each cycle of production, a surplus that the capitalists appropriate in the money form of profit, exactly equals the surplus labor value extracted from the workers in the process of production. This seems quite dramatically to prove the correctness of Marx's claims, at least in the simple case in which there is equal organic composition of capital in all lines of production.

But it occurred to me that one can equally well set up iron-value equations or corn-value equations [or Botox, Gummi Bear, apples, or broccoli value equations], and that every single result provable about labor-value equations can, without exception, be proved in each of those alternate systems of equations. The distinction between labor and labor-power, which Marx thought was the key to unraveling the mystery, plays no role in the construction of the equations. There is of course no meaningful distinction between iron and iron-power or corn and corn-power, but that does not in any way invalidate the conclusions drawn in those systems of equations.

Now, when I arrived at this result, I did not conclude that Marx was wrong in claiming that capitalism rests on the exploitation of the working class. Not at all. I concluded that we need to find a more successful way of modeling what happens in capitalism, a way that captures the historical separation of workers from the means of production and that cannot be replicated for iron, corn, or any other non-labor input into the productive process. My rather tentative and [admittedly] rudimentary efforts can be found in the essay to which I have several times alluded, "A Critique and Reinterpretation of Marx's Labor Theory of Value" {Wolff 1984}.

Let me repeat. I do not think that Marx contradicted himself. Quite to the contrary, I think when we cast his claims in mathematical form we can demonstrate that many of them (not all, to be sure) are correct. The problem is, all of the same claims, without exception, are also true of iron-values, corn-values, and so forth.

So it really does not matter to me whether you construct models with net negative output for some input, because whatever you prove thereby can be replicated for labor-values simply by adjusting the example and the notation appropriately. Thus, the supposed contradictions you generate can be generated as well, under the same assumptions, for labor-values.

There is a question to which I do not give much thought, but that agitates many people interested in this stuff. If I reject the Labor Theory of Value as Marx formulated it, can I call myself a Marxist? Well, Marx is long dead and the copyright has run out on that term, so I think it is in the public domain. I call myself a Marxist for two reasons. The first is that he remains my principal inspiration and guide in my ongoing efforts to understand the world in which I live. The second is that it irritates people.

It remains only to thank you, Alan Freeman, and Chris Byron for taking the time to engage with me on these matters. I have enjoyed the back-and-forth and have learned from it.

All the best,
Bob

E-MAIL MESSAGE TO ROBERT PAUL WOLFF
ANDREW KLIMAN
MAY 13, 2014

Dear Bob,

Thanks for another very quick reply.

I agree that I am focusing on the restriction you have imposed, that there is never a negative physical surplus (or negative net output) of any produced commodity, not even momentarily. And I agree that this is probably not "what separates us." I am not focusing on the restriction in order to pinpoint or discuss what separates us. I am focusing on it in order to make clear that

a. the "death spiral" justification for the restriction is untenable: economies can and do physically reproduce themselves when the restriction does not hold true;
b. the physicalist analytical framework implies that there can be positive surplus X-value but negative profit, and vice versa, if this restriction is not imposed; and
c. it follows from (b) that it has not been and cannot be proven, within the physicalist analytical framework, that exploitation of workers (positive surplus X-value) is the exclusive source of profit.

As far as I can see, your latest reply does not address any of these points. I hope we can reach agreement on them, so that we can then move on.

To explain what I think separates us, I will begin by rephrasing a passage near the end of your reply in a form that we—Alan Freeman and I, and perhaps Chris Byron as well—can accept:

> Let me repeat. I do not think that Marx contradicted himself. Quite to the contrary, I think when we cast *what we take to be* his claims in *the particular* mathematical form *that the physicalist analytical framework requires—that is, when per-unit prices and "values" of outputs are constrained to equal per-unit prices and "values" of inputs, and prices and "values" are determined wholly independently*—we can demonstrate that many of them [not all, to be sure] are ~~correct~~ *compatible with the implications of the physicalist models*. The problem is, all of the same claims, without exception, are also ~~true of~~ *compatible with the implications of the physicalist models when one replaces so-called "labor-values" with* iron-values, corn-values, and so forth.
>
> So it really does not matter to me whether you construct models with net negative output for some input, because whatever you prove thereby *to be an implication of the physicalist models when the "values" are iron-values, corn-values, and so forth* can be replicated for *physicalist* "labor-values" simply by adjusting the example and the notation appropriately. Thus, the ~~supposed~~ contradictions *between Marx's conclusions and the implications of the physicalist models* you generate can be generated as well, under the same assumptions, for *physicalist* "labor-values."

When recast in this neutral manner—such that it does not presuppose that Marx has been interpreted correctly or that compatibility with the physicalist analytical framework is tantamount to truth—what this passage says is basically what we said in our co-authored reply of a few days ago {chap. 13 of this book}:

> The above argument has demonstrated that, if one wishes to argue that "capital rests on the exploitation of the working class," it is not possible do so validly by means of Wolff's version of the physicalist model. Freeman and Kliman's previous demonstrations have shown that it is also not possible to do so validly by means of physicalist versions of "the labor theory of value."

The original version of your passage seems to suggest that Marx's conclusion that surplus labor is the exclusive source of profit is simply incorrect. It's not correct when we use corn-values, etc., but neither is it correct when we use "labor-values." My amended version suggests something quite different, precisely because it does not presuppose that Marx has been interpreted correctly or that compatibility with the physicalist analytical framework is tantamount to truth.

If these presuppositions are incorrect, then it is possible that a non-physicalist interpretation and formalization of Marx's arguments replicates the conclusions of his that the physicalist models cannot replicate—"under the same assumptions." And it is further possible that this non-physicalist interpretation and formalization interprets Marx correctly. It follows that it is possible that the arguments of Marx that have been declared logically invalid (since his conclusions, it is alleged, are not deducible from his premises) are in fact logically valid.

We contend, and we think we have demonstrated beyond reasonable doubt, that these things are not only possibly true but actually true as well. This is what we contend regarding all of the alleged internal inconsistencies in the quantitative dimension of Marx's value theory, including the inconsistency that allegedly renders untenable his own, original version of his exploitation theory of profit. Thus, as we said in our co-authored reply,

> if one wishes to argue that "capital rests on the exploitation of the working class," . . . there is a valid way to make such an argument—Marx's way.
>
> But Marx's argument is logically valid *only* if it is interpreted properly, not misinterpreted in the physicalist manner. On the basis of the non-physicalist interpretation of which we are proponents, the temporal single-system interpretation of Marx's value theory (TSSI), it does indeed follow validly that surplus labor is the exclusive source of (real) profit.[3] A decade of debate confirmed this result beyond reasonable doubt.[4]

This isn't the place to set out the details of the TSSI or to place to reproduce all the proofs and our defenses of them, which is why I've included the footnotes to the passage just quoted. What I can do here is illustrate a key difference between physicalist interpretations and the TSSI. The question I will address is, "Does it matter which specific value-forming substance we 'choose'?" We agree that it doesn't matter *within the physicalist framework.* I want to show that it does matter within a non-physicalist and temporalist (i.e., dynamic) framework.

Consider a corn model in which returns to scale are constant. Corn is produced by means of seed corn and labor. Let A be the quantity of seed corn that is planted at the start of the year, L be the quantity of labor performed during the year, and X be the quantity of corn output harvested at the end of the year. Also, let $V_{c(s)}$ and $V_{c(e)}$ be the per-unit values of corn at the start and end of the year, respectively, and let V_L be the value added by each unit of labor.

The general form of the value-determination equation is

$$V_{c(s)}A + V_L L = V_{c(e)}X$$

In the physicalist framework, the per-unit value of the output is constrained to equal the per-unit values of the seed-corn input. Thus, $V_{c(s)} = V_{c(e)} = V^*$, and the value-determination equation becomes

$$V^*A + V_L L = V^*X$$

so that

$$\frac{V^*}{V_L} = \frac{L}{X - A}$$

This is the case whether we choose corn, or whether we choose labor, as the value-forming substance.

In a temporalist framework, there is no constraint that $V_{c(s)}$ must equal $V_{c(e)}$. However, if corn is the value-forming substance, then $V_{c(s)} = 1$ and $V_{c(e)} = 1$, so the value-determination equation becomes

$$A + V_L L = X$$

so that

$$V_L = \frac{X - A}{L}$$

and thus

$$\frac{V_{c(e)}}{V_L} = \frac{L}{X - A} \quad (\text{since } V_{c(e)} = 1)$$

Thus, in a temporalist framework *in which corn is the value-forming substance*, the relative per-unit values of corn and labor are the same as those of the physicalist framework.

But what about a temporalist framework in which *labor* is the value-forming substance? In this case, $V_L = 1$, so the value-determination equation becomes

$$V_{c(s)}A + L = V_{c(e)}X$$

and thus

$$\frac{V_{c(e)}}{V_L} = \frac{V_{c(s)}A + L}{X}$$

Now, the right-hand side of this last equation does not generally equal $L/X{-}A$. Hence, in a temporalist framework in which labor is the value-forming substance, the relative per-unit values of corn and labor are, in general, not equal to

a. the relative physicalist per-unit values; or
b. the relative temporalist per-unit values when corn is the value-forming substance.

It follows from (a) that, if Marx did not constrain output values to equal input values, then the results of physicalist models cannot properly be assumed to be the actual implications of his theory.

It follows from (b) that the specific value-forming substance *does* matter within a non-physicalist and temporalist framework.

Best wishes,
Andrew

LAST ONE, I PROMISE
ROBERT PAUL WOLFF
MAY 14, 2014

Well, I said our last exchange was the final one, but here we are again. This one really is the last one. I think I at least am finally clear where Andrew and Alan Freeman and I part company, and since it at the initial stage of basic premises, there is really nothing more to be said.

{Here, Wolff reproduced Kliman's preceding e-mail message and responded as follows.}

Dear Andrew,

I am rushing to write this while preparing to leave for Seattle where, on Saturday, my wife's grandson will be bar mitzvah'd. As I am sure you will understand, this event takes precedence over merely settling the fate of capitalism.

Let me pass over your rewriting of some of what I have written and come directly to the eight lines of equations in the second half of your message. You introduce what you call the temporalist framework by distinguishing between the value of a unit of corn at the start of the year (which I take it means as input) from the value of a unit of corn at the end of the year (which, again, I assume means as output.) The key to your analysis is your insistence that corn and other commodities that are both inputs into and outputs of production may have values as inputs that differs from their values as outputs.

However, in your fourth equation, which you say represents the situation, in a temporalist framework, where corn is the "value-forming substance," there is only a term for labor (represented in the equation by the letter *L*), not a term for labor at the start of the year and another term for labor at the end of the year. If there were such terms, then the temporalist framework representations of a labor-value and corn-value analysis would be identical.

But, you may object, there is no labor industry; labor is not a produced commodity. So the distinction between the value of labor at the start and at the end of the production process makes no sense.

And suddenly it dawned on me why we have been unable to come to an agreement. To put it simply, you and the Sraffians agree that labor is, as economists like to say, *exogenous* to the system. It is given, it is not produced. I, on the other hand, think that the only way to capture Marx's brilliant insight into the real nature of capitalism is to treat labor as a *produced commodity*.

Well, you may once more object, if labor is a produced commodity, why doesn't the labor-producing industry earn the economy-wide rate of profit? But that is not an objection to my analysis. It is the whole point of my analysis! Let me explain. As I read *Capital*, Marx sees capitalism as thoroughgoingly mystified, precisely in order to conceal from view the fact that it rests on exploitation. One aspect of this mystification is capitalism's treatment of the worker. In the marketplace, that "very Eden of the rights of man," as Marx puts it with brilliant irony, the worker stands "as owner of the commodity 'labour-power' face to face with other owners of commodities, dealer against dealer." But of course this is a delusion, a mystification, as Marx goes on to show us, for as soon as he steps into the factory he is no longer treated as the producer of commodities, but as a wage-slave, chained to the machine.

The point of my effort to model labor as a produced commodity which yet does not earn a profit when it is sold was to find some way of capturing, in the equations, the anomalous status of labor in a capitalist economy. I freely acknowledge that I may have failed, but that is what I was trying to do.

From my point of view, you and the Sraffians against whom you argue agree on the one premise that I reject—you both assume that labor is exogenously given. Thirty years ago and more, when I was working on these ideas, Sraffa and his followers were the only game in town, or so I thought [I was unaware of your work—perhaps you had not then begun to publish it]. Consequently, I directed my arguments against their modern reformulation of Marx's critique of capitalism. Now that we have had this interesting series of exchanges, I finally realize that you share with Sraffa the very assumption that I rejected. Not surprisingly, therefore, I am no more able to come to an agreement with you than I was with them.

In light of this fundamental difference between us about the premises of our alternative analyses of capitalism, I do not think there is any further we can go, so I am going to call it a tie and leave the field of battle. I wish you good fortune in your ongoing struggle with the Sraffians. Perhaps if you and I are more fortunate than we have any right to expect, there will be barricades where may meet and join forces.

All the best,
Bob

E-MAIL MESSAGE TO ROBERT PAUL WOLFF
ANDREW KLIMAN
MAY 14, 2014

Dear Bob,

Once again, consider a corn model in which returns to scale are constant. Corn is produced by means of seed corn and labor. Let A be the quantity of seed corn that is planted at the start of the year and X be the quantity of corn output harvested at the end of the year. Also, let $V_{c(s)}$ and $V_{c(e)}$ be the per-unit values of corn at the start and end of the year, respectively.

But now assume that some labor is performed to plant the seed, and some labor is performed to harvest the corn output, but no labor is performed in between. So let $L_{(s)}$ and $L_{(e)}$ be the value added by each unit of labor at the start and end of the year, respectively, and let $V_{L(s)}$ and $V_{L(e)}$ be the value added by each unit of labor at the start and end of the year, respectively.

The general form of the value-determination equation is

$$V_{c(s)}A + V_{L(s)}L_{(s)} + V_{L(e)}L_{(e)} = V_{c(e)}X \tag{15.1}$$

In a temporalist framework in which *corn* is the value-forming substance, $V_{c(s)} = V_{c(e)} = 1$, so the value-determination equation becomes

$$A + V_{L(s)}L_{(s)} + V_{L(e)}L_{(e)} = X \tag{15.2}$$

By subtracting the first two left-hand side terms, then dividing by $L_{(e)}$, then dividing by $V_{c(e)} = 1$, we obtain

$$\frac{V_{L(e)}}{V_{c(e)}} = \frac{(X - A) - V_{L(s)}L_{(s)}}{L_{(e)}} \tag{15.3}$$

In a temporalist framework in which *labor* is the value-forming substance, $V_{L(s)} = V_{L(e)} = 1$, so the value-determination equation becomes

$$V_{c(s)}A + L_{(s)} + L_{(e)} = V_{c(e)}X \tag{15.4}$$

By dividing by X, we obtain an expression for $V_{c(e)}$. Since $V_{c(e)} = 1$, the reciprocal of this expression is $V_{L(e)}/V_{c(e)}$. Taking the reciprocal, we obtain

$$\frac{V_{L(e)}}{V_{c(e)}} = \frac{X}{V_{c(s)}A + L_{(s)} + L_{(e)}} \tag{15.5}$$

The right-hand side expressions in (15.3) and (15.5) are not equal, in general.

For example, assume that $A = L_{(s)} = L_{(e)} = 1$ and that $X = 2$. Then, according to (15.3), $V_{L(e)}/V_{c(e)} = 1 - V_{L(s)}$. But according to (15.5), $V_{L(e)}/V_{c(e)} = 2/(V_{c(s)} + 2)$, which does not generally equal $1 - V_{L(s)}$ even when $V_{c(s)} = 1/V_{L(s)}$. If $V_{c(s)} = 1/V_{L(s)}$, then $1 - V_{L(s)} = 2/(V_{c(s)} + 2)$ if and only if $V_{L(s)} = 0.5$.[5]

Thus, the conclusion you draw in your latest blog post is incorrect:

> [If there were] a term for labor at the start of the year and another term for labor at the end of the year . . . then the temporalist framework representations of a labor-value and corn-value analysis would be identical.

Because it is incorrect, the specific value-forming substance *does* matter within a non-physicalist and temporalist framework.

Have fun at the Bar Mitzvah and a safe trip,

Andrew

E-MAIL MESSAGE TO ANDREW KLIMAN
ROBERT PAUL WOLFF
MAY 14, 2014

Andrew,

I do not seem to be able to get you to step outside your conceptual framework for a moment.

Once you start thinking of labor as a produced commodity, every conclusion you draw can be duplicated for labor values. How? Obvious. Just switch the notation. All the equations remain the same, but what the symbols refer to changes.

But you don't consider labor a produced commodity. Exactly. That is what I said in my last response. Clearly, it would be a mistake for me to persist in treating labor as a produced commodity and then expect you to think that I had somehow refuted you with my equations. It would be the same mistake you are making by continuing to treat labor as exogenously given and then thinking that your equations refute me.

Now, we can argue about how Marx thought about the matter. Or we can argue about what the truth of the matter is (assuming, as I do, that those two are not necessarily identical, even though they turn out to be the same remarkably often—that is why Marx was a great thinker).

But given what separates us, that seems to me the only sensible argument for us to have, no?

Cheers,
Bob

E-MAIL MESSAGE TO ROBERT PAUL WOLFF
ANDREW KLIMAN
MAY 14, 2014

Dear Bob,

You write, "I do not seem to be able to get you to step outside your conceoptual framework for a moment." Actually, you can't get me to step outside of *Marx's* conceptual framework (as I understand it). The TSSI is not my "my take" on Marx. It is not an "approach" or a self-standing conceptual framework in its own right. It is an *exegetical* interpretation of two aspects of Marx's value theory. As an exegetical interpretation, it stands or falls on how well it is able to make the quantitative dimension of Marx's value theory, especially his arguments that have been alleged to be internally inconsistent, make sense.

You wrote on your blog, "I am simply saying that (Marx's) theoretical analysis of this fundamental fact (that profit comes solely from exploitation) is wrong, that a different theoretical analysis is required" {chap. 12 of this book}. The discussion between us began when we challenged this claim. And this is what the discussion has been about all along. At least on my end, the ultimate issue under consideration has never deviated from the logical validity of *Marx's own, original* argument in support of his conclusion that surplus labor is the exclusive source of profit. Everything I've written has been written in an effort to resolve this ultimate issue.

Let me recap what I think are the main results that have emerged from our discussion of this issue:

1. It has not been shown that there is anything wrong with Marx's own, original argument. What has been demonstrated is only that the physicalist theoretical framework is *incompatible* with his conclusion. But it has not been shown (as distinct from presupposed) that the physicalist theoretical framework is Marx's framework. It has therefore not been shown that a different theoretical analysis is *required.*
2. You tried to show, but it has not been shown, that an alternative exegetical interpretation of Marx's argument (the TSSI) cannot replicate Marx's conclusion on the basis of (its construal of) his own, original premises and reasoning. This lends additional support to our counterclaim that a different theoretical analysis is not *required.*
3. Your different theoretical analysis, meant to replicate Marx's conclusion by different means, has been shown not to do so. It has therefore not been shown that a different theoretical analysis that leads to Marx's conclusion is *possible.*

For decades, I've been battling attempts to make Marx's own, original value theory disappear. Each of us is entitled to have his/her own theories. Marx is entitled to his theories, too (unless there is a legitimate, honest-to-goodness, incontrovertible proof that there is no way to construe them such that they become logically valid and not definitively falsified empirically). But there is attempt after attempt to make his value theory—in its original form—disappear. It is made to disappear when it is said to be plagued by logical errors that require it to be rejected or corrected, as you and many, many others have said in a variety of ways for more than a century. And it is made to disappear when debates over the logical consistency of his value theory get deflected into debates over what you think vs. what I think vs. what Alan {Freeman} thinks. What Marx thinks has disappeared.

I'm not saying that it is wrong to have the latter kind of debate. I'm saying that it is a different debate, and it should not be permitted to crowd out the first one until that is settled. The world's access to Marx's own, original theory as a living theory is at stake.

As I wrote a number of years ago in *Reclaiming Marx's "Capital": A Refutation of the Myth of Inconsistency*,

> In recent years, Marx's critics have found it increasingly difficult to defend the allegations of inconsistency against the TSSI critique. Thus they generally try to avoid this issue altogether. Instead, they now prefer to debate the pros and cons of Marx's work and of alternative approaches to Marxian economic analysis. In other contexts, these are of course important and interesting topics, but to discuss them here and now is to fall into a diversionary trap, at the very moment when correction of the record has become a real possibility. I will be glad to discuss these topics with Marx's critics once the record has been set straight and they have done their part to help set it straight. This book, however, purposely refrains from offering a positive case for Marx's ideas or for Marxian economic analysis informed by the TSSI. (pp. xiii–ix {of Kliman 2007})

So, I will be glad to discuss with you whether I personally happen to think that labor is a produced commodity once the record has been set straight and you have done your part to help set it straight. I realize that readers of your blog might not be interested, but I do think the record needs to be set straight in the public domain, since what you wrote that we have challenged appeared in the public domain.

(By the way, if you object to my equating you to the critics of Marx, I'm sorry; I don't mean to offend you. I didn't mean to offend them either. I just mean that things like "his theoretical analysis of this fundamental fact is wrong, . . . a different theoretical analysis is required" are criticisms.)

In conclusion, let me emphasize that I am taking no position on whether labor is a produced commodity. I'm not saying that you're wrong and that Marx is right, or vice versa. I'm simply saying that you're entitled to your theory; Alan is entitled to his theory; and Marx is also entitled to his theory. And I'm pleading with you—and especially Alan—to not let the debate you want to have crowd out the debate about whether a different theoretical analysis from Marx's is *required*. The world's access to Marx's own, original theory as a living theory is at stake.

Best wishes,
Andrew

E-MAIL MESSAGE TO ANDREW KLIMAN
ROBERT PAUL WOLFF
MAY 14, 2014

OK, Andrew. I give up. It is clear that I cannot get you to engage in a conversation in which my interests, ideas, or take on Marx are accorded more than glancing notice by you. I do not think Marx is inconsistent, as I have explained several times, but let it go. I will be true to Marx's memory in my way, and you can be true to his memory in yours (yes, yes, I know, you don't think that is what you are doing—never mind).

Frankly, I thought an interesting and useful conversation was getting under way with Alan {Freeman}, but it looks as though that is not to be.[6]

Feel free to claim total victory on your blogsite. I am much too old to care!

Be well,
Bob

E-MAIL MESSAGE TO ROBERT PAUL WOLFF
ANDREW KLIMAN
MAY 14, 2014

Dear Bob,

You write, "It would be the same mistake you are making by continuing to treat labor as exogenously given and then thinking that your equations refute me."

I plead innocent. First, I don't accept that labor is exogenously given except in the same sense in which the seed corn and corn output are exogenously given. That is, the equation system does not determine the physical quantity of labor—or the physical quantity of seed corn, or the physical quantity of corn output. But the equations treat the value added by a unit of labor—and the value of the seed corn, and the value of the corn output—as unknowns.

In the temporalist value equation in which labor is the value-forming substance, the value added by a unit of labor is stipulated to equal 1 not because labor is not a produced commodity, but because the value added by a unit of the substance that forms value is one unit of value. After all, in the physicalist and temporalist value equations in which corn is the the value-forming substance, the value added by a unit of corn is stipulated to equal one even though corn is regarded there as a produced commodity.

Second, I have not claimed to refute "you" with these equations. I claim to have refuted the following statement, which is about an equation of *mine*: "[If there were] a term for labor at the start of the year and another term for labor at the end of the year . . . then the temporalist framework representations of a labor-value and corn-value analysis would be identical." And I claim that it follows from this refutation that the specific value-forming substance does matter within a non-physicalist and temporalist framework. You supposed that I would object to distinguishing between the value added by a unit of labor at the start and at the end of the production period, but I did not object.

I introduced that distinction, and showed that "the temporalist framework representations of a labor-value and corn-value analysis" are *not* identical.

You also write, "Once you start thinking of labor as a produced commodity, every conclusion you draw can be duplicated for labor values. How? Obvious. Just switch the notation. All the equations are remain the same, but what the symbols refer to changes."

This, together with the "exogenously given" statement, makes me suspect that you are confusing determination of physical quantities of inputs and output with determination of their values. But I can't be sure until I see the equations with switched notation. What you say is obvious isn't obvious to me.

If one wishes to consider all inputs and outputs as produced, and one wishes to specify the determination of their magnitudes, it seems to me that one needs *physical production functions* that relate physical outputs to the amount of physical inputs needed, and behavioral equations that specify how much of each output produced at time t is used as an input at times $t + k_1$, $t + k_2$, etc., in each line of production.

Best wishes,
Andrew

NOTES

1. X is the commodity that serves as the measure of value. In our counterexample, X was Botox, and there was a physical surplus of it. But X could equally well have been Gummi Bears, in which case we would have produced a counterexample that Wolff specifically allowed, one in which there was not a surplus of X in every year. If we make Gummi Bears the measure of value, its per-unit value remains 1, and the per-unit values of Botox and labor will still both equal 1. The surplus-value will be the same as in the original example (except that it will be surplus Gummi-Bear-Value rather than surplus Botox-Value). The only changes we need to make, in order to get the exact same numerical results, are to the prices in the two cases on p. 5 of our original response. In the first case, the prices of Gummi Bears and Botox will now be 1 and 29/30, respectively, rather than 1.05 and 1. In the second case, the prices will now be 1 and 31/30, respectively, rather than 0.95 and 1.

2. If Wolff were to insist on an internally inconsistent interpretation of his premises, on which it is both necessary and unnecessary that there be a physical surplus of X in every cycle of production, we could not disprove his claims in a formal sense, since absolutely every possible conclusion about everything is compatible with self-contradictory premises. But his argument would be absurd.

3. See Kliman (2001) {chap. 2 of this book}, chap. 10 of Kliman (2007), and Kliman and Freeman (2006, 2008, 2009) {chaps. 6, 8, and 9 of this book}.

4. See Kliman and Freeman (2008) and Freeman and Kliman (2009) {chaps. 8 and 11 of this book}.

5. {In a follow-up message, Kliman wrote, “Actually, technically speaking, there’s another case in which the last two expressions are equal, $V_{L(s)} = -1$. This doesn’t affect my conclusion. A”}

6. {Wolff and Freeman had exchanged messages on the topic of whether labor is a produced commodity.}

Bibliography

Antichrist Productions. 2012. *Reclaiming Marx's Capital: The Movie.* www.youtube.com/watch?v=7ajFOyBr8Bg&feature=youtu.be.

Bortkiewicz, Ladislaus von. 1952. Value and Price in the Marxian System, *International Economic Papers* 2, 5–60.

Chiang, Alpha C. 1974. *Fundamental Methods of Mathematical Economics*, 2nd ed. New York: McGraw-Hill.

Desai, Meghnad. 1991. The Transformation Problem. In Caravale, Giovanni A. (ed.), *Marx and Modern Economic Analysis*, Vol. 1. Aldershot, UK: Edward Elgar.

Dmitriev, V. K. 1974. *Economic Essays on Value, Competition and Utility.* Cambridge: Cambridge University Press.

Duménil, Gérard. 1980. *De la Valeur aux Prix de Production: Une réinterprétation de la transformation.* Paris: Economica.

———. 1983. Beyond the Transformation Riddle: A Labor Theory of Value, *Science & Society* 47:4, 427–50.

Duménil, Gérard, and Dominique Lévy. 2000. The Conservation of Value: A Rejoinder to Alan Freeman, *Review of Radical Political Economics* 32:1, 119–46.

Ernst, John R. 1982. Simultaneous Valuation Extirpated: A contribution to the Critique of the Neo-Ricardian Concept of Value, *Review of Radical Political Economics* 14:2, 85–94.

Foley, Duncan K. 1982. The Value of Money, the Value of Labor Power and the Marxian Transformation Problem, *Review of Radical Political Economics* 14:2, 37–47.

———. 1997. Recent Developments in the Labor Theory of Value. Presented at the International Working Group in Value Theory Mini-conference at the Eastern Economic Association conference, April, Washington, D.C.

———. 1999. Response to David Laibman, *Research in Political Economy* 17, 229–33.

———. 2000. Recent Developments in the Labor Theory of Value, *Review of Radical Political Economics* 32:1, 1–39.

Freeman, Alan. 1996. A General Refutation of Okishio's Theorem and a Proof of the Falling Rate of Profit. In Freeman, Alan, and Guglielmo Carchedi (eds.), *Marx and Non-equilibrium Economics*. Cheltenham, UK: Edward Elgar.

———. 1996. Price, Value and Profit—a Continuous, General, Treatment. In Freeman, Alan and Guglielmo Carchedi (eds.), *Marx and Non-equilibrium Economics*. Cheltenham, UK: Edward Elgar.

Freeman, Alan, and Guglielmo Carchedi (eds.). 1996. *Marx and Non-equilibrium Economics*, Cheltenham, UK: Edward Elgar.

Freeman, Alan, and Andrew Kliman. 2000. Two Concepts of Value, Two Rates of Profit, Two Laws of Motion, *Research in Political Economy* 18, 243–67.

———. 2009. No Longer a Question of Truth? The Knell of Scientific Bourgeois Marxian Economics and a Positive Alternative, *Marxism 21* 6:3, 302–17.

Freeman, Alan, Andrew Kliman, and Julian Wells (eds.). 2004. *The New Value Controversy and the Foundations of Economics*. Cheltenham, UK: Edward Elgar.

Freeman, Alan, et al. 2010. Open Letter to the Editorial Board of the *Review of Radical Political Economics*. Oct. 15. Available at www.academic.edu/10937571/Letter_to_the_editorial_board_of_RRPE

Giussani, Paulo. 1991–1992. The Determination of Prices of Production, *International Journal of Political Economy* 21:4, 67–86.

Howard, M. C., and J. E. King. 1992. *A History of Marxian Economics: Volume II, 1929–1990*. Princeton, NJ: Princeton University Press.

Kliman, Andrew, 1996. A Value-theoretic Critique of the Okishio Theorem. In Freeman, Alan, and Guglielmo Carchedi (eds.), *Marx and Non-equilibrium Economics*. Cheltenham, UK: Edward Elgar.

———. 1997. A Contribution to the Ongoing Inquiry into the Existence of Marx's Marxism. Submitted for Discussion to the International Working Group in Value Theory Mini-conference at the Eastern Economic Association Conference, April, Washington, D.C.

———. 2001. Simultaneous Valuation vs. the Exploitation Theory of Profit, *Capital & Class* 25:1, 97–112.

———. 2002. Stigler and Barkai on Ricardo's Profit Rate Theory: Some Methodological Considerations Thirty-five Years Later. Presented at the Eastern Economic Association Meetings, March, Boston.

———. 2003. Deriving a Negative PNP. Available at akliman.squarespace.com/neg-pnp.

———. 2007. *Reclaiming Marx's "Capital:" A Refutation of the Myth of Inconsistency*. Lanham, MD: Lexington Books.

Kliman, Andrew, and Freeman, Alan. 2006. Replicating Marx: A Reply to Mohun, *Capital & Class* 30:1, 117–26.

———. 2008. "Simultaneous Valuation vs. the Exploitation Theory of Profit: A Summing Up," *Capital & Class* 32:1, 107–17.

———. 2009. The Truthiness of Veneziani's Critique of Marx and the TSSI, *Marxism 21* 6:2, 335–66.

Kliman, Andrew, and Ted McGlone. 1988. The Transformation nonProblem and the nonTransformation Problem, *Capital & Class* 35, 56–83.

———. 1999. A Temporal Single-System Interpretation of Marx's Value Theory, *Review of Political Economy* 11:1, 33–59.

Krantz, Steven G. 2005. *Differential Equations Demystified: A Self-Teaching Guide.* New York: McGraw-Hill.

Laibman, David. 1999a. Okishio and His Critics: Historical Cost versus Replacement cost, *Research in Political Economy* 17, 207–27.

———. 1999b. The Profit Rate and Reproduction of Capital: A Rejoinder. *Research in Political Economy* 17, 249–54.

———. 2000. Two of Everything: A Response, *Research in Political Economy* 18, 269–78.

Lee, Chai-On. 1993. Marx's Labour Theory of Value Revisited, *Cambridge Journal of Economics* 17:4, 463–78.

———. McGlone, Ted, and Andrew Kliman. 1996. One System or Two? The Transformation of Values into Prices of Production vs. the "Transformation Problem." In Freeman, Alan, and Guglielmo Carchedi (eds.), *Marx and Non-Equilibrium Economics*, Cheltenham, UK: Edward Elgar, 206–24.

Maldonado-Filho, Eduardo. 1997. Release and Tying up of Productive Capital and the "Transformation Problem." Presented at Eastern Economic Association Conference, April, Washington, D.C. Available at www.iwgvt.org/files/97Maldonado.pdf.

Marx, Karl. 1973. *Grundrisse: Foundations of the Critique of Political Economy.* London: Penguin.

———. 1990a. *Capital: A Critique of Political Economy,* Vol. I. London: Penguin.

Marx, Karl. 1990b. Postface to the Second German Edition. In Marx, Karl, *Capital: A Critique of Political Economy,* Vol. I. London: Penguin, 94–103.

———. 1991a. *Capital: A Critique of Political Economy,* Vol. III. London: Penguin.

———. 1991b. *Karl Marx, Frederick Engels: Collected Works,* Vol. 33. New York: International Publishers.

Mohun, Simon. 2003. On the TSSI and the Exploitation Theory of Profit, *Capital & Class* 27:3, 85–102.

Mohun, Simon, and Roberto Veneziani. 2007. The Incoherence of the TSSI: A Reply to Kliman and Freeman, *Capital & Class* 31:2, 139–45.

———. 2009. The Temporal Single-System Interpretation: Underdetermination and Inconsistency, *Marxism 21* 6:3, 277–301.

Mongiovi, Gary. 2002. Vulgar Economy in Marxian Garb: a Critique of Temporal Single System Marxism, *Review of Radical Political Economics* 34:4, 393–416.

Morishima, Michio. 1973. *Marx's Economics: A Dual Theory of Value and Growth.* Cambridge: Cambridge University Press.

Moseley, Fred. 1993. Marx's Logical Method and the "Transformation Problem." In Moseley, Fred (ed.), *Marx's Method in Capital: A Reexamination.* Atlantic Highlands, NJ: Humanities Press, 157–83.

Okishio, Nobuo. 1961. Technical Changes and the Rate of Profit, *Kobe University Economic Review* 7, 85–99.

———. 1963. A Mathematical Note on Marxian Theorems, *Weltwirtschaftliches Archiv* 91, 287–99.

———. 1993a. A Mathematical Note on Marxian Theorems. In Okishio, Nobuo, *Nobuo Okishio—Essays on Political Economy: Collected Papers*. Frankfurt am Main: Peter Lang, 27–39.

———. 1993b. Three Topics on Marxian Fundamental Theorem. In Okishio, Nobuo, *Nobuo Okishio—Essays on Political Economy: Collected Papers*. Frankfurt am Main: Peter Lang, 77–94.

Potts, Nick. 2014. An Unacceptable Misrepresentation: Dismissing Marx's Value Theory by Deliberately Distorting the Temporal Single System Interpretation of Marx, *World Review of Political Economy* 5:1, 96–116.

Ramos, Alejandro. 1997. Labor, Money, Labor-Saving Innovation, and the Falling Rate of Profit. Presented at the International Working Group in Value Theory Mini-conference at the Eastern Economic Association Conference, April, Washington, D.C.

Robinson, Joan. 1967. *An Essay on Marxian Economics*, 2nd ed. London: Macmillan.

Roemer, John. 1981. *Analytical Foundations of Marxian Economic Theory*. Cambridge: Cambridge University Press.

Sinha, Ajit. 2009. Book Review: *Reclaiming Marx's "Capital" A Refutation of the Myth of Inconsistency* (by Andrew Kliman), *Review of Radical Political Economics* 41:3, 422–27.

Skillman, Gil. 1997. Technical Change and the Equilibrium Profit Rate in a Market with Sequential Bargaining, *Metroeconomica* 48:3, 238–61.

Steedman, Ian. 1977. *Marx after Sraffa*. London: New Left Books.

———. 2003. Marx After Sraffa and the Open Economy. Discussion Papers in Economics, Manchester Metropolitan University, Working Paper 2003–02.

Sweezy, Paul M. 1970. *The Theory of Capitalist Development: Principles of Marxian Political Economy*. New York: Modern Reader Paperbacks.

Veneziani, Roberto. 2002. Dynamics, Disequilibrium, and Marxian Economics. Unpublished Working Paper, London School of Economics and the Università degli Studi di Siena.

———. 2004. The Temporal Single-System Interpretation of Marx's Economics: A Critical Evaluation, *Metroeconomica* 55:1, 96–114.

———. 2005. Dynamics, Disequilibrium, and Marxian Economics: A Formal Analysis of Temporal Single-system Marxism, *Review of Radical Political Economics* 37:4, 517–29.

Wolff, Richard, Antonino Callari, and Bruce Roberts. 1984. A Marxian Alternative to the Traditional "Transformation Problem," *Review of Radical Political Economics* 16: 2–3, 115–35.

Wolff, Robert Paul. 1981. A Critique and Reinterpretation of Marx's Labor Theory of Value, *Philosophy & Public Affairs* 10:2, 89–120.

———. 1984. *Understanding Marx: A Reconstruction and Critique of Capital*. Princeton University Press.

———. 1988. Moneybags Must Be So Lucky: *On the Literary Structure of Capital*. Amherst, MA: University of Massachusetts Press.

Index

About the Editors

Nick Potts is a professor of economics at Southampton Solent University (United Kingdom). He received his PhD degree from the University of London under the supervision of Lord Meghnad Desai. He serves on the editorial boards of *Capital and Class* and Lexington Books' series *Heterodox Studies in the Critique of Political Economy*. His research applies Marx's value theory and analysis of capitalism to the economic issues of today, including globalization, the environment, the Euro, knowledge-based production, and the latest global economic crisis.

Professor Potts's recent publications include "The Missing C that Threatens to Flood Us All," *International Journal of Social Economics*; "Valuation in the Presence of Stocks of Commodities," *Critique of Political Economy*; "Marx and the Crisis," *Capital and Class;* "Keynesian Economics: In Search of Unnatural Stability," *Critique: Journal of Socialist Theory*; and "An Unacceptable Misrepresentation: Dismissing Marx's Value Theory By Deliberately Distorting The Temporal Single System Interpretation of Marx," *World Review of Political Economy*.

Andrew Kliman is professor emeritus of economics at Pace University in New York and editor of the Lexington Books series *Heterodox Studies in the Critique of Political Economy*. A member of Phi Beta Kappa, he holds BA and PhD degrees in economics from the University of Maryland and the University of Utah, respectively. Politically, he works with Marxist-Humanist Initiative.

Professor Kliman is the author of *Reclaiming Marx's "Capital": A Refutation of the Myth of Inconsistency* (2007) and *The Failure of Capitalist Production: Underlying Causes of the Great Recession* (2012), and a co-editor of and contributor to *The New Value Controversy and the Foundations of*

Economics (2004). His work has appeared in numerous scholarly journals, including the *Beiträge zur Marx-Engels-Forschung,* the *Cambridge Journal of Economics, Capital and Class, Historical Materialism, Marxism 21, Political Economy, Research in Political Economy*, and *Review of Political Economy*, and several edited collections. His current book projects include a study of Marx's concept of socialist society, an empirical study of inequality in the United States, and a study guide and commentary to Marx's *Capital.*